D1606128

THE RULE OF LAW AND THE LAW OF WAR

This book has been awarded
The Adèle Mellen Prize
for its distinguished contribution to scholarship.

THE RULE OF LAW AND THE LAW OF WAR
Military Commissions and Enemy Combatants Post 9/11

161001

Leonard Cutler

Studies in Political Science
Volume 25

The Edwin Mellen Press
Lewiston•Queenston•Lampeter

Library of Congress Cataloging-in-Publication Data

Cutler, Leonard.
  The rule of law and the law of war : military commissions and enemy combatants post 9/11 / Leonard Cutler.
    p. cm. -- (Studies in political science ; v. 25)
  Includes bibliographical references and index.
  ISBN 0-7734-6209-0 (hardback)
    1. Military courts--United States. 2. Terrorists--Legal status, laws, etc. 3. Prisoners of war--Legal status, laws, etc. 4. War on Terrorism, 2001- I. Title. II. Studies in political science (Lewiston, N.Y.) ; v. 25.

KF7661.C88 2005
343.73'0143--dc22

                                                              2005040455

This is volume 25 in the continuing series
Studies in Political Science
Volume 25 ISBN 0-7734-6209-0
SPSc Series ISBN 0-7734-7434-X

A CIP catalog record for this book is available from the British Library

The Edwin Mellen Press   The Edwin Mellen Press
     Box 450   Box 67
Lewiston, New York   Queenston, Ontario
USA 14092-0450   CANADA L0S 1L0

The Edwin Mellen Press, Ltd.
Lampeter, Ceredigion, Wales
UNITED KINGDOM SA48 8LT

Printed in the United States of America

This book is dedicated to GG, Sheila, Ethan and Maya.

TABLE OF CONTENTS

PREFACE

It would be difficult to imagine a more timely work or one more meticulously researched. In these chapters Dr. Cutler hones in on the continuing debate over the right to indefinitely detain American Citizens classified as enemy combatants (Padilla and Hamdi) and the right to hold non-citizen enemy combatants (Rasul and Al-Odah) at Guantanamo Bay in Cuba without opportunity to challenge the basis for their detention in any court of the United States. The author's dissection and analysis of the Federal Court decisions in these matters is superb and confirms the outstanding research that characterizes the entire work. Aside from the hundreds of pertinent footnotes throughout, the appendices contain all of the controlling Presidential orders, Department of Defense Regulations and Congressional Resolutions and other directives to satisfy the most avid general reader or researcher. September 11, 2001, and its aftermath have presented daunting challenges to our nation. This book addresses itself to one of those challenges, namely the manner in which we balance our national security interests with the civil liberties of captured enemy combatants, foreign, or non-foreign. Dr. Cutler begins with a necessary discussion and historical perspective on military commissions dating from the Revolutionary War. His emphasis however, is properly placed on World War II cases such as Yamashita and Quirin, plus others that still serve or are cited as useful precedents today. Next he details the Presidents', the Department of Defense and Congressional actions in the form of orders, and regulation in the aftermath of 9/11. Major emphasis is placed on both the Joint Resolution, the Authorization for Use of Military Force, the establishment of Military Commissions and Department of Defense orders subsequent to 9/11. Chapter III examines fundamental fairness issues in the post 9/11 procedures of military commissions noting in particular the omissions of the right to habeas corpus relief; the heavily encumbered right to civilian counsel; and the highly restrictive appeal process, all of which depart from Federal practice in both civilian and military courts. Chapter IV, inter alia, provides an in depth review of the Padilla and Hamdi cases. Both are American citizens and both were detained indefinitely. Hamdi however was captured in a foreign theatre of war while Padilla was arrested within this country. There are other distinguishing factors in these two cases, highlighted before careful analysis of the Supreme Court decision in Hamdi and its "non-decision" in Padilla in Chapter V. The final chapter discusses the Executive's response to the Supreme Court decision in the Hamdi case by the establishment of Combatant Status Review Tribunals. These tribunals provide rules to permit detainees to contest their status as enemy combatants and for the creation of administrative review boards to annually determine whether a detainee remains a threat to the United States.

The author states that "it is highly misleading to conclude that because military commissions are comprised exclusively of commissioned and experienced officer judges – that they will automatically be unfair – historical experience demonstrates to the contrary," and he gives several examples to aptly demonstrate the point. Nonetheless, critics maintain that despite the many similarities between court martial trials and the military commission orders as revamped by the DoD Rules, Regulations, and Procedures of 2004, the lack of independent civilian review is a serious impediment to the doctrine of fundamental fairness. Furthermore, they argue that the scope of collateral review of military commission decisions must be clearly enunciated. The same, of course, can be said of the restrictions on the right to counsel. Of the several "rights" not afforded enemy combatants, the lack of effective representation by counsel most probably generate the loudest cries for reform. The pressure for reform to include unrestricted right to counsel will doubtless continue. (It is perhaps somewhat problematic whether civilian counsel with no military background and with minimal trial experience could represent, under extant rules, an enemy combatant any more effectively than an experienced military career officer. As currently provided for, under the restrictions currently in place, civilian lawyers with "heavy hitting" credentials are not likely to be flocking to Guantanamo.)

It is regrettable that the three decisions Hamdi, Padilla and the Rasul/Al-Odah were not fully dispositive of the serious issues raised by the author. Padilla in particular was a disappointment to anyone hoping for a resolution to the question of the legality of indefinite detention of an American citizen. When the court ruled on jurisdictional grounds that his petition for habeas corpus had to be brought in South Carolina rather than a New York court, should the "technicality" have prevailed over expedience in the matters of national security vis-à-vis civil liberties? In the Padilla case, the author suggests justice would have been better served if the jurisdictional "technicality" had given way to the speedier solution. Was the Supreme Court merely postponing the all but inevitable release of Padilla?

The author's careful review of the decisions in these and related cases is most impressive. As noted, his research throughout is extraordinary! In his last chapter he reasonably concludes that "legislation is warranted to establish standards and procedures for preventively detaining U.S. citizens and non-citizens as enemy combatants" and believes relevant issues that need to be addressed by Congress include: the threshold level of terrorist activity that warrants preventative detention; the standard of proof needed to justify preventive detention; the type of hearing that must be conducted to classify a detainee as an enemy combatant; the length of time that detention can continue; what rights of appeal do enemy combatants have, and if so, when and to whom?

Continuing congressional inaction may be anticipated because the Executive's responsiveness to the Hamdi and Rasul decisions may ameliorate congressional concerns. Another may be the Congress's reluctance to extend more "rights" to captured enemy combatants when terrorists are beheading American citizens and released detainees are reportedly again fighting coalition forces. Although congressional action remains problematic the author makes a persuasive argument that Congress should act. If each member would take the time to read this important scholarly book however chances for swift congressional action might well be greatly improved.

James P. King
B/Gen USMC (Ret) (JAG)
Judge NYS Court of Claims (Ret)

ACKNOWLEDGEMENTS

A small group of highly supportive and talented individuals helped to make the vision of this book a reality, and to them I owe a considerable amount of gratitude. Professor Richard Ognibene, my friend, colleague and former Dean at Siena College, encouraged me to write and complete the book, and his support was much appreciated as a motivating factor.

I received immeasurable assistance from Dr. Linda Richardson, Vice President for Academic Affairs of Siena College who answered my requests for resource assistance with utmost professionalism and amiability. Ellen Johnson from Faculty Support Services of Siena College, was an invaluable aide to me and truly guided the manuscript with her suggestions for clarification and improvement, and was instrumental in its preparation and completion. Michele Monforte was diligent and thorough in her role as copy editor/proof reader.

The following scholars whose reviews and critiques markedly improved the manuscript earn my appreciation and I wish to acknowledge their contributions: Hon. James P. King, Adjunct Professor of Law, Albany Law School, and retired Brigadier General/Senior Marine Judge Advocate of the Marine Corps, and retired New York State Court of Claims Judge graciously agreed to write the Preface and patiently guided me through the processes of the UCMJ and the Military Court System; Dr. Steven J. Lamy, Director of the International Studies Program of the University of Southern California who stimulates my life as an intellectual sounding board; and Professor Art Wolf, Director of Legislative and Constitutional Studies, Western New England College of Law, who provided thoughtful constructive feedback.

Despite all of the extensive expert assistance given to me there may very well exist errors in the writing of the book, and if so, I alone am fully responsible.

CHAPTER I

Military Commissions in Historical Perspective

On September 11, 2001, two commercial American airliners were hijacked and purposely flown into the Twin Towers of the World Trade Center in New York City, killing all passengers, crew, and the hijackers, as well as over three thousand people on the ground. Within an hour, another hijacked airliner hit the Pentagon in Washington with similar tragic consequences. A fourth airliner presumably headed for the White House or U.S. Capitol crashed in a field near Pittsburgh killing all on board.

In response to these horrific acts of terrorism committed against the United States, President George W. Bush proclaimed a national emergency and issued a military order, which for the first time in United States history permits the government to hold and prosecute by military commission stateless members of an organization in an undeclared war.[1]

> To protect the United States and its citizens, and for the effective conduct of military operations and prevention of terrorist attacks, it is necessary for individuals subject to this order . . . to be tried for violations of the laws of war and other applicable laws by military tribunals.[2]

The attacks of September 11, involving the murder of several thousand people from eighty-seven countries, and the massive destruction of the World Trade Center, the Pentagon, and commercial aircraft, were of unprecedented proportion and represent grave breaches of international law and the law of war. Even though Osama bin Laden's terrorist network, al-Qaida, and others responsible for these devastating actions do not constitute a state under the law of nations, the violence associated with their behavior and the extent of organization involved in successfully completing their mission of mass casualty terrorism provide ample justification for arguing that these were acts of war.

The President's Order initially targeted for commission trials of representatives of al-Qaida or members of the Taliban, yet it makes clear that its reach is not limited in the effort to fight and punish global terrorism. Cooperative and collaborative efforts have been undertaken by the Administration with friendly governments in the Philippines, Malaysia, and Singapore to root out terrorist groups, and in other countries where al-Qaida cells are thought to be located, such as Indonesia, Yemen, and Somalia.

In the war against Iraq, the President eluded to the linkage between Saddam Hussein and al-Qaida in his State of the Union speech in January 2003, saying: "Evidence from intelligence sources, secret communications and statements by people now in custody reveal that Saddam Hussein aids and protects terrorists, including members of al-Qaida." The President painted a catastrophic picture of what would happen if Saddam supplied chemical or biological weapons to al-Qaida or helped them develop their own:

> Imagine those 19 hijackers who committed the September 11 attacks with other weapons and other plans, this time armed by Saddam Hussein. It would take one vial, one canister, one crate slipped into this country to bring a day of horror like none we have ever known.[3]

Terrorists are not members of established armed forces for the purpose of the law of war[4] and they do not comply with the acceptable rules as lawful combatants.[5] Those who are directly involved in such acts of war, like the September 11 terrorist attack, violate the laws of war, and if captured, may be tried by a nation in its national courts or by a military commission under that nation's jurisdiction.

The focus of this section of the study is to examine the nature and purpose of military commissions in American history and to provide the historical context for their role as anticipated by the Bush Administration.

* * * * * * * * * *

Military Commissions in Historical Perspective

A military commission is a special court run by the military not the civilian judiciary, and convened to adjudicate extraordinary cases usually involving foreigners and usually during wartime. They derive their authority from the United States Constitution and the powers vested in them by statutory law.[6]

Congress has provided for military commissions in Article 21 of the Uniform Code of Military Justice (10 U.S.C. Sec. 821), which provides:

> The provisions of this chapter conferring jurisdiction upon courts-martial do not deprive military commissions, provost courts, or other military tribunals of concurrent jurisdiction with respect to offenders or offenses that by statute or by the law of war may be tried by military commission, provost court, or other military tribunals.[7]

A military commission is distinguishable from a court martial in that a court martial is a trial of a member of the military service governed by the Uniform Code of Military Justice.[8] United States service members charged with a war crime may also be tried in federal court.[9]

A military commission is a form of military tribunal. The correct use of the term "military commission" has been the subject of considerable debate, and has taken many forms and borne many names.[10]

The Revolutionary War to Mexican War Cases

Precedent for the use of military commissions dates back to the period of the Revolutionary War. General George Washington, in 1780, appointed a board of officers to try Major John Andre, a British spy who slipped behind American lines to gather secret information for Benedict Arnold.[11] In the war against the Creek Indians in 1818, military trials were used to try persons not otherwise subject to military jurisdiction.[12]

The original formal creation of American military commissions is traced to Major General Winfeld Scott during the Mexican-American War (1846-48). Military commissions were used when volunteer American troops went out of

4

control once below the Rio Grande to deal with the offenses of Mexican guerilla fighters and the fractious local populace in Mexico.

History reports no criticism of General Scott's use of these panels to administer justice against enemy belligerents and citizens harboring such combatants. Trying Mexican guerilla fighters who were not part of the Mexican army before military commissions is an early precedent for bringing contemporary foreign terrorists before such tribunals today.[13]

The Civil War Cases

During the Civil War when President Lincoln suspended the writ of habeas corpus, martial law was declared and military commissions were established to deter and punish those determined to be disloyal to the preservation of the Union. The following proclamation was issued by the President:

> That during the existing insurrection, and as a necessary means for suppressing the same, all rebels and insurgents, their aiders and abettors, within the United States, and all persons discouraging volunteer enlistments, resisting militia drafts, or guilty of any disloyal practice, affording aid and comfort to rebels, against the authority of the United States, shall be subject to martial law, and liable to trial and punishment by courts martial or military commission.
> Second. That the writ of habeas corpus is suspended in respect to all persons arrested, or who now, or hereafter during the Rebellion shall be, imprisoned in any fort, camp, arsenal, military prison, or other place of confinement, by any military authority, or by the sentence of any court martial or military commission.[14]

There were over 2,000 cases tried by military commissions during the war and post the period of Reconstruction. A few of the more important cases include:

- On May 22, 1865, T. E. Hogg and others were tried by a Military Commission, for 'violations of the laws and usages of civilized war,' the specifications charging that the accused 'being commissioned, enrolled, enlisted or engaged' by the Confederate Government, came on board a United States merchant steamer in the port of Panama 'in the guise of peaceful passengers' with the purpose of capturing the vessel and converting her into a Confederate cruiser. The Commission found the accused guilty and sentenced them to be hanged. The reviewing authority affirmed the judgments, writing an extensive opinion on the question whether violations of the law of war were alleged, but modified the sentences.[15]

- On January 17, 1865, John Y. Beall was tried by a military commission for 'violation of the laws of war.' The opinion by the reviewing authority reveals that Beall, holding a commission in the confederate Navy, came on board a merchant vessel at a Canadian port in civilian dress and, with associates, took possession of the vessel in Lake Erie; that, also in disguise, he unsuccessfully attempted to derail a train in New York State, and to obtain military information. His conviction by the Commission was affirmed on the ground that he was both a spy and a 'guerilla,' and he was sentenced to be hanged.[16]

- On January 17, 1865, Robert C. Kennedy, a Captain of the Confederate Army, who was shown to have attempted, while in disguise, to set fire to the City of New York, and to have been seen in disguise in various parts of New York State, was convicted on charges of acting as a spy and violation of the law of war 'in undertaking to carry on irregular and unlawful warfare.' He was sentenced to be hanged, and the sentence was confirmed by the reviewing authority.[17]

- On September 19, 1865, William Murphy, 'a rebel emissary in the employ of and colleagued with rebel enemies' was convicted by a military commission of 'violation of the laws and customs of war' for coming within the lines and burning a United States steamboat and other property.[18]

- Soldiers and officers 'now or late of the Confederate Army; were tried and convicted by military commission for being secretly within the lines of the United States forces; for recruiting men within the lines, and for lurking about the posts, quarters, fort functions and encampments of the armies of the United States; although not as a spy.'[19]

However, serious constitutional questions were raised when the government prosecuted one Lambden P. Milligan, a civilian and member of the "Sons of Liberty," who was sentenced to death by an army court for allegedly disloyal activities in Indiana. Specifically, Milligan was found guilty of conspiracy against the government, giving aid and comfort to the enemy, inciting insurrection, disloyal practices and violation of the law of war. Milligan appealed to the circuit court in Indiana for his release under the 1863 Habeas Corpus Act. The federal circuit court split on the question of whether civilian courts had jurisdiction over appeals from military tribunals. The United States Supreme Court ruled that the law of war can never be applied to citizens in states which have upheld the authority of the government, and where the courts are open and their process unobstructed.[20] The Court pointed out in painstaking detail that Milligan, a citizen and twenty year resident in Indiana, had never been a resident of any of the states in rebellion, and was not an enemy belligerent either entitled to the status of prisoner of war or subject to the penalties imposed upon unlawful belligerents.[21] Milligan is not a limitation upon the trial of U.S. citizens by military commission; it is a bar on the application of martial law, which employs military commissions in areas where the government of the United States or a state is operational.

President Lincoln's Assassination

In 1865 the Attorney General found that co-conspirators charged in the assassination of President Lincoln could be tried by military commission, despite the fact that the courts were operating in Washington, D.C.[22] His opinion emphasized the difference between "open and active participants" in war and "secret, but active participants" in violation of the law of war.[23]

Joseph Holt, the Judge Advocate General of the Army headed the prosecution team that tried those who were involved in the conspiracy to assassinate President Lincoln, and it is significant to note that the fairness and thoroughness of the proceedings is striking when one reads the trial record of the Hunter Commission, as the nine officers were known, who tried those who conspired to kill the President.

Defendants were all represented by counsel, entitled to call witnesses in their defense and over 350 witnesses testified.[24] Given the tragic nature of the crime, where the crime occurred, and where the Hunter commission sat, the fairness and impartiality of this tribunal is particularly noteworthy. Furthermore, since not all the conspirators were sentenced to death demonstrates the ability of such a body to make just determinations.[25]

Dr. Samuel Mudd was tried and sentenced to life in prison for aiding and abetting after the fact the conspiracy by providing medical assistance, lodging, and horses to John Wilkes Booth and a co-conspirator.[26] Dr. Mudd later received a full pardon for his work in battling yellow fever in the prison. His great-grandson filed an application with the Army Board for Correction of Military Records asserting his great-grandfather was innocent of the charges and that the military commission lacked jurisdiction to try a citizen of Maryland when the courts were fully functional. The Board recommended the conviction be set aside, but the Secretary of Defense denied the application. The United States District Court for the District of Columbia dismissed the appeal, finding that "if Dr. Samuel Mudd was charged with a law of war violation, it was permissible for him to be tried before a military commission even though he was a United States and Maryland citizen and the civilian courts were open at the time of the trial."[27]

World War II Cases

In the twentieth century military commissions had their most extensive application for the prosecution of war crimes at the end of World War II. In 1946, the Supreme Court approved a commission conviction of the commanding general of the Japanese Army in the Philippines, Tomoyuki Yamashita,[28] who was charged with permitting his troops to engage in brutal atrocities against civilians and prisoners of war, and wanton destruction of public and private property, including religious monuments. He was convicted and sentenced to death by hanging.[29]

General Yamashita petitioned for a writ of habeas corpus, and argued to the Supreme Court that the military commission lacked appropriate jurisdiction to try him after the cessation of hostilities, and that among other things, he did not commit or order his troops to commit any of the offenses directed at the civilian population for which he was charged.

The Court disagreed, affirming the power of the President, pursuant to his authority as Commander-in-Chief in Article II of the Constitution, and the power delegated to him by the Congress to administer a system of military justice for the trial and punishment of enemy combatants who have violated the law of war.[30] The Court defined the existence of a state of war to extend from its declaration by Congress to the proclamation of peace which means that the legitimate authority of the military commission did not cease with the cessation of hostilities, but carries with it the inherent power to guard against the immediate renewal of the conflict, and to remedy, at least in ways Congress has recognized the evils which military operations produced.[31]

The *Quirin* Case

A most important case during World War II involved eight German saboteurs who landed in a group of four from a U-Boat at Amagansett, Long Island on June 13, 1942, and four more who landed four days later at Ponte Vedra Beach, Florida. Their mission was to blow up rail centers, bridges, locks on the Ohio River, the New York water supply system, and a number of industrial plants. After they came ashore they removed their naval uniforms and buried them along with a supply of explosives and incendiaries. Because one of the leaders decided to turn himself in, the FBI was able to arrest all eight within two weeks.[32]

On July 2, less than a week after the eight men had been apprehended, President Roosevelt issued a proclamation carrying this title: Denying Certain Enemies Access to the Courts of the United States.[33] The first paragraph is highly significant because it states "the safety of the United States demands that all enemies who have entered upon the territory of the United States as part of an invasion or predatory incursion, or who entered in order to commit sabotage espionage or other hostile or war like acts should be promptly tried in accordance with the law of war."

Reference to the "law of war" is of value in the context of military commissions because it provides far more flexibility in utilizing the principles and procedures of Roosevelt's proclamation than had the President cited the "Articles of War" which would have triggered statutory procedures established by the Congress for courts martial.[34]

The second paragraph of the proclamation refers to the President acting as "Commander-in-Chief of the Army and Navy of the United States, by virtue of the authority vested in me by the Constitution and statutes of the United States." He was acting with joint authority granted constitutionally and statutorily by the Congress. The second paragraph also contained a provision that denied any of the eight captured prisoners access to a civil court because the President did not want to permit them an opportunity for judicial review.

The military order of July 2 appointed the seven military members of the Commission, the prosecutors, and defense counsel and directed the body to meet on July 8, or as soon thereafter as practicable, to try the offenses against both the law of war and Articles of War.

The Commission would make its own rules for conducting its proceedings ensuring the necessity for a full and fair trial of the defendants. The Commission could admit evidence "as would in the opinion of the President of the Commission have probative value to a reasonable man." The reasonable man test would evolve with clarity over the course of the proceedings as the Commission issued its rulings.

Under the requirements of a court martial pursuant to Articles of War a unanimous vote was necessary. The military order for the Commission with respect to sentencing including death, required "at least two-thirds of the members of the Commission." Additionally, the July 2 order required all records of the trial, including any judgment or sentence, to be directly transmitted to the President for his action because he was to be the final reviewing authority for these proceedings.

In the midst of the trial the accused petitioned the United States District Court for leave to bring habeas corpus proceedings. On July 28 the District Judge issued a brief statement denying permission for relief refusing to consider *Ex Parte Milligan* as controlling for the petitioner.[35]

The case immediately moved to the United States Supreme Court where the defendants embraced the following contentions: (1) that the offense charged against them was not known to the laws of the United States; (2) that it was not one "arising in the land and naval forces;" and (3) that the tribunal trying them had not been constituted in accordance with the Articles of War.

After two days of oral argument the Court issued a brief per curiam decision on July 31, which determined that the military tribunal was properly constituted. On October 27, almost three months later, Chief Justice Stone and his colleagues issued a full decision explaining the legal and constitutional bases for the per curiam.

The unanimous court decision began its consideration of military commissions by reaffirming a basic principle, that the government may act only through a valid grant of constitutional authority. The Court found that Article 1 powers of Congress "to provide for the common defense, to raise and support armies, to provide and maintain the navy, to make rules for the government, and regulation of the land and naval forces, to define and punish piracies and felonies committed on the high seas and offenses against the law of nations" along with the Necessary and Proper clause, firmly authorized Congress to create military commissions.

The Court found similarly with respect to the President under the Article II powers as Commander-in-Chief and Chief Executive.[36] In upholding the President's order the Court declared:

> By his order creating the present Commission he has undertaken to exercise the authority conferred upon him by Congress, and also such authority as the Constitution itself gives the Commander-in-Chief to direct the performance of those function which may constitutionally be performed by the military arm of the nation in the time of war.[37]

After upholding the constitutionality of the military commission the Court next addressed the scope of the jurisdiction. In their jurisdictional challenge, the defendants argued that their conduct, while perhaps criminal, was not an "offense against the law of war," and therefore, their case was not properly before a military commission. In rejecting this challenge, the *Quirin* Court drew the distinction between the common law notion of lawful and unlawful belligerents.

Citing over a dozen international authorities on military law, the *Quirin* Court recognized that there is universal agreement among the nations with respect to the "law of war" and "lawful and unlawful combatants." The most fundamental distinction is that unlawful combatants, if captured, are subject to trial and punishment by military commissions for acts which render their belligerency unlawful. As for determining what acts give rise to unlawful belligerency, the Court reviewed the history of war dating from the eighteenth century and cited many factors. A central element was the common law crime of spying. Those who during the time of war pass surreptitiously from enemy territory into our own, discarding their uniforms upon entry for the commission of hostile acts, have the status of unlawful combatants. For the *Quirin* Court, the saboteurs were so plainly within the bounds of the international common law definition of unlawful combatants that their argument that they were not properly before a military commission was summarily dismissed.[38]

The Court next distinguished the *Milligan* decision from that of the German saboteurs. Milligan was a U.S. citizen who resided in Indiana for twenty years, was never in military or naval service, was not a resident of one of the rebellious states or a prisoner of war, and therefore jurisdiction could not be applied under the laws and usages of war to citizens in states which have upheld the authority of the government, and where the courts are open and their process unobstructed.[39] Most importantly, the Court refused to define with "meticulous care" the ultimate boundaries of military commissions to try persons who are charged with violating the law of war. It was sufficient to state that the defendants were "plainly within these boundaries."[40]

What was not addressed by the Court was the question of whether the *Ex Parte Quirin* decision would justify the President to act unilaterally as Commander-in-Chief if Congress were to restrict or withdraw the authority statutorily for the President to act as he did under the circumstances. The Court intentionally avoided addressing that issue.

There has been an opportunity in recent history to criticize the Supreme Court for its assembling in special session in the summer of 1942 to decide a case without ever receiving briefs in advance and without knowledge about how the secret trial was conducted or how it would eventually turn out. The highly compressed schedule, including taking a case directly from a district court without action by the D.C. Circuit Court of Appeals, and issuing a decision within a day of completion of oral argument, certainly gave the appearance of a rush to judgment.

The Court has been widely criticized for issuing a brief per curiam and then taking three months to release its full opinion that contained its full legal reasoning. The drafting of the full decision occurred after the execution of six of the saboteurs. The decision could not, and did not, in any way suggest that there had been any violations of justice in this instance, although it is obvious from the absence of either concurrence, or dissents, that unanimity was essential.

As Chief Justice William Rehnquist, in his 1998 study, *All the Laws But One*, suggests, *Quirin* is one example of how the Supreme Court throughout history has given the green light to restrictions on civil liberties while war is underway, whereas it is far less willing to do so once the hostilities have ceased. This point is well validated with respect to Lincoln's actions during the Civil War, and Roosevelt's during World War II. These two illustrations provide examples of an old maxim of Roman Law, *Inter Arma Silent Leges*, which loosely translated means: in time of war the laws are silent.[41]

Besides the trials of the German saboteurs and Yamashita in World War II, subsequent military tribunals were used to prosecute approximately 2600 members of the Axis for violations of the laws of war, to include the murder of captured American soldiers at the Battle of the Bulge.[42] Surviving high-ranking war criminals in the German military and government were tried by a special international tribunal in Nuremberg, Germany, at the so-called Nuremberg trials. The Japanese leaders were tried at the International Military Tribunal for the Far East.[43]

The general principles of law concerning military commissions that are developed from these cases include: (a) if Congress formally declares war, the President as Commander-in-Chief is recognized with the authority to create military commissions; (b) defendants before the military commissions are specifically assigned procedural safeguards as determined by the President; and (c) military commissions are legitimate to redress the atrocities produced by war crimes, even if hostilities have ceased at the time of trial.

Summary

Although there is no explicitly articulated language in the Constitution and minimal mention in legislative code that clearly establishes military commissions, there is extensive historical precedent from the period of the earliest Presidential administration to that of Franklin D. Roosevelt in World War II that ensures a basis for their existence and legitimacy.

The Constitution provides the Congress with the power to declare and define war, and the power to define and punish "Piracies and Felonies committed on the high seas and Offenses against the Law of Nations."[44] The definition and punishment of war crimes are constitutionally the direct responsibility of Congress, and the historically and legally approved mechanism for discharging this duty is the military commission.

The President's authority to convene military commissions emanates from his position as Commander-in-Chief of the Armed Forces and his duty to faithfully execute the laws of the nation.[45] The President and the military commanders representing him employ the commission as the occasion requires for the investigation and punishment of violations of the laws of war and other offenses not cognizable by court-martial.[46] In our military law the distinctive name of military commission has been adopted for the exclusively war court which is a distinct tribunal from the court martial of the Articles of War.[47]

The President has been delegated the authority to set rules of procedure for military commissions in both a trial and post trial setting.[48] Military commissions historically have been composed of commissioned officers of the armed services, although legally they could be composed otherwise, for example, in part by civilians or of enlisted personnel. In the absence of any law fixing the number of members of a military commission they may legally be composed of any number in the discretion of the convening authority. A commission of a single member would be as strictly legal as would be one of thirteen members.[49]

A military commission (except where otherwise authorized by statute) assumes jurisdiction of offences committed within the field of command or the theater of war. A military commission cannot (in the absence of specific statutory authority) legally assume jurisdiction of or impose punishment for an offense committed either before or after the war. The President may, however, with congressional approval, employ military commissions to try accused war criminals in occupied territories despite the fact that actual hostilities have ceased.[50]

The classes of persons who may be subject to the jurisdiction of military commissions include: (1) individuals in the enemy's army who have been guilty of violating the laws of war; (2) inhabitants of the enemy's nation occupied and held by the right of conquest; (3) inhabitants of places and districts under martial law; (4) officers and soldiers of our own army, or persons serving with it in the field who in time of war, become chargeable with crimes not cognizable, or triable by the criminal courts or under the Articles of War.[51] Case law has determined that military commissions could try as enemy belligerents those accused of violating the law of war even if they were U.S. citizens.[52]

The offences cognizable by military commissions may be classified as: (1) Crimes and statutory offenses cognizable by State or U.S. courts, and which would properly be tried by such courts if open and acting.[53] Case law has determined that the law of war permits a United States citizen to be tried before a military commission even though the State or U.S. courts are open at the time of trial;[54] (2) Violations of the laws and usages of war cognizable by military tribunals only; (3) Breaches of military orders or regulations for which offenders are not legally triable by court-martial under the Articles of War.[55] Case law has determined that the law of war permits the use of military commissions even in the absence of a formal declaration of a state of war.[56]

As a general rule military commissions have allowed the prisoner: attendance of counsel, consideration of special pleas if any are offered, receipt of all material evidence desired to be introduced, full argument, findings and sentence after adequate deliberation, provision of a fully authenticated record of the commissions proceedings to the convening authority, and operation by the established rules and principles of law and evidence. Sentences have included death, imprisonment and fine. Death has commonly been by hanging, imprisonment has been imposed for a term of months or years for life, or during the war.[57] As in the case of a court martial, and as held by the Supreme Court in *Ex Parte Vallandigham*,[58] the proceedings or sentences of military commissions are not subject as such to be appealed from, or to be directly revised by, any civil tribunal. The proper reviewing authority is the Commander-in-Chief or his delegated commander in the field.[59]

Military commissions have played a consistent role in our constitutional and historic tradition, and their use has been supported by the Congress and upheld by the United States Supreme Court. Such commissions have been constitutionally recognized agencies for meeting urgent governmental responsibilities relating to war without Congress specifically declaring war.[60]

Notes

[1] Proclamation No. 7463, 66 Fed. Reg. 48, 199 (Sept. 14, 2001) and the Military Order on the Detention, Treatment, and Trial of Certain Non-Citizens in the War Against Terrorism, (November 13, 2001); § 1(a), 66 Fed. Reg. 57, 833 (November 16, 2001). *See* Appendix A.

[2] *Id.* § 1(e).

[3] *See* President's Address Before a Joint Session of the Congress on the State of Union, *39 Weekly Comp. Pres. Doc. 109*, January 28, 2003. According to a staff report to the National Commission on Terrorist Attacks on the United States there was "no credible evidence that Iraq and al Qaeda cooperated on attacks against the United States, and . . . that any ties existed between al Qaeda and Iraq." *See Staff Statement No. 15, Overview of the Enemy,* June 2004 at 5.

[4] *See* David B. Rivkin, Jr., Lee A. Casey and Darin Bartram, *Bringing Al-Qaida to Justice: The Constitutionality of Trying Al-Qaida Terrorists in the Military Justice System*, Heritage Foundation, Legal Memorandum No. 3, November 5, 2001.

[5] *See* Spencer J. Crona and Neal A. Richardson, "Justice for War Criminals of Invisible Armies: A New Legal and Military Approach to Terrorism," *21 Okla. City U.L. Rev.* 349 (1996).

[6] *See* Articles I and II of the Constitution. Article I, Section 8, grants to Congress the powers: "To provide for the common Defense" (clause 1) and "To define and punish piracies on the high seas, and offenses against the Law of Nations; To declare War, grant letters of Marque and Reprisal, and make Rules concerning Captures on Land and Water; To raise and support Armies . . .; To provide and maintain a Navy; To make Rules for the Government and Regulation of the land and naval Forces;" (clauses 10-14). Article II confers on the President the "Executive Power" (Section 1) and makes him the "Commander in Chief of the Army and Navy" (Section 2). Additionally, Congress has statutorily authorized the President in Article 106 of the UCMJ to try anyone acting as a spy before a military commission (*See* 10 U.S.C. § 836. Article 104 of the UCMJ which authorized trial by military commissions of any person who aids, or attempts, to aid, the enemy with communication, supplies, money or other things; or without proper authority, knowingly harbors or protects or gives allegiance to, or communicates or corresponds with or holds any intercourse with the enemy, directly, or indirectly.) (*See* 10 U.S.C. § 834) and powers that may be vested in them by statutory law (*e.g.*, Authorization for use of Military Force, PL 107-40).

[7] This language is designed to retain the common law jurisdiction of military commissions. In *Application of Yamashita,* 327 U.S. 1 (1946) the Court discussed Article of War 15, which contained substantially the same language as UCMJ Article 21. It explained that Article 15 was adopted in 1916 in response to other amendments of the Articles of War which granted jurisdiction to courts-martial to try offenses and offenders under the law of war. Thus, the Court stated:

> [I]t was feared by the proponents of the 1916 legislation that in the absence of a saving provision, the authority given by Articles [of War] 12, 13, and 14 to try such persons before courts-martial might be construed to deprive the non-statutory military commission of a portion of what was considered its traditional jurisdiction. To avoid this, and to preserve that jurisdiction intact, Article 15 was added to the Articles. . . . By thus recognizing military commissions in order to preserve their traditional jurisdiction over enemy combatants unimpaired by the Articles [of War], Congress gave sanction, as we held in *Ex Parte Quirin*, to any use of the military commission contemplated by the common law of war. *Id.* at 19-20 (footnote omitted).

[8] 10 U.S.C. § 801-941 (West 1985, Supp. 1996).

[9] The War Crimes Act of 1996, codified at 18 U.S.C. § 2441, subjects persons suspected of perpetrating a violation of the Geneva Conventions and other international conventions to criminal punishment if the perpetrator or victim is either a U.S. service member or a U.S. national. Article 18 of the UCMJ, 10 U.S.C. § 818, provides general court martial jurisdiction over "any person who by the law of war is subject to trial by a military tribunal and may adjudge any punishment permitted by the law of war."

[10] *See Madsen v. Kinsella*, 343 U.S. 341 at 348 (1952) in which the Supreme Court examined the history of military commissions and determined: Since our nation's earliest days, such commissions have been constitutionally recognized agencies for meeting many governmental responsibilities related to war. They have been called our common law war courts. Neither their procedure nor their jurisdiction has been prescribed by statute. It has been adopted in each instance to the need that called it forth. In this decision the Supreme Court upheld the trial of a military spouse (civilian) by a military commission. The spouse was convicted of murdering her husband while he was stationed in U.S. occupied Germany following World War II.

[11] The Board found that the facts charged were true, and that when captured Major Andre had in his possession papers containing intelligence, for the enemy, and reported their conclusion that 'Major Andre . . . ought to be considered as a Spy from the enemy, and that agreeable to the law and usage of nations . . . he ought to suffer death.' Major Andre was hanged on October 2, 1780. Proceedings of a Board of General Officers Respecting Major John Andre, Sept. 29, 1780, printed at Philadelphia in 1780. *See generally*, W. Winthrop, *Military Law and Precedents* (2nd ed. 1920 reprint) at 832. There were other trials in the Revolutionary War. *See also* Maj. Timothy C. MacDonnell, *Military Commissions and Courts Martial: A Brief Discussion Between the Constitutional and Jurisdictional Distinctions Between the Two Courts*. Army Law 19 (March 2002).

[12] Winthrop, *supra* n.10 at 832. *See also* Maj. Michael D. Lacey, *Military Commissions. A Historical Survey,* Army Law 41 (March 2002).

[13] Military tribunals were employed in the war with Mexico despite the fact that Congress never formally declared war. The war broke out when Texas, an American settled province of Mexico that had broken away in 1836, was annexed by the United States in 1845. Congress adopted the Act of Congress of May 13, 1846 which did not formally declare war, but recognized a defacto "state of war as existing by the act of the Republic of Mexico." *See* Maj. Michael A. Newton, *Continuum Crimes: Military Jurisdiction over Foreign Nationals who Commit International Crimes*, 153 *Mil. L. Rev.* 1, 20 (1996). *See also, General Orders*, No. 20 of February 19, 1847, reprinted in Appendix I of Military Government and Martial Law. Among the offenses tried by military commission were "assassination, murder, poisoning, rape, or the attempt to commit either, malicious stabbing or maiming, malicious assault or battery, robbery, theft, the wanton desecration of churches, cemeteries, and the destruction, except by order of a superior officer, of public or private property, whether committed by Mexicans or other civilians in Mexico against individuals of the U.S. military forces, or by such individuals against such individuals, or against Mexicans or civilians; as well as the purchase by Mexicans or civilians in Mexico, from soldiers, of horses, arms, ammunition, equipments or clothing."

[14] *See* Presidential Proclamation of September 24, 1862 cited in *Ex Parte Milligan*, 71 U.S. (4 Wall) 2, 15-16 (1866). Military Commissions were used during the Civil War to try Confederate

soldiers who had shed their uniforms in attempts to take over civilian ships or commit acts of sabotage.

[15] *See Ex Parte Quirin*, 317 U.S. 1, n.10 at 32 (1942).

[16] *Id.* n.10 at 33.

[17] *Id.*

[18] *Id.* n.10 at 32-33.

[19] *Id.* For reference to other cases where military commissions were employed during the Civil War, *see* Winthrop, *supra* n.9 at 1310-11.

[20]*Ex Parte Milligan*, 71 U.S. (4 Wall) 121 (1866). The Supreme Court did not take up the case until active hostilities had ceased and civil order had generally returned.

[21] *Id.* at 127. The Supreme Court offered the following additional reasoning. "It will be borne in mind that this is not a question of the power to proclaim martial law, when war exists in a community and the courts and civil authorities are overthrown. Nor is it a question what rule a military commander, at the head of his army, can impose on states in rebellion to cripple their resources and quell the insurrection. . . . Martial law cannot arise from a threatened invasion. The necessity must be actual and present; the invasion real, such as effectively closes the courts and deposes the civil administration." Future President James Garfield who presented Milligan's brief wrote about a decision supporting Milligan: It will establish forever this truth, of inestimable value to us and to mankind, that a republic can wield a vast engine of war without breaking down the safeguards of liberty; can suppress insurrection, and put down rebellion, however formidable, without destroying the bulwarks of law; can by the might of its armed millions, preserve and defend both nationality and liberty. *See* William Rehnquist, *All the Laws But One: Civil Liberties in Wartime* (New York: Alfred A. Knopf, 1988) at 22.

[22] *Military Commissions*, 11 Op. Atty Gen. 297; 1865 U.S. AG LEXIS 36 (July 1865).

[23] 11 Op. Atty Gen. 297; 1865 U.S. AG LEXIS 36, § 13-14. The Attorney General opined:
The law and usage of war contemplate that soldiers have a high sense of personal honor. The true soldier is proud to feel and to know that his enemy possesses personal honor, and will conform and be obedient to the laws of war. In a spirit of justice, and with a wise appreciation of such feelings, the laws of war protect the character and honor of an open enemy. When by the fortunes of war one open enemy is thrown into the hands and power of another, and is charged with dishonorable conduct and a breach of the laws of war, he must be tried according to the usages of war. Justice and fairness say that an open enemy to whom dishonorable conduct is imputed, has a right to demand a trial. If such a demand can be rightfully made, surely it cannot be rightfully refused. It is to be hoped that the military authorities of this country will never refuse such a demand, because there is no act of Congress that authorizes it. In time of war the law and usage of war authorize it, and they are a part of the law of the land.

[24] *See* John Dean, "Military Tribunals: A Long and Mostly Honorable History," *Find Law's Writ*, December 7, 2001 at 2.

[25] *Id.*

[26]*Mudd v. Caldera*, 134 F. Supp. 2d 138, 140 (2001). The court decided that. . . . It was not Mr. Lincoln who was assassinated but the Commander-in-Chief of the Army for military reasons. I find no difficulty, therefore, in classing the offense as a military one and with this opinion arrive at the necessary conclusion that the proper tribunal for the trial of those engaged in it was a military one.

[27] *Id.* at 146 (reading together *Ex Parte Milligan and Ex Parte Quirin*).

[28] See In re *Yamashita*, 327 U.S. 1 (1946).

[29] *Id.* at 5-6. In *Yamashita*, the Military Commission heard 286 witnesses and over 3000 pages of testimony in a period just over five weeks.

[30] *Id.* at 11.

[31] *Id.* at 12. Although a formal state of war had been proclaimed by Congress, peace had not been agreed upon or proclaimed. Therefore the President retained full war power as Commander-in-Chief to appoint and put into effect military tribunals, even after hostilities had ceased, but before the official end of the war when peace was officially proclaimed.

[32]*Ex Parte Quirin*, 317 U.S. 1 (1942).

[33] Presidential Proclamation No. 2561, July 2, 1942, 7 Fed. Reg. 5101, 56 Stat. 1964. It is of interest to note that the military order issued by President Roosevelt in 1942 which establishes a military commission to try the eight German saboteurs served as a model for President Bush in establishing a military commission to try terrorists post September 11.

[34] The law of war in traditional international law "prescribes the rights and obligations of belligerents and defines the status and relation, not only of enemies . . . whether or not in arms . . . but also of persons under military government and martial law and persons simply resident or being upon the theatre of war, and which authorizes their trial and punishment when offenders." Such laws and customs would be especially taken into consideration by Military Commissions. See Winthrop, *Military Law and Precedents,* Supra, at 773 and Louis Fisher *Military Tribunals: The Quirin Precedent.* Congressional Research Service, March 26, 2002 at 5.

[35] *Ex Parte Quirin*, 47 F. Supp. 431 (D.D.C. 1942).

[36] *Ex Parte Quirin*, 317 U.S. at 25-26.

[37] *Id.* at 28. Indeed, this very same language is cited by the court in the *Padilla* case providing broad support for the President as Commander-in-Chief. *Padilla v. Bush*, 233 F. Supp. 2d 564, 595-96 (S.D.N.Y. 2002). The Fourth Circuit in *Hamdi v. Rumsfeld*, 296 F.3d 278, 281-82 (4th Cir. 2002), ruled that the President has broad authority as Commander-in-Chief to declare someone an unlawful combatant. The U.S. Supreme Court in *Hamdi v. Rumsfeld*, 542 U.S. __ (2004), 124 S. Ct. 2633 (2004), No. 03-6696, acknowledged that the President as Commander-in-Chief did have the authority to designate citizens as enemy combatants, relying upon the congressional authorization for the use of Military Force and *Quirin* as precedent. See Chapter IV at 88 for a discussion of *Padilla*, and Chapter V at 150 for the discussion of the U.S. Supreme Court decision in *Hamdi*.

[38] *Id.* at 29-37.

20

[39] *Ex Parte Milligan,* 71 U.S. 2 (1866) at 121. Four of the justices concurred in the result, but based their decision on construction of a statute suspending the writ of habeas corpus. In a strongly worded opinion by Chief Justice Salmon P. Chase, the four concurring justices affirmed the power of Congress to provide for trial and punishment by military commission even in states where civilian courts were open, and concluded that the power superceded any of the amendments in the Bill of Rights. *Id.* at 132, 137-138. In *Quirin,* one of the defendants claimed U.S. citizenship. Assuming this to be the case, the *Quirin* Court stated, "Citizenship in the United States of an enemy belligerent does not relieve him from the consequences of a belligerency which is unlawful because in violation of the law of war." *Quirin* at 37. The *Quirin* Court opined that Milligan, as a non-belligerent, was not subject to the law of war, and therefore not amenable to trial by a military commission.

At least with respect to citizens, the *Quirin* Court seems to have drawn a distinction based on the status of the offender. The *Quirin* defendants were combatants, that is, members of the German armed forces, who sneaked behind enemy lines and shed their uniforms with the intent to commit sabotage against U.S. defense facilities. Lambden Milligan, on the other hand, was never a member of the enemy forces (although he was, allegedly, a member of a secret society in the north that intended to overthrow the government). His offenses were otherwise similar to those of the *Quirin* defendants: communicating with the enemy and conspiring to seize government munitions and to free confederate prisoners of war.

[40] *Id.* at 46.

[41] *See* Rehnquist, *All the Laws But One: Civil Liberties in Wartime,* (New York: Alfred A. Knopf, 1988) *supra* at 222, 224-25. It is also of significance to note the action taken by Hawaiian authorities after the bombing of Pearl Harbor in declaring martial law, the closing of the civil courts, and the application of military tribunals to prosecute ordinary crimes. *See also,* Tony Mauro, *Historic High Court Ruling is Troublesome Model for Modern Terror Trials,* American Lawyer Media (November 19, 2001). Five years later, in *Duncan v. Kahanamoku,* 327 U.S. 304 (1946), the Supreme Court announced that martial law could not justify replacing civil courts with military tribunals.

[42] *See* Jan E. Aldykiewicz, "Authority to Court Martial Non-US Military Personnel for Serious Violations of International Humanitarian Law Committed During Internal Armed Conflicts," 167 *Mil. L. Rev.* 74 (2001).

[43] The international tribunal was created, and the crimes within its jurisdiction spelled out, in the London Charter of August 8, 1945. The tribunal consisted of representatives from the major allied powers—the United States, the U.S.S.R., Great Britain, and France. The accused were charged with a combination of offenses labeled: crimes against humanity, crimes against peace ("planning, preparation, initiation or waging of a war of aggression . . . ") and war crimes. The tribunal lasted from November 20, 1945 to October 1, 1946. Twelve of the twenty-two defendants were convicted and sentenced to death, seven were convicted and sentenced to terms in prison ranging from ten years to life and three were acquitted. *See* Charter of the International Military Tribunal, Aug. 8, 1945, art. 16, 82 U.N.T.S. 279; Charter of the Military Tribunal for the Far East, Jun. 19, 1946 art. 9, 4 Bevans 20. For a critique of some aspects of the Nuremberg trials regarding standards of proof and rules of evidence, *see* H. K. Thompson, Jr., and Henry Strutz, *Doenitz at Nuremberg: A Reprisal* (New York: Amber Pub. Corp., 1976).

[44] U.S. Const. art. I, § 8, cl. 10.

[45] U.S. Const. art. II.

[46] *See* 11 Op. Atty. Gen. 305.

[47] *See* Winthrop at 833.

[48] 10 U.S.C. § 836.

[49] *See* G. O. 20 of 1847 (Gen. Scott).

[50] *In re Yamashita,* 327 U.S. 1 (1946) *supra* n.31.

[51] *See* Winthrop at 838.

[52] *Ex Parte Quirin supra* n.35 and *Johnson v. Eisentranger,* 339 U.S. 763 (1950); *also see, Madsen v. Kinsella,* 343 U.S. 341 (1952) *supra* n.10 upholding the jurisdiction of military commissions to try civilians in occupied territories.

[53] *See* Winthrop at 839.

[54] *See Mudd v. Caldera,* 134 F. Supp. *Id.* 138, 140 (2001) *supra* n.26.

[55] *See* Winthrop at 839.

[56] *See The Prize Cases,* 67 U.S. (6 Mem.) 635, 668, 670 (1863). The court declared "If war be made by invasion of a foreign nation, the President is not only authorized but bound to resist force with force. He does not initiate war, but is bound to accept the challenge without waiting for any special legislative authority." Further, . . . whether the President in fulfilling his duties as Commander-in-Chief in suppressing an insurrection . . . is to accord to them the character of belligerents, is a question to be decided by him, and this Court must be governed by the decisions and acts of the political department of the Government to which the power was entrusted.

[57] *See* Winthrop at 843.

[58] 1 Wallace 243.

[59] *See* Winthrop at 846.

[60] *Madsen v. Kinsella,* 343 U.S. 341 (1952).

CHAPTER II

Military Commissions, Al-Qaida and the Law of Partial War

After the simultaneous terror attacks of September 11, 2001, on New York, Washington D.C., and Pennsylvania, the United States Congress in a demonstration of bipartisan unity passed The Joint Resolution, the Authorization for Use of Military Force,[1] which was supported by every member of the Senate and, with one exception, every member of the House of Representatives. Among other things it authorized the President:

> Under the Constitution to take action to deter and prevent acts of international terrorism against the United States . . . [and] authorized . . . to use all necessary and appropriate force against those nations, organizations, or persons he determines planned, authorized, committed, or aided the terrorist attacks that occurred on September 11, 2001 or harbored such organizations or persons, in order to prevent any future acts of international terrorism against the United States by such nations, organizations or persons.[2]

The Preamble to the Resolution establishes that the acts of September 11 were attacks against the United States, and were acts of war that render it both necessary and appropriate that the United States exercise its right to self-defense and this is reinforced by the actions taken in the United Nations and regional defense organizations who responded in similar fashion.[3] It can be reasonably suggested that Congress's authorization to use "all necessary and appropriate force" includes both a legal and practical ratification for the Military Order of November 13, 2001, as a vital component of the war against terrorism.[4]

The focus of this section of the study is to examine the role of President Bush as Chief Executive and Commander-in-Chief under Article II of the United States Constitution to issue his military orders on military commissions in an age of international terrorism, and the jurisdiction of United States Courts to

24

determine the sovereignty of Guantanamo Bay where the military commissions will operate.

* * * * * * * * * *

The United States Supreme Court in the *Quirin* decision made clear that a state of war was necessary before individuals arrested in the United States could be subjected to trial by military commissions, yet it did not specifically discuss how the state of war was to come about.

The Constitution grants to Congress the formal power to "declare war."[5] That phrase is highly distinguishable from the power to make war, to employ military force, which is constitutionally vested in the President as Chief Executive and Commander-in-Chief of the armed forces.[6] A few basic principles are discernable, both from the Constitution's text and from historical practice: (1) the Commander-in-Chief clause relates to war powers and is a shared duty and power with Congress; (2) the President is able to exercise his duties as Commander-in-Chief so as to give him extraordinary powers, powers that by and large are limited by the workings of the political process; (3) this limitation is because the courts speaking generally, either refuse to, or uphold when they do rule, exercises of the power. The Commander-in-Chief power is open ended, malleable, and limited far more by politics then it is by law.

Early American Experience—Helvidius/Pacificus Dispute

Originally, as perceived by Alexander Hamilton in *Federalist 69*, the President would exercise his Commander-in-Chief authority "to nothing more than the supreme command and direction of a military and naval forces, as first General and first Admiral of the Confederacy," while that of the British King extends to the declaring of war and to the raising and regulating of fleets and armies, which means that the clause had only military significance. Hamilton clearly rejected the view that the authority extended to the declaring of war and to the raising and regulating of fleets of armies, powers which would belong to the Congress.

As to the actual meaning of declaring of war, the provision became a matter of dispute for Hamilton and James Madison in the Helvidius/Pacificus debate, over whether President Washington had the power, on his own authority, to issue a proclamation of neutrality with respect to the war between Britain and Jacobin France in 1793. Although the proclamation's author, Attorney General Randolph, had purposively avoided using the word neutrality, it was challenged by French sympathizers as having extended beyond the President's legitimate constitutional authority. Its defense was taken by Hamilton who wrote under the pseudonym Pacificus in several articles that appeared in the Gazette of the United States. Hamilton's central argument is that the Commander-in-Chief provision of Article II is a grant of power and by inference there are other powers that are implied in this general grant of authority including control over the direction of foreign policy, which is inherently an executive function.[7] He cites his position in the following context:

> This serves as an example of the right of the executive, in certain cases, to determine the condition of the nation, though it may, in its consequences, affect the exercise of the power of the legislature to declare war. Nevertheless, the executive cannot thereby control the exercise of that power. The legislature is still free to perform its duties, according to its own sense of them; though the executive, in the exercise of its constitutional powers, may establish an antecedent state of things, which ought to weigh in the legislative decision. The division of the executive power in the Constitution creates a *concurrent* authority in the cases to which it relates.[8]

The President has all the power that the facts of international intercourse may at anytime make conveniently applicable if the Constitution does not vest them elsewhere in clear precise terms. This normally means that the initiative in the foreign field rests with the President. He is able to confront the Congress with faits accomplis at will, although Congress is under no constitutional obligation to back up such faits accomplis or to support the policies giving rise to them.

Jefferson was supportive of the proclamation but he was very concerned about Hamilton's constitutional perspectives and he called on Madison to refute them. "Nobody answered him and his doctrines are taken for confessed. For God's sake my dear Sir, take up your pen, select the most striking heresies and cut him to pieces in face of the public."[9] Madison responds as Helvidius in his letter, which also appeared in the Gazette. His constitutional attack on Hamilton focuses on the attempt to link the Presidency to that of the British crown.

> Thus it appears that by whatever standard we try this doctrine, it must be condemned as no less vicious in theory than it would be dangerous in practice. It is countenanced neither by the writers on law; nor by the nature of the powers themselves; nor by any general arrangements, or particular expressions, or plausible analogies, to be found in the constitution.
> Whence then can the writer have borrowed it?
> There is but one answer to this question.
> The power of making treaties and the power of declaring war, are *royal prerogatives* in the *British government*, and are accordingly treated as *executive prerogatives* by British *commentators. . . .*[10]

Madison's view is that the right to determine foreign policy of the United States is with Congress by virtue of its power to declare war, and that the powers of the President in the area of foreign policy are instrumental and involve no greater range of discretion then the determination of matters of fact. The duties of advocacy required of Madison that he show that if a power was claimable for the President on sound constitutional grounds, Congress was constitutionally obligated by the President's exercise of it, for it could then follow that, if the President's proclamation was valid, it took from Congress the power to decide between war and peace, a conclusion manifestly at variance with Congress's possession of the war declaring power. The proclamation therefore was not valid, nor was the conception of the presidential power on which it was based, a constitutionally tenable one.[11]

These early constitutional disagreements between Helvidius/Pacificus included the question of whether a formal declaration of war was necessary for any U.S. military action. During the conflict between the United States and the

Barbary Pirates, for instance, the Jefferson Administration took the position that a declaration by Congress was necessary before the United States could seize Algerian vessels on the high seas. Alexander Hamilton took particular exception to this view writing that a state of war, "between two nations, is completely produced by the act of one . . . it required no concurrent act of the other." He further noted that the Constitution did not incorporate such a rule claiming that "the framers of it would have blushed at a provision, so repugnant to good sense, so inconsistent with national safety and inconvenience . . . [W]hen a foreign nation declares or openly and avowedly makes war upon the United States, they are then by the very fact, already at war, and any declaration on the part of Congress is nugatory: it is at least unnecessary."[12]

Hamilton's view was recognized by the Supreme Court in the so-called Quasi-war, a naval war that erupted between France and the United States in 1797. In instances involving the disposition of ships captured by the U.S. Navy during the conflict, the Court acknowledged that a limited war could be waged in the absence of a formal declaration but was covered by extant federal statutes. The first court opinion, *Bas v. Tangy*, written by Justice Samuel Chase stated: "Congress is empowered to declare a general war or Congress may wage a limited war; limited in place, in objects and in time. If a general war is declared its extent and operation are only restricted and regulated by the jus belli forming a part of the law of nations; but if a partial war is waged, the extent and operation depend on our municipal [domestic] laws."[13]

Discussing the war power of Congress in the *Talbot* case, Chief Justice John Marshall wrote:

> The whole powers of war being by the Constitution of the United States, rested in Congress . . . Congress may authorize general hostilities, in which case the general laws of war apply to our situation; or partial war, in which case, the laws of war as they actually apply to our situation, must be noticed.[14]

The act of Congress considered by the Court authorized the capture of armed vessels acting either under the authority of the French government, or under the pretense of authority for the purpose of committing depredations on commercial vessels.[15] A reasonable interpretation in this instance from Chief Justice Marshall's discussion is that the War Powers Clause enabled Congress to authorize hostilities against a particular military activity without having to declare a full-scale war against a state in the traditional law of war sense.[16]

What we learn from these early experiences is that all war powers are available to the government when there is a formal declaration of war exercised by the United States Congress. However, there may be the use of partial or limited war with appropriate measures utilized in the absence of such a formal action taken by the Congress. The measures appropriate to such levels of hostilities include the right to subject unlawful combatants to military courts for trial purposes. Since the laws of war dealing with unlawful combatants are so basic to any level of hostilities dealing with questions of who may lawfully take part in a conflict and how they must be treated upon capture or defeat, they always apply when the United States is involved in an armed struggle.

It has been argued that the devastating acts of September 11 were of such proportion in both their purpose and effect as to be considered war crimes, and as such commenced an armed conflict which provided President Bush with support to legally subject the unlawful combatants, members and supporters of al-Qaida and the Taliban, to trial by military commissions where Congress authorized hostilities even though it had not formally declared war. What this means is that catastrophic terrorist acts are of such magnitude that they rise to the level of war crimes.[17]

* * * * * * * * *

Title 10, U.S. Code

In his order authorizing military commissions to try the September 11 terrorists President Bush cited the Joint Resolution adopted by the Congress authorizing him to take all appropriate measures against the terrorists and Title 10 of the U.S. Code, which authorized President Roosevelt to use military tribunals to try the German saboteurs in WWII. President Bush specifically referenced sections 821 and 836 of Title 10.

Section 818, qualifying section 821 says, "General courts-martial also have jurisdiction to try any person who by the law of war is subject to trial by a military tribunal and may adjudge any punishment by the law of war."

Section 821 says: "The provisions of this chapter conferring jurisdiction upon courts-martial do not deprive military commissions, provost courts, or other military tribunals of concurrent jurisdiction with respect to offenders or offenses that by statute or by the law of war may be tried by military commissions, provost courts or other military tribunals."

Section 836 gives the President exclusive authority to set procedures for such trials: "Pretrial, trial, and post trial procedures, including modes of proof, for cases arising under this chapter triable in courts-martial, military commissions and other military tribunals, and procedures for courts of inquiry, may be prescribed by the President by regulations which shall, so far as he considers practicable, apply the principles of law and rules of evidence generally recognized in the trial of criminal cases in the United States district courts, but which may not be contrary to, or inconsistent with, this chapter."[18]

President Bush confronted several uncharted waters with few navigational aids at his disposal in issuing the November 13 Military Order because, as discussed previously, Congress had not formally declared war, and critics questioned whether the acts committed by al-Qaida were war crimes and violations of the law of war. Furthermore, Sections 821 and 836 do not specifically authorize the President to create military commissions. Rather, authority is provided to set procedures after the military commission has been established through some other law making source.

About Al-Qaida

Al-Qaida (the Base) is a transnational non-state terrorist organization principally founded by Osama bin Laden and a group of his loyal supporters,

ered in Afghanistan and Peshamar, Pakistan in the late
m 1991 to approximately 1996 the leadership of al-Qaida
the Sudan where bin Laden helped to finance the
government's war against separatists in the south. He was successful in
developing an operational infrastructure that supported terrorism while
maintaining a presence in over fifty nations. Bin Laden was successful during this
period in setting up training camps and weapons and supply depots in Sudan that
he used to support al-Qaida. In 1996 al-Qaida was sponsored by the Taliban
government of Afghanistan and at all relevant times members remained
supremely loyal to their emir (or prince) Osama bin Laden.

Al-Qaida violently opposed the United States for several reasons. First, the
United States was regarded as an "infidel" because it was not governed in a
manner consistent with the group's extremist interpretation of Islam. Second, the
United States was viewed as providing essential support for other "infidel"
governments and institutions, particularly the governments of Saudi Arabia and
Egypt, the nation of Israel, and the United Nations organization, which were
regarded as enemies of the group. Third, al-Qaida opposed the involvement of the
United States armed forces in the Gulf War in 1991 and in Operation Restore
Hope in Somalia in 1992 and 1993. In particular, al-Qaida opposed the continued
presence of American military forces in Saudi Arabia (and elsewhere on the Saudi
Arabian peninsula) following the Gulf War. Fourth, al-Qaida opposed the United
States Government because of the arrest, conviction and imprisonment of persons
belonging to the organization of its affiliated terrorist groups or those with whom
it worked. For these and other reasons, Osama bin Laden declared a jihad, or holy
war, against the United States, which would be carried out through al-Qaida and
its affiliated organizations.

One of the principal goals of al-Qaida was to drive the United States
armed forces out of Saudi Arabia (and elsewhere on the Saudi Arabian peninsula)
and Somalia by violence. Members of al-Qaida issued <u>fatwahs</u> (rulings on Islamic
law) indicating the such attacks were both proper and necessary.

Al-Qaida functioned both on its own and through some of the terrorist organizations that operated under its umbrella, including: Egyptian Islamic Jihad, which was led by Ayman al-Zawahiri, and at times, the Islamic Group (also known as "el Gamaa Islama" or simply "Gamaa't"), and a number of jihad groups in other countries, including the Sudan, Egypt, Saudi Arabia, Yemen, Somalia, Eritrea, Djibouti, Afghanistan, Pakistan, Bosnia, Croatia, Albania, Algeria, Tunisia, Lebanon, the Philippines, Tajikistan, Azerbaijan, and the Kashmiri region of India and the Chechnyan region of Russia. Al-Qaida also maintained sleeper cells and personnel in a number of countries to facilitate activities, including in Kenya, Tanzania, the United Kingdom, Germany, Canada, Malaysia, and the United States.

Al-Qaida had a command and control structure, which included a majlis al-shura (or consultation council), which discussed and approved major undertakings, including terrorist operations. It had a "military committee" which considered and approved "military" matters such as proposed targets for attack and support operations, a Sharia and "political committee" responsible for the issuance of the fatwahs authorizing terrorist attacks; a "finance committee" which undertook fundraising and budgetary support for training camps, housing costs, living expenses and travel; a "foreign purchases committee" responsible for acquiring weapons, explosives and technical equipment; a "security committee" responsible for physical protection, intelligence collection and counter intelligence, and an "information committee" responsible for propaganda. Because of the many attributes of the traditional nation state that al-Qaida possessed it has been labeled a "virtual state"[19] with the added ability to evade the norms of international law since it has no fixed boundaries. The al-Qaida virtual state had a military, treasury, a foreign policy, and links with other nation states and terrorist organizations.[20]

Since at least 1989, al-Qaida sponsored, managed, and/or financially supported training camps in Afghanistan, which were used to instruct members and associates of al-Qaida and its affiliated terrorist groups in the use of firearms, explosives, chemical weapons, and other weapons of mass destruction. In addition to providing training in the use of various weapons, these camps were used to conduct operational planning against United States targets around the world and experiments in the use of chemical and biological weapons. These camps were also used to train others in security and counterintelligence methods, such as the use of codes and passwords, and to teach members and associates of al-Qaida about traveling to perform operations. For example, al-Qaida instructed its members and associates to dress in "Western" attire and to use other methods to avoid detection by security officials. The group also taught its members and associates to monitor media reporting of its operations to determine the effectiveness of their terrorist activities.

About the Taliban

The Taliban is a fundamentalist Islamic group that assumed control of a large part of Afghanistan and became the defacto government of Afghanistan after the departure of Soviet troops in 1989. The Taliban's senior leader was Mullah Mohammed Omar and its political leader was Mullah Mohammed Rabani. The principal opposition to the Taliban were mostly Uzbek and Tajik Afghan tribes from Northwestern Afghanistan. Despite support from Iran, Turkey, Russia, Uzbekistan, Kazakhstan, Kyrgyzstan and Tujikistan, these tribes were soundly defeated on the battlefield in almost every battle with the Taliban, which was backed diplomatically by Pakistan, Saudi Arabia and the United Arab Emirates. Most of the international community, including the United States and the United Nations, refused to recognize the Taliban regime.

Al-Qaida and Taliban Belligerency Status

In the days immediately following the September 11 attacks, a conclusive body of evidence pointed directly to the al-Qaida organization as the perpetrators of the attacks and to the Afghanistan Taliban as the state supporter of the terrorist organization. President Bush offered the Taliban government a time certain ultimatum to turn over the al-Qaida leader and to shut down all terrorist camps in Afghanistan. In a speech to a joint session of Congress on September 20, 2001, the President demanded:

> And tonight, the United States of America makes the following demands on the Taliban: Deliver to the United States authorities all the leaders of al-Qa'eda who hide in your land . . . [c]lose immediately and permanently every terrorist training camp in Afghanistan, and hand over every terrorist, and every person in their support structure, to appropriate authorities. Give the United States full access to terrorist training camps, so we can make sure they are no longer operating. These demands are not open to negotiation or discussion. The Taliban must act, and act immediately. They will hand over the terrorists, or they will suffer their fate.[21]

The Taliban leadership refused to comply and the United States in conjunction with NATO and numerous allies conducted a military campaign in Afghanistan, which deposed the Taliban, destroyed the al-Qaida camps and dismantled most of the terrorist infrastructure in that nation by the end of December 2001. Approximately 1,000 al-Qaida and Taliban fighters were turned over to the United States for disposition because they were either too dangerous to release or were suspected of committing war crimes. About 660 were transported to Guantanamo Bay in Cuba for internment, while others were to be held in custody in Afghanistan until specific charges were levied against them for associated war crimes.

Every violation of the law of war is a war crime. A deliberate attack on non-combatant civilians violates the law of war and customary law of war. The deliberate kidnapping and killing of non-combatant civilians on September 11 were violations of the Geneva Conventions of 1949.[22] The law of war applies to nonstate actors who may be part of rebel groups or may be part of rebel groups within the nation.[23] Further, a reasonable argument can be made that the al-Qaida who planned and conducted the September 11 attacks were involved in the commission of acts of war without complying with the laws of war for recognition as a belligerent and therefore were acting as unlawful belligerent.[24]

They failed to satisfy any of the requirements for being treated as lawful combatants, such as wearing a uniform or other fixed emblem(s) recognizable at a distance or carrying their arms openly.[25] Additionally, there is the fact that al-Qaida terrorists fought alongside the Taliban forces in an internationally recognized conflict in Afghanistan against United States military forces and those of our allies, which satisfy requirements under the law of war and the Constitution that a state of war exists.

As to the captured Taliban fighters, the United States determined that they were likewise not entitled to prisoner of war status under the Geneva Conventions because of their failure to comply with the Conventions' criterion which requires lawful combatants to wear distinctive military insignia, i.e., uniforms which would make them distinguishable from the civilian population at a distance.[26] In finding that the Taliban "have not effectively distinguished themselves from civilian population," the United States also added that the Taliban fighters had further forfeited any special status because they had "adopted and provided support to the unlawful terrorist objectives of the al-Qaida. While the latter finding would not necessarily indicate that the Taliban fighters would not be entitled to prisoner of war status, the former finding would. The Bush administration indicated that all detainees were to be designated as 'enemy combatants' and were to be treated in accordance with the humanitarian concerns set out in the Geneva Conventions even though they were not entitled to the additional protections the Geneva Conventions gives to prisoners of war."[27]

Given the fact that the al-Qaida and Taliban detainees are not prisoners of war, and assuming that sufficient evidence is available to believe that particular individual(s) have committed war crimes, than the appropriate forum available for prosecution predicated upon the November 13, 2001 Military Order issued by President Bush, is the military commission. That order specifically applies to certain "non citizens" who engaged in terrorist acts against the United States or who aided or abetted in terrorist acts against the United States.[28]

An individual determination will have to be made whether the detainee(s) are members(s) of al-Qaida, the Taliban, or both, and the position of the individuals within each organization. It would probably be impractical to include all common foot soldiers of the Taliban under the rubric of "enemy combatant" for the purpose of detention, charge and prosecution by military commission. The case of Taliban leaders who may have harbored terrorists is far different from that of the rank and file. Knowing participation in the harboring of al-Qaida operatives would certainly provide a stronger justification for the application of a military commission.

A question exists as to whether mere membership in al-Qaida, without more, is sufficient for identification as an "enemy combatant" subject to the jurisdiction of military commissions. It would seem that any foreign citizen who can be linked by competent evidence to the September 11 attacks against civilians can be considered an "enemy combatant" subject to the jurisdiction of a military commission.

Jurisdiction of United States Courts

Challenging the constitutionality of properly constituted military commissions to try the al-Qaida terrorists for war crimes will undoubtedly prove unsuccessful. The American Bar Association (ABA) Task Force on Terrorism and Law concluded that the terror attacks of September 11, 2001 were violations of the law of war that would justify the use of military tribunals.[29]

Similarly, the New York State Bar Association in its *Report on Military Commissions* concluded that the "use of the November 13 orders—the President's convening of military commissions under defacto wartime emergency conditions to try non citizens outside the United States for alleged violations of the law of war is a valid exercise of his constitutional war powers as Commander in Chief and Chief Executive that finds ample support in case law and historical tradition."[30]

There are currently over 550 detainees from over forty countries who are being held by the United States Government at a site identified as Camp Delta at the United States Naval Air Station in Guantanamo Bay in Cuba. These prisoners were captured after the war in Afghanistan and neighboring Pakistan during Operation Enduring Freedom in the wake of the September 11 terrorist attacks. The Department of Defense has designated the war detainees as enemy combatants who do not qualify for prisoner of war status under the Geneva Conventions. Although approximately 190 prisoners have been released so far, many of the remaining detainees are still in legal, political, and geographical limbo because they have been held without formal charges having been presented against them despite the recent U.S. Supreme Court decision in *Rasul* and *Al-Odah*.[31] They have also been denied access to legal counsel.

The detainees sought to invoke the jurisdiction of United States courts to challenge their incarceration. The United States Court of Appeals for the District of Columbia Circuit ordered that the territory where they were held is not part of the sovereignty of the United States,[32] and the United States Court of Appeals for the Ninth Circuit ruled that Guantanamo is clearly under the jurisdiction of the United States and that the detainee(s) were entitled to protections of United States law.[33] The United States Supreme Court granted certiorari in the District of Columbia Circuit Court of Appeals decision and reversed that decision.[34]

The detainees have argued that they are not enemy combatants or enemy aliens, and have never been members of al-Qaida or any other terrorist group. Prior to their detention, they claim that they did not commit any violent act against any American person, nor espouse any violent act against any American person or property. They insist that they had no involvement, direct or indirect, in either the terrorist attacks on the United States of September 11, 2001, or any act of international terrorism attributed by the United States to al-Qaida or any terrorist group.[35]

The D.C. Court of Appeals and Guantanamo Jurisdiction

The D.C. Court of Appeals addressed whether the Supreme Court's decision in *Johnson v. Eisentrager*,[36] which interpreted events that began in China during the closing days of the war between the United States and Japan, is applicable or distinguishable from Guantanamo.

Eisentrager, using the pseudonym Ludwig Ehrhardt, ran a German intelligence office based in Shanghai known as Bureau Ehrhardt. After Germany's surrender on V-E Day, May 8, 1945, but before the surrender of Japan on August 15, 1945, twenty-one German nationals in China assisted Japanese forces fighting against the United States. Eisentrager and his fellow spies signed agreements to assist the Japanese in exchange for money and food, and supplied Japanese forces with intercepts of U.S. naval communications, German made aircraft parts, and thousands of propaganda leaflets aimed at U.S. troops.

In the early part of 1946 Eisentrager and twenty-six other German intelligence officers, press agents, and diplomats accredited to the Japanese puppet government in Nanking had been rounded up by the American military mission in China. A United States military commission headquartered in Shanghai tried and convicted them for violating the laws of war and transferred them to Landsberg prison in Germany which was under the control of the United States Army.[37]

The defendants disputed the jurisdiction of the military commission since China was not under United States occupation. They contended that they should be tried in a Chinese court but the commission overruled their position.

On April 26, 1948, Eisentrager on behalf of himself and the twenty others, sought writs of habeas corpus in the United States District Court for the District of Columbia, claiming violations of the Constitution, other laws of the United States, and the 1929 Geneva Convention.[38] The district court dismissed for lack of jurisdiction, but a three-judge panel of the court of appeals reversed on the ground that the Constitution applied not only to United States territory but also to the conduct of U.S. government officials anywhere.[39]

The Supreme Court, agreeing with the district court, held that "the privilege of litigation" had not been extended to the German prisoners. The prisoners therefore had no right to petition for a writ of habeas corpus: "These prisoners at no relevant time were within any territory over which the United States is sovereign, and the scenes of their offense, their capture, their trial and their punishment were all beyond the territorial jurisdiction of any court of the United States."[40]

The *Eisentrager* Court also stressed that judicial review of the claims of aliens seized overseas by the military in time of war would interfere with the President's authority as Commander-in-Chief which has been deemed throughout our history as essential to wartime security.[41]

The Court stated that judicial proceedings would create a conflict "between judicial and military opinion" which would be highly comforting to enemies of the United States and which would diminish the prestige of any field commander as he was called to account in his own civil court, and would "direct his efforts and attention for the military offensive abroad to the legal defensive at home."[42]

The D.C. Circuit Court of Appeals acknowledged that the Supreme Court throughout its opinion referred to the *Eisentrager* prisoners as enemy aliens. "The Guantanamo detainees distinguish themselves from the German prisoners on the ground that they have not been charged and that the charges in *Eisentrager* are what rendered the prisoners enemies." The court agreed that none of the Guantanamo detainees were within the category of "enemy aliens," at least as *Eisentrager* used the term. They were nationals of Kuwait, Australia, or the United Kingdom. "Our war in response to the attacks of September 11, 2001, obviously is not against these countries. It is against a network of terrorists operating in secret throughout the world and often hiding among civilian populations."[43]

Nonetheless the Guantanamo detainees had much in common with the German prisoners in *Eisentrager*. They too were aliens, they too were captured during military operations, they were in a foreign country when captured, they were now abroad, they were in the custody of the American military, and they never had any presence in the United States.

Under *Eisentrager* the detainees are precluded from seeking habeas corpus relief in the courts of the United States. Constitutional rights including the right to a jury trial are not held by aliens outside the sovereign territory of the United States regardless of whether they are enemy aliens. The practical consequence is that no court in this country has jurisdiction to grant habeas relief to the Guantanamo detainees even if they have not been adjudicated enemies of the United States. "The Constitution does not entitle detainees to due process, and it does not permit the jurisdiction of our courts to test the constitutionality or the legality of restraints on their liberty."[44]

In a separate concurring opinion Judge Randolph Winter wrote:

> It is also of no moment that the detainees were captured without Congress having declared war against any foreign state.... The military actions ordered by the President with approval of Congress are continuing; those military actions are part of the war against the al-Qaida terrorist network, those actions constitute war.[45]

The Ninth Circuit Court of Appeals and Guantanamo Jurisdiction

In an opinion written by Judge Stephen Reinhardt and joined by Senior United States District Judge for the Northern District Milton Shadur, sitting by designation, the Ninth Circuit panel concluded that *Johnson v. Eisentrager* permitted the District Court for the Central District of California jurisdiction to hear the writ of habeas corpus because the prisoners were within the jurisdiction of the United States court system.

The panel stated that in times of national emergency it is the obligation of the Judicial Branch to ensure our nation's constitutional rules and principles and to prevent the "Executive Branch from running roughshod over the rights of citizens and aliens alike."[46] The majority could not accept the government's argument that the Executive possessed unchecked authority to detain individuals

40

indefinitely on territory under the "sole jurisdiction and control of the United States,"[47] without allowing for some form of recourse in the courts, or access to counsel. There existed no precedent for such a policy and *Eisentrager* neither required or authorized such action.[48] The panel position was that indefinite detention violated American jurisprudence, as well as, Article 5 of the Third Geneva Convention.[49]

The government maintained that habeas jurisdiction over Gherebi's petition was foreclosed by *Eisentrager* because the conditions were equivalent in terms of application of "enemy combatant" status in both cases. The driving issue on appeal related to the legal status of Guantanamo.

The government contended that the United States did not maintain sovereignty over Guantanamo because of the 1903 Lease agreement and the 1934 treaty continuing the agreement which ceded to the U.S. complete jurisdiction and control over the Base, but also recognized the continuance of ultimate sovereignty in Cuba, which meant that it fell outside U.S. sovereign territory.

The panel did not read *Eisentrager* as ruling that the prerequisite for the exercise of jurisdiction was sovereignty rather than territorial jurisdiction. The United States had throughout the twentieth century exercised "complete jurisdiction and control"[50] over the Base, and "we have acted as if we intend to retain the Base permanently, and have exercised the exclusive, unlimited right to use it as we wish, regardless of any restrictions contained in the Lease or continuing Treaty."[51]

The panel argued that *Eisentrager* strongly implied that territorial jurisdiction is sufficient to support habeas jurisdiction. Sovereignty therefore was not an essential prerequisite for habeas jurisdiction, rather territorial jurisdiction was enough.[52] The opinion stated that since we subject persons who commit crimes at Guantanamo to trial in United States Courts,[53] it was clear that the United States exercised exclusive control over Guantanamo and that by virtue of its exercise of such jurisdiction, habeas rights existed for all persons located at the Base.[54]

The panel further opined that even if *Eisentrager* required sovereignty, its decision that habeas jurisdiction existed would be the same because Guantanamo was part of the sovereign territory of the United States and both the language of the Lease and Treaty and the practical reality of U.S. authority and control over the Base supported that answer.[55] The United States possessed and exercised virtually all the attributes of sovereignty while Cuba retained only a residual or reversionary sovereignty interest, contingent on a possible future United States decision to surrender its complete jurisdiction and control.[56] The U.S. had acquired full dominion and control over Guantanamo as well as the right to purchase land and the power of eminent domain. The panel stated "that until such time as the United States determined to surrender its rights, it exercised full and exclusive executive, legislative and judicial control over the territory and Cuba retained no rights of any kind to do anything with respect to the Base."[57]

Since the United States insisted on using its right to use the territory for any and all purposes, and refused to recognize any limitation in its rights provided in the Lease and the continuing Treaty, sovereignty was complete over Guantanamo.[58] It would appear that there was no stronger example of the United State's exercise of "Supreme power" or the adverse nature of its occupying power, than this country's purposeful actions contrary to the terms of the Lease and over the vigorous objections of a powerless lessor.[59]

The panel would not accept the government's theory that it could imprison Gherebi indefinitely along with hundreds of other citizens of foreign countries, friendly nations among them, and "to do with the detainees whatever we pleased," without compliance with any rule of law, without permitting counsel, and without acknowledging any judicial forum in which its actions could be challenged. The panel stated that "prior to the current detention of prisoners at Guantanamo, the U.S. government never before asserted such a grave and startling proposition."[60] The government's position was without parallel and so extreme that it raised the gravest concerns under both American and international law.[61]   .

The panel refused to defer its decision until after the Supreme Court declared the pending Guantanamo detainee case in which certiorari had been granted.[62] The majority argued that the Supreme Court had always encouraged the Courts of Appeal to resolve issues properly before them in advance of their determination by the Supreme Court, reasoning that having a variety of considered perspectives will aid the Court's ultimate resolution of the issue in question.[63] The panel concluded that the district court erred in its holding based on *Johnson v. Eisentrager*, that no district court would have jurisdiction over Gherebi's habeas petition.

In her dissent Judge Susan Graber argued that the Ninth Circuit was bound by existing Supreme Court precedent, and since the issues were so important and difficult and the Supreme Court had decided to revisit them, "we should await the Supreme Court's imminent decision."[64] In Judge Graber's view the Supreme Court, and only the Supreme Court may, modify the sovereignty rule established in *Eisentrager*.[65] Guantanamo was the sovereign territory of Cuba and the treaty explained that "the United States recognizes the continuance of the ultimate sovereignty of the Republic of Cuba over the above described areas of land and water."[66] The United States, by terms of Article III of the Lease, is an occupier, which means it is a tenant rather than a landlord of Guantanamo.[67]

Judge Graber addressed the ability and willingness of the United States to violate the terms and conditions of the Lease and Treaty: "The fact that Cuba lacks the political or military might necessary to hold the United States responsible for breaching the Lease does not mean that the United States has not breached the Lease or that the Lease ceased to exist."[68] The ability to violate terms of an agreement with impunity does not render a party legally free to ignore the agreement and even if the United States violated the Lease, it simply is big enough and strong enough that Cuba has been unable to enforce its legal entitlements.[69]

Judge Graber's dissent forcefully addressed the issue of separation of powers. She suggested that both parties to the Guantanamo Lease and Treaties maintained that Guantanamo was a sovereign part of Cuba. Since the majority announced that the United States annexed Guantanamo "it has seriously compromised the very capacity of the President to speak with one voice in dealing with other governments."[70] Such an action has created an inconsistency in our nation's foreign policy, with "the Executive, which has primary responsibility in this field declaring that the United States is not sovereign over Guantanamo, and the Judiciary, which has no political accountability, declaring that it is."[71] This kind of action runs contrary to the intent of the framers of our Constitution, in her view, and treads upon a sensitive area of constitutional allocation of powers, where the need for the United States to speak with one voice in dealing with foreign nations is vital.[72] Judge Graber admonished the majority to back off and step lightly in this situation, and suggested that its ruling was an unwise and unwarranted extension of judicial authority in an arena belonging primarily to the executive branch.[73]

Judge Graber concluded her dissent by stating that the Ninth Circuit should defer to hear the Supreme Court's answer to the issue of whether the United States courts lack jurisdiction to consider challenges to the legality of the detention of foreign nationals captured abroad in connection with hostilities and incarcerated at the Guantanamo Bay Naval Base, Cuba.[74] In her view, if there was to be any change in the law it must come from the Supreme Court. If the court failed to provide a change, than it was left to the political branches of government, namely the Congress and executive branch, to act.

On November 10, 2003, when the United States Supreme Court granted cert for the *Rasul* and *Al-Odah* appeal, it agreed to only "examine the jurisdictional question at this stage,"[75] and would not consider whether the detentions were unconstitutional. Solicitor General Theodore B. Olson in the brief filed on behalf of the government insisted that these were not appropriate cases to be heard by the Supreme Court, and that the determination of sovereignty of a particular territory is not a question on which a court may second guess the political branches. Olson's position is clearly reflected in the six justices' majority opinion written by Justice Robert M. Jackson in *Eisentrager*. Jackson wrote that it would be difficult to devise more effective fettering of a field commander than to allow the very enemies he is ordered to reduce to submission to call him to account in his own civil courts.[76]

The lawyers for the Guantanamo detainees are asking the Supreme Court to adopt Justice Hugo Black's dissenting opinion in *Eisentrager*, which was joined by Justices Douglas and Burton. It contended that the Constitution should follow the American flag. Black argued that conquest by the United States, unlike conquest by many other nations, does not mean tyranny.

They also note that there are three key distinctions between their case and *Eisentrager's*. The first is that the Germans were tried by military commission, while the Guantanamo detainees had not faced any legal proceeding, military or civilian. Secondly, while Jackson's opinion rested on the fact that the Germans as citizens of a hostile power were enemy aliens under international law, the two Britains, two Australians, and twelve Kuwaitis contesting their detention at Guantanamo were citizens of friendly allies. Lastly, they argued China and Germany were clearly outside United States sovereignty, while Guantanamo through the lease to the United States has given it both jurisdiction and control.

Summary

While the Constitution grants to the Congress the power to declare war, the power to conduct war and employ military forces is vested in the President as Commander-in-Chief of the armed forces and Chief Executive of the nation. The President is able to exercise his duties as Commander-in-Chief so as to provide him with extraordinary powers that are principally limited by the nature of the political process more so than the legal system.

From early historical precedent and case law we learn that the role of the President as Commander-in-Chief has had a profound effect on the determination of our nation's condition in foreign affairs, and in his exercise of the Commander-in-Chief power he has controlled the authority of Congress in declaring war. The

Helvidius/Pacificus dispute as played out in the Quasi-War between France and the United States stands for the principle that when a foreign nation openly and avowedly makes war upon our nation, we are then by that very fact, in a state of war thereby making a formal declaration by Congress to that effect unnecessary.

We learn further from Chief Justice John Marshall that in a partial or limited undeclared war there are necessary measures appropriate to the level of hostilities that may be undertaken by government involving the right to subject unlawful combatants to military courts for trial purposes, because the laws of war dealing with unlawful combatants are basic to any level of conflict.

Although the Congress did not formally declare war after the September 11 attack on the United States, it did issue a Joint Resolution authorizing President Bush to use "all necessary and appropriate force against any organization ... individuals he determines, planned, committed, aided, approved the attacks or even those who harbored such individuals or members of such organizations." Congress has declared, in effect, a "partial war" which is legal and is supported by both legal and historical precedent.

While the Joint Resolution made no explicit reference to convening military commissions or forums and procedures with which to deal with enemy combatants, such a right in emergency circumstances or de facto wartime conditions is implicit in the authorization for the use of military force.

The President in his Military Order of November 13, 2001 authorizing the establishment of military commissions to try the September 11 terrorists cited the Joint Resolution of Congress, as well as, Title 10 of the U.S. Code, Section 821 and Section 836, which served as functional equivalents for the use of military commissions in the period of World War II.

In the immediate aftermath of September 11, a mounting body of evidence pointed directly to Osama bin Laden and the al-Qaida terrorist organization as the principal perpetrators for the murders of the thousands of civilians and the attempted murder of civilian and military leadership of the United States in one stroke. The Taliban served as the state supporter of the al-Qaida terrorist organization. In addition to killing the nation's leaders, al-Qaida sought to disrupt the economy by destroying the heart of New York City's financial district.[77]

In the absence of a formal declaration of war it may be arguable as to whether the alleged acts committed by al-Qaida were war crimes and violations of the law of war. Every violation of the law of war is a war crime. A deliberate attack on non-combatant civilians violates the law of war and the customary law of war, and the kidnapping and killing of non-combatant civilians on September 11, 2001 violated the Geneva Convention of 1949. Further, the al-Qaida who planned and conducted the September 11 attacks were involved in the commission of acts of war without complying with the laws of war for recognition as a belligerent, and therefore they were acting as unlawful belligerents. By fighting alongside the Taliban forces in an internationally recognized conflict in Afghanistan against the United States military forces and those of our allies, the al-Qaida satisfied requirements under the laws of war and the Constitution that a state of war exists.

Likewise the Taliban fighters who supported al-Qaida did not effectively distinguish themselves from the civilian population thereby failing to comply with the Geneva Convention requiring lawful combatants to wear distinctive military insignia, and since the Taliban fighters adopted and provided support to the unlawful terrorist objectives of the al-Qaida they satisfied the requirements under the laws of war and the Constitution as unlawful belligerents.

Since neither the al-Qaida terrorists nor Taliban fighters conformed to the requirements of the law of war, and since they are responsible for breaches of the law of war, they are not entitled to the status of prisoners of war. Since the al-Qaida and Taliban detainees are not prisoners of war, and assuming that sufficient evidence is available to believe that particular individuals(s) committed war crimes, than the appropriate forum for prosecution based on the November 13, 2001 Military Order of President Bush, is the military commission.

Challenging the constitutionality of properly constituted military commissions to try al-Qaida terrorists and the Taliban fighters will prove to be unsuccessful. The American Bar Association and the New York State Bar Association have concluded that the attacks on September 11, 2001 were violations of the law of war and that military tribunals were appropriate to try non-citizens outside the United States for the alleged commissions of such acts. Additionally, the action taken by President Bush on November 13 is a valid exercise of his constitutional war powers as Commander-in-Chief and Chief Executive that finds ample support in case law and historical tradition.

Recent rulings by United States District Courts, the D.C. Court of Appeals and the Ninth Circuit Court of Appeals conflicted as to whether the federal courts have jurisdiction over prisoners who are being held as detainees in Guantanamo Bay, Cuba. Relying upon a United States Supreme Court decision from 1950, *Johnson v. Eisentrager,*[78] the D.C. Court of Appeals held that enemy aliens who have not entered the United States are not entitled access to United States courts, while the Ninth Circuit ruled that our federal courts do have jurisdiction to hear the writ of habeas corpus because the prisoners were within the jurisdiction of the United States Court system. Cuba leased Guantanamo Bay to the United States at the turn of the twentieth century, but it has continued to retain sovereignty over that area.

The United States Supreme Court's 2004 decision examined only the jurisdictional question, whether habeas corpus actions can be brought before United States courts, not the more substantive due process issues and those that impact upon the Geneva Convention.[79]

48

Notes

[1] *See* Authorization for Use of Military Force Joint Resolution, Public Law 107- 40, 115 Stat. 224. September 18, 2001, Appendix B.

[2] *See* Jeffrey F. Addicott, *Winning the War on Terror: Legal and Policy Lessons from the Past,* Lawyer and Judges Publishing Co. 2002 at 30.

[3] The Joint Resolution of Congress was preceded by recognition from NATO's North Atlantic Council that the attack was covered by Article V of the Washington Treaty, which states that, "an armed attack against one or more of the allies in Europe or North America shall be considered an attack against all." The North Atlantic Treaty Organization declared (for the first time in the history of the security treaty) that the acts of barbarism if directed from abroad amounted to an armed attack against a member state and called upon member nations to provide assistance. See statement of North Atlantic Council (Sept. 12, 2001), 40 ILM 1267 (2001). Also on September 12, the United Nations Security Council recognized the United States' right to self-defense, U.N.S.C. Res. 1368, U.N. SCOR, 56th Sess., 4370th mtg., at 1, U.N. Doc. S| RES| 1368 (2001); *see also,* S.C. Res. 1373, U.N. SCOR, 56th Sess., 4385th mtg., U.N. Doc. S| RES| 1373 (2001). Similarly, the Organization of American States (OAS) interpreted the attacks as acts of "armed attacks;" recognized the inherent right of the United States to act in self-defense; and invoked the collective self-defense provision of the Inter-American Treaty of Reciprocal Assistance, Sept. 2, 1947, T.I.A.S. no. 1838, 21 U.N.T.S 77, art. 3. *See* Terrorist Threat to the Americas, OAS Doc. RC. 24| Res. (1/01/2001); Security Treaty between Australia, New Zealand and the United States of America, Sept. 1, 1951, art. IV, 3 U.S.T. 3420, 3423, 131 U.N.T.S 83, 86, "Australia offered combat military forces and invoked art. IV of the ANZUS Treaty declaring September 11 an attack on Australia."

[4] *See* Military Order on the Detention, Treatment, and Trial of Certain Non-Citizens in the War Against Terrorism, (November 13, 2001); § 1(a), 66 Fed. Reg. 57,833 (Nov. 16, 2001). *See* Appendix A.

[5] U.S. Const. art. I, § 8, cl. 11.

[6] U.S. Const. art. II, § 2.

[7] Works (Hamilton, ed.) VII 10-12.

[8] *Id.* at 14.

[9] Writings (Ford ed.) vol. 1, 338 Madison accepted Jefferson's request very reluctantly as is evidenced in his letter of July 23, 1793: "As I intimated in my last I have forced myself into the task of a reply. I can truly say I find it the most grating one I ever organized." Writings (Hunt ed.) at 138-139.

[10] Edward S. Corwin, *President, Office and Powers,* 4th Revised Edition, New York University Press, 1962, at 180.

[11] *Id.* at 182.

[12] *See* Alexander Hamilton, "The Examination," No. 1, 17 Dec. 1801, reprinted in 3 *The Founder's Constitution,* Kurland and Lerner eds., 1987.

[13] *See Bas v. Tingy,* 4 U.S. 37, 43 (1802).

[14] *Talbot v. Seeman*, 5 U.S. 1 (1801) at 28. Of course, this leaves open the question, how "far" do they apply? Marshall provided no clear answer, but the opinion did recognize that their application need not be explicit in Congress's authorizing act. *See also*, Congress's declaration in the Mexican War, where Congress did not "declare war." Rather, it recognized that "by the act of the Republic of Mexico, a state of war exists between that government and the United States." *See also, Prize Cases supra* Chapter I, n.56 at 21.

[15] *Id.* at 29.

[16] *Id.* Therefore, according to Talbot, the Constitution seems to recognize imperfect or "quasi" war. The War Powers clause permits Congress to authorize the use of force against specific types of predatory military activities without formally declaring war.

The Supreme Court has also ruled that the United States could be considered to be "at war" without a formal declaration in the case of undeclared or "limited" war with Indian tribes. *See Montoya v. United States* 180 U.S. 261, 267 (1901) "We recall no instance where Congress has made a formal declaration of war against an Indian nation or tribe; but the fact that Indians are engaged in acts of general hostility to settlers especially if the government has deemed it necessary to dispute a military force for their subjection is sufficient to constitute a state of war." *See* Rivkin, Casey and Bartram, *Bringing al-Qaida to Justice: The Constitutionality of Trying Al-Qaida Terrorists in the Military Justice System, supra* Chapter I, n.4 at 16.

[17] In remarks prepared for testimony before Congress, Attorney General John Ashcroft specifically referred to what he described as the "President's authority as Commander-in-Chief to lead our nation in times of war as authority for a wide range of terrorism-related investigation and detention measures, and . . . in taking such steps the executive branch did not consider itself under obligatory congressional oversight in relation to those core executive powers." Thus, said the Attorney General, "our fight against terrorism is not merely or primarily a criminal justice endeavor. It is a defense of our nation and citizens." Attorney General John Ashcroft, Testimony before the Senate Committee on the Judiciary, at http://www.usdoj.gov/ag/testimony/2001/1206/transcriptssenatejudiciarycommittee.htm, December 6, 2001 and Testimony before the House Committee on the Judiciary at http://www.usdoj.gov/ag/testimony/2001/agcrisisremarks9_24.htm, Sept. 24, 2001.

The FBI defines terrorism as "the unlawful use of force or violence against persons or property to intimidate or coerce a government, the civilian population, or any segment thereof, in furtherance of political or social objectives," Terrorist Research and Analytical Center, U.S. Dept. of Justice, Terrorism in the United States 1982-1992 at 20 (1992). *See* Christopher M. Evans, *Terrorism on Trial: The President's Constitutional Authority to Order the Prosecution of Suspected Terrorists by Military Commission,* 51 *Duke L. J.* 1831 (2002).

[18] The Supreme Court concluded that identical language in the predecessor provision to section 821 Article 15 of the Articles of War – "authorized trial of offenses against the laws of war before such commissions." (*Ex Parte Quirin* 317 U.S. at 29). Given the text and history of section 821, it must be read as preserving the broad traditional jurisdiction exercised by military commissions before they were expressly mentioned in statutory law. *See also,* in *Application of Yamashita, supra* Chapter I, n.7 at 16.

[19] *See* Jeffrey F. Addicott, *Winning the War on Terror: Legal and Policy Lessons from the Past,* Lawyer and Judges Publishing Co. 2002 at 12. *See also* "National Commission on Terrorist Attacks on the United States," *Staff Statement No. 15, Overview of the Enemy,* June 2004 at 3.

50

[20] *Id.*

[21] *Id.* at 32, and see "Bush Issues Ultimatum to the Taliban, Calls Upon Nations of World to Unite and Destroy Terrorism," *Congressional Quarterly*, September 22, 2001 at 2226.

[22] *See* Common Article 3 of the Geneva Convention of 1949 and U.S. Army Field Manual [FM] 27-10 Article 499 which defines war crimes as the "technical expression for a violation of the law of war by any person or persons, military or civilian." *See* Convention Relative to the Protection of Civilian Persons in the Time of War 6 U.S.T. 3516, T.I.A.S. 3365, 75 U.N.T.S. 287.

[23] *See* Common Article 3 of 1949 Geneva Conventions, *e.g.,* Convention Relative to the Protection of Civilian Persons in Time of War, 6 U.S.T. 3516, T.I.A.S. 3365, 75 U.N.T.S. 287. *See also,* The 1977 Protocols Additional to the Geneva Conventions, 16 I.L.M. 1391 (The U.S. has not ratified the 1977 Protocols, but recognizes that parts of them reflect customary law of war); David Bederman, International Law Frameworks, New York, 2001 at 230-231. *See* "American Bar Association Task Force on Terrorism and the Law," *Report and Recommendations on Military Commissions*, January 4, 2002 at 7. The authors report that most conflicts since World War II have been internal between a rebel or insurgent group and the state itself. States have not wanted to provide legitimacy for acts of violence for non state actors preferring to treat them and their acts as criminal. Al-Qaida is not an internal dissident group, but rather a well organized and resourced organization operating globally. Al-Qaida has also acted as a piratical group that feigned civilian status, condemned by the laws of war as banditry and sabotage. The conventions and customary law of war are designed to protect innocent victims. They do so by establishing standards of treatment for various combatants, including civilians, as well as lawful combatants who have been captured. That does not mean that these protections should be turned into a shield against the jurisdiction of a court for the trial of war crimes of an unprecedented nature. *See* Ruth Wedgwood, "Al-Qaida, Terrorism and Military Commissions," *American Journal of International Law,* Vol. 96 No 2. April 2002 at 328-37. *See also* Professors Curtis A. Bradley and Jack Goldsmith, "The Constitutional Validity of Military Commissions," 5 *Green Bag* 2d 249 (2002) who argue that al-Qaida "is a sufficiently organized and hostile organization to be subject to the law of war. If the September 11 attacks were committed by traditional state actors during this armed conflict, they would clearly violate international law prohibitions on attacking civilian populations and destroying their property. There is precedent for applying the laws of war to groups not directly acting on behalf of nation states, such as guerilla groups and insurgents."

[24] *See* U.S. Army Field Manual [FM] 27-10, The Law of Land Warfare (1956) paras. 80-82. *See* Convention (No. IV) Respecting the Laws and Customs of War on Land, with Annex of Regulations, October 18, 1907. Annex, art. 1 36 Stat. 2277 T.S. No. 539 (Jan. 26, 1910) (The Hague Convention).

[25] FM 27-10 paragraph 60(b) indicates that "[p]ersons who are not members of the armed forces as defined in [the Geneva Conventions], who bear arms or engage in other conduct hostile to the enemy thereby deprive themselves of many of the privileges attaching to the members of the civilian population." This means that they are responsible for breaches of the law of war, but are not entitled to the status of prisoners of war. This provision applies to al-Qaida terrorists who were engaged in armed hostilities against the United States, however it isn't that clear for those members of al-Qaida who did not actively participate in the conflict as to whether they are considered unlawful belligerents. Similar questions can be raised about members of the Taliban who do not bear arms, and what of American citizens who live in the United States and donate money to the al-Qaida terrorism network. Do they violate the law of war?

[26] FM 27-10 para. 504 (9) lists as a war crime, in addition to the "grave breaches" of the Geneva Convention, the "[u]se of civilian clothing by troops to conceal their military character during hostilities." *See also*, the 1874 Brussels Convention, Project of an International Declaration Concerning the Laws and Customs of War, August 27, 1874, art. 9, 65 Brit. & Foreign St. Papers 1005 (1873-74) reprinted in the Laws of Armed Conflicts (Dietrich Schindler & Jiri Toman eds, 3d rev. ed. 1988).

[27] *See* Addicott *supra* at 63. *See also*, William J. Haynes II, Department of Defense General Counsel, Council on Foreign Relations, cfr.org/publication php=5312 in which he stated that "under the laws and customs of war, an enemy combatant is one who may be detained for the duration of an armed conflict. *See* Geneva Conventions Relative to POWs at Article 5. The determination as to their status is to be made by a separate military board (competent tribunal) and not by the President of the United States. There has been substantial experience with Article 5 tribunals in the recent Persian Gulf War when thousands of individuals came under their jurisdiction. *See Operational Law Handbook*, JA 422 (Charlottesville 1977) at 18-8. *See also*, Geneva Conventions Relative to POWs at Articles 12, 22.

[28] Military Order on the Detention, Treatment, and Trial of Certain Non-Citizens in the War Against Terrorism (November 13, 2001) op. cit. *See* Appendix A.

[29] *See* Task Force report at 15 wherein it was concluded that "There is historical authority supporting the President's establishment of military commissions in wartime, under the Constitution and laws of the United States. Additionally The President's constitutional authority to use military commissions is least open to question . . . when he consults with and has the support of Congress."

[30] *See* New York State Bar Association Coordinating Committee on Federal Anti-Terrorism Measures, *Report on Military Commissions,* June 20, 2002 at 15.

[31] *See Rasul et al. v. Bush* and *Al-Odah et al. v. United States*, 542 U.S. ___(2004), Nos. 03-334, 03-343. The case is discussed in full detail in Chapter V at 160-165.

[32] *Rasul et al. v. Bush* and *Al Odah et al. v. United States*, 321 F.3d 1134 (D.C. Cir. 2003). The United States has occupied the Guantanamo Bay Naval Base under a lease with Cuba since 1903, as modified in 1934. Lease of Lands for Coaling and Naval Stations, Feb. 23, 1903, U.S. Cuba, T.S. No. 418 (6 Bevans 1113) ("1903 Lease"); Relations With Cuba, May 9, 1934, U.S. Cuba, T.S. No. 866 (6 Bevans 1161) ("1934 Lease"). In the 1903 Lease, "the United States recognizes the continuance of the ultimate sovereignty of the Republic of Cuba" over the naval base. 1903 Lease, art. III. The term of the lease is indefinite. 1903 Lease, art. I; 1934 Lease, art. III ("So long as the United States of America shall not abandon the said naval station at Guantanamo or the two governments shall not agree to modification of its present limits, the station shall continue to have the territorial area that it now has. . . .")

"The text of the leases shows that Cuba, not the United States, has sovereignty over Guantanamo Bay, which does not justify any court to assert habeas corpus jurisdiction at the behest of an alien held at a military base leased from another nation."

In an earlier suit filed by a coalition of clergy, lawyers and professors, writs of habeas corpus were sought on behalf of those detained at Camp X-Ray in Guantanamo. The petitioners alleged, inter alia, that those imprisoned were held in violation of the Geneva Conventions. The U.S. District Court for the Central District of California dismissed the action, finding that the petitioners lacked standing, that the Court lacked jurisdiction to entertain the claims, and that no federal court could exercise jurisdiction over the claims. Indeed, as the district court explained, the Guantanamo detainees are similar "[i]n all respects" to the prisoners in Eisentrager. *See Coalition of Clergy v. Bush*, 189 F. Supp. 2d 1036 (C.D. Cal. 2002) at 1048.

[33] *Gherebi v. Bush*, No. 03-55785, (9th Cir. 2003).

[34] *See Rasul et al. v. Bush* and *Al-Odah et al. v. United States*, 542 U.S. __ (2004), Nos. 03-334, 03-343.

[35] *Rasul v. Bush*, 215 F. Supp. 2d 55, 56, n.12 at 67 (D.D.C. 2002).

[36] *Johnson v. Eisentrager*, 339 U.S. 763 (1950).

[37] *Id.* at 765-66.

[38] *Id.* at 767.

[39] *Eisentrager v. Forrestal* 174 F.2d 961 (D.C. Cir. 1949).

[40] *Johnson v. Eisentrager*, 339 U.S. at 778 (1950).

[41] *Id.* at 774.

[42] *Id.* at 788.

[43] *Al Odah et al. v. United States*, Pet. App. at 10a.

[44] *Id.* at 12a. It is of interest to note that the detainees do not deny that if they were in fact categorized as enemy aliens, if they engaged in international terrorism, or if they were affiliated with al-Qaida, the courts would not be open to them.

[45] *Id.* at 27a. *See Campbell v. Clinton*, 203 F.3d 19, 29-30 (D.C. Cir. 2000) (Randolph, J. Concurring on the Judgment).

[46] *Gherebi v. Bush*, No. 03-55785, (9th Cir. 2003) at 8.

[47] *Id.*

[48] *Id.* at 9.

[49] Article 5 of the Third Geneva Convention provides:
    Should any doubt arise as to whether persons, having committed a belligerent act and having fallen into the hands of the enemy, belong to any of the categories enumerated in Article 4 [defining POWs], such persons shall enjoy the protection of the present Convention until such time as their status has been determined by a competent tribunal.
    Geneva Convention Relative to the Treatment of Prisoners of War, Aug. 12, 1949, Articles 5, 6 U.S.T. 3316, 75 U.N.T.S. 135. *See also,* Geneva Conventions, *supra,* Chapter II, n.23 at 50. In a recent article Lieutenant Colonel William Lietzau, a principal legal advisor to Secretary of Defense Rumsfeld on Guantanamo, comments on a Central Command Regulation of February 7, 1995 entitled "Captured Persons: Determination of Eligibility for Enemy Prisoner of War (EPW) status" which would completely reverse what happens to prisoners detained at Guantanamo Bay. The regulation states that "A person who has committed a belligerent act . . . shall be treated as an EPW until such time as his status has been determined by a Tribunal." The prisoner must have an

interpreter "who shall be competent in English and Arabic (or other language understood by the Detainee)." The tribunal should be chaired by a military lawyer— known as a "judge advocate"— trained to act in courts-martial, and witnesses must testify under oath. The detainee has the right to be present, to cross-examine witnesses, and to look at documents. Unless the evidence shows he does not deserve it, the prisoner must be given full EPW status.

Colonel Lietzau is quoted as saying he is not surprised by the Centcom regulation although he has not seen it, "and as with many things in this war, the order has become somewhat moot." He argues that the law of war has always developed in response to changes, in the way wars are waged, and the nature of war on terror requires the law to "adapt and advance," although he believes some form of due process is necessary to determine the captive's status. *See* David Rose, "Guantanamo Bay on Trial," *Vanity Fair*, January 2004, 88-92, 132-136, and Enemy Prisoners of War, Retained Personnel, Civilian Internees and Other Detainees, Army Reg. 190-8, §§ 1-5, 1-6 (1997).

[50] *Gherebi v. Bush*, No. 03-55785 (9th Cir. 2003) at 18.

[51] *Id.*

[52] *Id.* at 21.

[53] *See*, for example, *United States v. Rogers*, 388 F. Supp. 298, 301 (E.D. Va. 1975), a U.S. civilian employee, working on the Naval Base at Guantanamo Bay under a contract with the Navy, was prosecuted in the Eastern District of Virginia for drug offenses committed on the Base in violation of 21 U.S.C. §§ 841, 846. In considering Rogers' motion to suppress under a Fourth Amendment claim, the court reasoned:

> By the lease, Cuba agreed that the United States should have complete control over criminal matters occurring within the confines of the base. It is clear to us that under the leasing agreement, United States law is to apply.

[54] *Id.* at 23.

[55] *Id.* at 25.

[56] *Id.* at 26.

[57] *Id.* at 32.

[58] *Id.* at 35.

[59] *Id.* at 38. *See Dura v. Reina*, 495 U.S. 676, 685 (1990).

[60] *Id.* at 46-47. On the last day of its 2004 term the United States Supreme Court issued an order remanding *Bush, President of the U.S. et al. v. Gherebi, Falen*, (03-1245) to the Ninth Circuit Court of Appeals for further consideration in light of *Rumsfeld v. Padilla*, 542 U.S. __ (2004), 124 S. Ct. 2711 (2004), Certiorari denied. A three judge panel of the Ninth Circuit subsequently ruled that the U.S. District Court for the District of Columbia was the appropriate venue for the Guantanamo detainees to challenge their detention. *See* Chapter V for further discussion of the *Padilla* Case at 157-160.

[61] *Id.* at 47.

54

[62] *See Rasul v. Bush,* and *Al Odah v. United States,* 321 F.3d 1134 (D.C. Cir. 2003), cert. granted, (Nov. 10, 2003), 124 S. Ct 534.

[63] *See United States v. Sperry Corp.,* 493 U.S. 52, 66 (1989) (noting that the Court benefit[s] from the views of the Court[s] of Appeals); *United States v. Mendoza,* 464 U.S. 154, 160 (1984) (noting that the Court benefits when several Courts of Appeal hear an issue prior to Supreme Court review), *E.I. Dupont de Nemours & Co. v. Train,* 430 U.S. 112, 135 (1977) lauding the "wisdom of allowing difficult issues to mature through full consideration by the courts of appeals" and (noting that having a variety of perspectives can "vastly simplif[y] our task").

[64] *Id.* at 59.

[65] *Id.* at 61.

[66] *Id.* at 62.

[67] *Id.* at 68-69.

[68] *Id.* at 71.

[69] *Id.*

[70] *Id.* at 76. *See also, Crosby v. Nat'l Foreign Trade Council,* 530 U.S. 363, 381 (2000).

[71] *Id.* at 77.

[72] *Id.*

[73] *Id.*

[74] *Id. See Rasul v. Bush,* 215 Supp. 2d 55 (D.D.C. 2002), and *Al Odah v. United States* 321 F.3d 1134 (D.C. Cir. 2003).

[75] *See Rasul v. Bush,* and *Al-Odah v. United* States, 321 F.3d 1134 (D.C. Cir. 2003), cert. granted 124 S. Ct. 534 (2003). See *also,* Linda Greenhouse, "Justices to Hear Case of Detainees at Guantanamo," *N.Y. Times,* November 11, 2003. Seventeen amicus curiae briefs were filed with the United States Supreme Court including: two former secretaries of the navy, 175 members of British Parliament, several retired federal appellate judges, a coalition of former U.S. prisoners of war, Amnesty International and the American Civil Liberties Union. All the briefs filed came down in support of those detained at Guantanamo Bay except one. The defense team assigned to represent accused terrorists before military commissions filed a brief staking out a middle ground.
In their brief, the five military defense attorneys assigned to represent the enemy combatants before military commissions support the president's wartime power to detain these accused terrorists indefinitely, but went to Court to recognize that habeas corpus jurisdiction exists for those who are tried by military commissions. The brief states "The Constitution cannot countenance an open-ended Presidential power, with no civilian review whatsoever, to try anyone the President deems subject to military tribunal, whose rules and judges have been selected by the prosecuting authority itself." *See* Vanessa Blum, "Military Lawyers Urge Role for High Court," *Legal Times,* January 21, 2004.

[76] *Johnson v. Eistrager,* 339 U.S. at 777–778 (1950).

[77] *See* John C. Yoo and James C. Ho, The New York University – University of Virginia Conference on Exploring The Limits of International Law: The Status of Terrorists, 44 *Va. J Int'l Law* 207 (Fall 2003). Four days before the Presidential election of 2004, Osama bin Laden appeared in a video message to the American people where he claimed direct responsibility for the September 11 attacks. He said as he watched Israeli aircraft bombing tower blocks in Lebanon in 1982, ". . . it occurred to me to punish the unjust the same way—to destroy towers in America so that it can taste some of what we are tasting and to stop killing our children and women. We decided to destroy towers in America. God knows that it had not occurred to our mind to attack the towers (World Trade Center), but after our patience ran out and we saw the injustice and the inflexibility of the American-Israeli alliance toward our people in Palestine and Lebanon this came to my mind." *See* Douglas Jehl and David Johnston, "In Video Message, Bin Laden Issues Warning to U.S." *New York Times* October 30, 2004, www.nytimes.com/2004/10/30/international /middleeast/30qaeda.html

[78] *Id.*

[79] *See* Chapter V for a full discussion of the Supreme Court decision in the case of *Rasul v. Bush,* and *Al-Odah v. United States* at 160-165.

CHAPTER III

Military Commissions Post 9/11: Procedures and Fundamental Fairness Issues

After months of internal review and consultation with a number of experts in and out of government, in and out of Washington, including Judge Advocates General and the general counsels of the Military department, the Secretary of Defense on March 21, 2002 issued Military Commission Order No. 1,[1] which includes rules and procedures that adopt considerable provisions of the UCMJ and civilian trial structure.[2]

The focus of this section of the study is to examine the principal substantive procedures issued by the Pentagon to make the military commissions fully operational. It is important to note that the process was evolutionary in nature since the original March 21, 2002 document was further refined and revised over the course of twenty-two months to be finalized in 2004. The final set of thirteen documents contains a detailed series of instructions for the special trials including a listing of crimes, the elements for trial by military commissions, the responsibilities of the Chief Prosecutor and support team prosecutors, responsibilities of Chief Defense Counsel and support team defense counsels, qualifications of Civilian Defense Counsel, reporting relationships for military commission personnel, sentencing, and procedures for the conduct of trials.[3]

* * * * * * * * * *

The Bush Administration's approach to military commissions is based upon two important principles. First, the President specifically wanted the option of a process that is distinct from the processes in the Federal Court and the Military Court system under the Uniform Code of Military Justice. The commissions are intended to be different because of the unusual national security situation the United States faces. Secondly, although each distinct provision may not compare to all the provisions of the federal court system or the court martial system, as a whole, the rules and procedures are designed to be fair, impartial and balanced and serve the needs of the justice in their application.

Rights of the Accused

The rights of the accused who is charged with a violation of the laws as discussed in Military Commission Order No. 1 include:

- The presumption of innocence;
- Guilt must be proven "beyond reasonable doubt;"
- Trials to be open to the public except when classified evidence is being introduced;
- Defendants are provided with a court-appointed military lawyer or the freedom to hire civilian lawyers who are authorized by the federal government to handle classified documents;
- Access to evidence that the prosecution plans to present at trial;
- Access to the evidence known to the prosecution tending to exculpate the accused;
- The right to remain silent;
- The right to testify, subject to cross examination;
- The right to obtain witnesses and documents for the defense;
- The right to present evidence and cross-examine the witnesses;
- The right to be present at every stage of the trial (except when proceedings are closed by the presiding officer) unless disruptive;
- Access to sentencing evidence;
- The right to submit a plea agreement;
- The appointment of interpreters to assist in the defense and a copy of all charges in English as well as a language the defendant understands; and

- No re-trial by a military commission once a verdict is final.

The Prosecution, Trial and Appeals Process

Other provisions related to the role of prosecution, the trial, and appeals process, as discussed in Military Commission Order No. 1 include:

- A panel of three to seven military officers without a separate jury tries the accused. The Secretary of Defense appoints the panel, all of whom must be commissioned officers in the military;

- Hearsay evidence deemed of "probative value to a reasonable person" is allowed;

- Evidence obtained from battlefield documents without reliable step-by-step chain of custody can be used by prosecutors;

- Two-thirds of the military officers on the panel must agree on findings of guilt;

- A unanimous decision of a seven-member panel is required for the death sentence;

- After the trial, there will be an automatic post-trial process of appeal and review;

- A review panel, appointed by the Secretary of Defense, will consider appeals from convicted defendants within thirty days of sentence. The panel will be made up of four military officers, one of whom has experience as a judge advocate. The rules permit the review panel to obtain civilian legal experts appointed by the President, in which case they may be commissioned as temporary military officers;

- The rules restrict the review panel to review issues of fact and law in accordance with the commission's rules, not pursuant to federal law or the Constitution. They may return the case to the commission for further proceedings, or they may advise the Secretary of Defense for disposition of the case. If the review panel sends the record of trial to the Secretary of Defense, he will then conduct an independent review and either remand the case for further proceedings or forward to the President with his recommendations for a final decision.

Listing of Crimes

More than 30 crimes have been laid out for prosecution before military commissions, a list that for the most part coincides with activities considered war crimes under international law. They include the following:

- Deliberate killings of civilians;
- Taking of civilian hostages;
- Using civilians as human shields;
- Torturing persons;
- Raping prisoners;
- Pillaging;
- Improper use of flags of truce or protective emblems; and
- Terrorism[4]

Each of these crimes carries a maximum penalty of death.

The list of rules and regulations provide many of the rights of the accused that have come to be identified with the concept of fundamental fairness specifically recognized with those afforded court-martial procedure under the UCMJ and required by the International Convention of Civil and Political Rights (ICCPR) to which the United States became a party in 1992.[5] Article 14 of the ICCPR provides standards and procedures that should be applied in all courts and tribunals and which President Clinton ordered be observed by all federal departments and agencies of the United States.[6] The convention has been respected with respect to application of basic rights in recently conducted tribunals in the former Yugoslavia and Rwanda.[7]

Fundamental Fairness Issues in WWII Commissions

Although the Congress has codified procedures to ensure fundamental fairness applicable to courts-martial there does not exist any comparable statute to address defendant rights before military commissions. Therefore the President may establish any rules of procedure and evidence that he determines to be appropriate.

Examining precedence from the period of World War II, President Roosevelt's military order in *Quirin* which referred to the trying of offenses against both the law of war and the Articles of War, liberated the commission from some of the restrictions established by Congress in the Articles of War. The commission would "have power to and shall, as occasion requires, make such rules for conduct of the proceeding, consistent with the powers of military commissions under the Articles of War, as it shall deem necessary for a full and fair trial of the matters before it." The power to "make such rules" freed the commission from procedures enacted by Congress and the *Manual for Courts-Martial.*[8]

As President of the Quirin military commission, General McCoy issued rulings in response to various questions raised by the two sides. Few rules had been agreed to in advance. The day before the trial began, the tribunal adopted a three-and-a-half-page, double-spaced statement of rules. Primarily this document dealt with the sessions not being open to the public, the taking of oaths of secrecy, the identification of counsel for the defendants and for the prosecution, and the keeping of a record. Only eight lines referred to rules of procedure: peremptory challenges would not be allowed, there would be one challenge for cause, and this concluding language: "In general, wherever applicable to a trial by Military Commission, the procedure of the Commission shall be governed by the Articles of War, but the Commission shall determine the application of such Articles to any particular question."[9] The commission could thus discard the procedures from the Articles of War or the *Manual for Courts-Martial* whenever it wanted to. As General Cramer told the commission at one point: "Of course, if the Commission pleases, the Commission has discretion to do anything it pleases; there is no dispute about that."[10]

There were lessons learned from the 1942 experience in *Quirin* which were not repeated in subsequent tribunal proceedings and these include: military tribunals should not be prosecuted by the Attorney General and the Judge Advocate General; the President should not be the appointing official; and, he should not receive the trial record directly from the tribunal. Instead, review of the trial record should be performed by trained and experienced experts within the Office of Judge Advocate General.

In another famous World War II military commission case, *In re Yamashita*,[11] the evidentiary rules and standards employed included:

> 16. Evidence. - a. The commission shall admit such evidence as in its opinion would be of assistance in proving or disproving the charge, or such as in the commission's opinion would have *probative value in the mind of a reasonable man.* In particular, and without limiting in any way the scope of the foregoing general rules, the following evidence may be admitted:
>
> (1) Any document which appears to the commission to have been signed or issued officially by any officer, department, agency, or member of the armed forces of any government, without proof of the signature or of the issuance of the document.
>
> (2) Any report which appears to the commission to have been signed or issued by the International Red Cross or a member thereof, or by a medical doctor or any medical service personnel, or by an investigator or intelligence officer, or by any other person whom the commission finds to have been acting in the course of his duty when making the report.
>
> (3) Affidavits, depositions, or other statements taken by an officer detailed for that purpose by military authority.
>
> (4) Any diary, letter or other document appearing to the commission to contain information relating to the charge.
>
> (5) A copy of any document or other secondary evidence of its contents, if the commission believes that the original is not available or cannot be produced without undue delay. . . .[12]

* * * * * * * * * *

Fundamental Fairness Issues - Military Commission Orders and Military Commission Instructions - 2004

There are several rights that are omitted from Defense Secretary Rumsfeld's *Rules, Regulations and Procedures for the Operation of Military Commissions* of individuals subject to the President's military order.

The first is the right to habeas corpus relief. This right permits the accused to be tried before a military commission to challenge the constitutionality of the November 13 order and the authority of the military commission to try the petitioner for the offense charged, but not the guilt or innocence of the accused, which is left to the military authorities, to exclusively review. The November 13 order precludes any remedy or proceedings by, or on behalf of, persons subject to the order in any court of the United States. The objective of this language appears to be the elimination of habeas corpus review by persons subject to the order. Under the Constitution of the United States, only the Congress, not the President or his delegated authority, the Secretary of Defense, can suspend the writ of habeas corpus.[13] In the *Quirin* decision, the Supreme Court held that habeas relief cannot be denied to those who were tried under the jurisdiction of military commissions. In interpreting language virtually identical to the November 13 order,[14] the Court determined that there was a right to judicial review "for determining (President Roosevelt's order's) applicability to the particular case and petitioner's contentions that . . . laws of the United States constitutionally enacted forbid their trial by military commission."[15]

It should be noted that the military commission in *Quirin* was conducted in Washington, D.C. and unlike the al-Qaida and Taliban detainees at the U.S. Naval Base at Guantanano, Cuba, and in Bagram, Afghanistan, the German saboteurs had access to federal courts. The Supreme Court has held that captured enemy belligerents who are not held on the sovereign territory of the United States cannot petition for habeas corpus relief.[16]

Another right, which is of concern because of its restrictive and highly constrained nature, is the accused's right to civilian counsel. To be eligible to participate, civilian attorneys must avow: "I understand that my communications with my client, even if traditionally covered by the attorney-client privilege, may be subject to monitoring or review by government officials using any available means, for security and intelligence purposes."[17] Further, "I will not discuss or otherwise communicate or share documents or information about the case with anyone except persons who have been designated as members of the defense team."[18]

The rules further require that civilian defense attorneys have a security clearance of "secret" or higher.[19] They must state that their qualifications as a civilian defense counsel do not guarantee their presence at closed military commission proceedings or guarantee access to any protected information.[20] The defense team, however, will have access to all secret evidence because the military defense counsels have clearance for such access. A potential concern is that such evidence may be restricted exclusively to someone in the military command.

The rules do require that the prosecution must provide defense counsel (civilian and military) with access to all evidence the prosecution intends to introduce at trial and access to evidence that the prosecution knows tends to exculpate the accused (Military Commission Order No.1, Procedures Accorded the Accused, Appendix C1). While the rules permit the prosecution, upon motion, to withhold evidence necessary to protect the interests of the United States, any information that is protected shall not be admitted as evidence for consideration by the commission if it is not presented to defense counsel (Military Commission Order No. 1. 6, Conduct of Trial, D, Evidence, (5) Protection of Information, (b) Limited Disclosure, Appendix C1).

Access to protected information by military counsel is appropriate unless it is automatically assumed that military counsel is less capable than civilian counsel of pursuing a vigorous defense. The rules applicable to both military and civilian defense counsel require that they work cooperatively and coordinate their efforts to ensure that they are capable of conducting the defense independently if it is necessary (Military Commission Instruction No. 5 Affidavit and Agreement, Annex B, Section II, D, Appendix C9).

The instructions originally imposed travel and communications restrictions of civilian counsel. "All work relating to the proceedings, including any electronic or other research, is to be performed at the site of the proceedings."[21] This provision was eliminated as a requirement by the Pentagon after the rules were fully vetted by outside legal consultants who took strong exception to this requirement.

The new rules require that the defendant pay any and all expenses of civilian defense counsel, even if the defendant is indigent; and the civilian lawyer must avow that the military proceedings will be her primary duty for the duration of the trial. The civilian lawyer cannot "delay or continue the proceedings for any reasons that arise in the course of my law practice or other professional or personal activities that are not related to military commission proceedings."[22]

Another revision to the legal rules addresses criticism concerning the privacy of lawyers and their clients. The revisions guarantee that a defense lawyer will know ahead of time if the government plans to listen in on attorney-client conversations, and permits the lawyer to inform her client that the conversation may not be private. It also assures that the government will not eavesdrop on any conversations defense lawyers may have among themselves. Any eavesdropping must be approved by the Commander of the combatant command with control of the detainee or the commander's designee, and only if it is likely to help gather information about terrorist activities or prevent new terrorist attacks. (Military Commission Order No. 3, Special Administrative Measures for Certain Communications Subject to Monitoring, Appendix C6).

It has been suggested that the combination of no government reimbursement for costs and the mandate that civilian counsels work primarily on the military tribunal case will serve as a principal deterrent to recruiting capable, competent, effective civilian legal representation. Furthermore, the government's monitoring and oversight of lawyer-client discussions is considered a chilling surveillance device that runs totally counter to fundamental fairness guarantees.[23]

There is a misunderstanding with respect to the procedures of military commissions as they relate to the right to monitor conversations between defense counsel and the accused. The impression given is that evidence derived from monitoring and overseeing lawyer client discussions will be used at trial. The rules, however, provide to the contrary, stating that "any evidence or information derived from such communication will not be used in proceedings against the accused who made or received the relevant information" (Military Commission Instruction No. 5 Affidavit and Agreement, Annex B, Section II, I Appendix C9). It is important to note that this requirement is an exclusionary rule which extends to all potential proceedings against the accused.

Probably the most dramatic departure from federal and military practice, and the source of the most criticism of the military commission process, involves the review of decision-making. In the regular military justice system, a case proceeds through three levels of appellate review, The Court(s) of Military Review in each service, The United States Court of Military Appeals, and in some instances, review by the United States Supreme Court.[24]

Under the Defense Secretary's Rules and Instructions, only a three-member panel will review the rulings of military commissions before the President or Secretary of Defense. The review panel may include a civilian and must include at least one individual with experience as a judge. The panel members have been selected by the Secretary of Defense and serve at his pleasure. They include former U.S. Attorney General Griffin Bell; former U.S. Transportation Secretary William Coleman Jr.; Edward Biester, a Pennsylvania jurist and former state attorney general; and Frank Williams, Chief Justice of the Rhode Island Supreme Court. They will be commissioned as Army major generals for their two-year term on the panel. One or more additional review panel members may be named at a later date. Review panel members will select among themselves the three members who will hear a specific case. (Military

Commission Instruction No. 9 Review of Military Proceedings, Section IV, B Appendix C13.)

Several organizations including the American Civil Liberties Union (ACLU) and Lawyers Committee for Human Rights have taken strong exception to the role and operation of the review panel. Tim Edgar, Legislative Counsel to the ACLU has stated: "The appellate structure is problematic because there is no appeal outside the military system. There will be no independent review."[25] However, in the Department of Defense News Briefing on military commissions, the Under Secretary of Defense, Douglas Feith, and the Department of Defense General Counsel, William J. Haynes, specifically offered the following comments on that issue:

Q.   Why specifically exclude the Supreme Court from the process?

Feith: I don't think that you'll find anything that excludes the Supreme Court. It's not within our power to exclude the Supreme Court from the process.

Q.   It says that under the UCMJ, you can appeal up to the Supreme Court. Here you appeal only to the President or Secretary of Defense after the review panel is done. They seem . . . they are the highest.

Feith: That is the only appeal provided for in the rules . . . prepared. As far as whether the Supreme Court gets involved, that's beyond our authority to say.

Haynes: Far be it from me to tell the Supreme Court not to do something. We anticipate that anybody that is tried will have vigorous, competent representation, and we expect that they will seek every avenue they can to protect the interests of their client.[26]

It would appear from this discussion that although the rules and procedures promulgated in Military Commission, Order No. 1 do not mandate review and appeal by the Federal Court System the civilian courts are not specifically prohibited from appellate review of military commission cases.

Critics have also suggested that the evidentiary rules and standards to be employed by military commissions amount to an inferior brand of justice because they permit the introduction of any evidence that "would have probative value to a reasonable person," and would permit the use of hearsay evidence and other evidence that would not be admitted in civilian trials.[27]

These very procedures are based upon long precedent of consistent historical practice in this country as well as internationally. The same standards were imposed by President Roosevelt in the *Quirin* case and were followed in *Yamashita* and hundreds of military commissions after World War II in order to simplify evidentiary proceedings, to eliminate cumbersome rules of evidence and to ensure that all evidence with probative value to the issue of guilt or innocence could be considered.

The evidentiary rules at Nuremberg and adopted by the Tokyo trials were specifically designed to be non-technical to allow for expeditious admissions of all evidence the Tribunal deems to have probative value; such evidence included hearsay, coerced confessions, and the findings of prior mass trials.[28]

This makes eminent practical sense given that during wartime and on the battlefield, the collection and maintenance of evidence cannot be done under the same laboratory-like conditions as those at a domestic crime scene. As White House counsel Alberto Gonzales has noted, there are circumstances in a war zone which often make it impossible to meet the authorization requirements for documents in a civilian court, yet documents from al-Qaida safe houses in Kabul might be expected to accurately determine the guilt of al-Qaida cell members hiding in the West. There is no reason the international community should frown on this standard; after all, it is the same standard applied by the UN-sponsored war crimes tribunals such as the tribunal for the former Yugoslavia.[29]

Fundamental Fairness and the Geneva Conventions

The fundamental fairness rights that are not included in the Defense Secretary's Rules or Instructions are elements of fundamental fairness that are afforded members of the United States military under the UCMJ. The Geneva Conventions adopted in 1949 required that the same due process rights guaranteed to United States members of the armed services to be tried in military courts be accorded to accused standing trial before military courts. The question of those rights is addressed in the 1977 First Additional Protocol to the Geneva Conventions.

Though not ratified by the United States, several of the provisions are so widely accepted that they are recognized as expressing norms of customary international law, which for the first century of our history as a nation the United States accepted as binding.[30] Among those provisions that qualifies them as customary international law is Article 75, which deals with the due process rights of "persons who are in the power of a Party to the conflict and who do not benefit from more favorable treatment under the Conventions."[31]

The list of basic fundamental fairness guarantees in Article 75 are:

1. In so far as they are affected by a situation referred to in Article 1 of this Protocol, persons who are in the power of a Party to a conflict and who do not benefit from more favorable treatment under the Conventions or under this Protocol shall be treated humanely in all circumstances and shall enjoy, as a minimum, the protection provided by this Article without any adverse distinction based upon race, color, sex, language, religion or belief, political or other opinion, national or social origin, wealth, birth or other status, or any other similar criteria. Each Party shall respect the person, honor, convictions and religious practices of all such persons.

2. The following acts are and shall remain prohibited at any time and in any place whatsoever, whether committed by civilian or by military agents:
   (a) Violence to the life, health, or physical or mental well-being of persons, in particular:
       (i)   Murder;
       (ii) Torture of all kinds, whether physical or mental
       (iii) Corporal punishment; and
       (iv) Mutilation;
   (b) Outrages upon personal dignity, in particular humiliating and degrading treatment, enforced prostitution and any form of indecent assault;
   (c) The taking of hostages;
   (d) Collective punishments; and
   (e) Threats to commit any of the foregoing acts.

3. *Any person arrested, detained or interned for actions related to the armed conflict shall be informed promptly, in a language he understands, of the reasons why these measures have been taken. Except in cases of arrest or detention for penal offences, such persons shall be released within the minimum delay possible and in any event as soon as the circumstances justifying the arrest, detention or internment have ceased to exist.* (emphasis added)

4. No sentence may be passed and no penalty may be executed on a person found guilty of a penal offense related to the armed conflict except pursuant to a conviction pronounced by impartial and regularly constituted court respecting the generally recognized principles of regular judicial procedure, which include the following:

   (a) The procedure shall provide for an accused to be informed without delay of the particulars of the offense alleged against him and shall afford the accused before and during his trial all necessary rights and means of defense;

   (b) No one shall be convicted of an offense except on the basis of individual penal responsibility;

   (c) No one shall be accused or convicted of a criminal offense on account of any act or omission which did not constitute a criminal offense under the national or international law to which he was subject at the time when it was committed; nor shall a heavier penalty be imposed than that which was applicable at the time when the criminal offense was committed; if, after the commission of the offense, provision is made by law for the imposition of a lighter penalty, the offender shall benefit thereby;

   (d) Anyone charged with an offense is presumed innocent until proved guilty according to law;

   (e) Anyone charged with an offense shall have the right to be tried in his presence.

   (f) No one shall be compelled to testify against himself or to confess guilt;

   (g) Anyone charged with an offense shall have the right to examine, or have examined the witnesses against him and to obtain the attendance and examination of witnesses on his behalf under the same conditions as the witnesses against him;

   (h) No one shall be prosecuted or punished by the same Party for an offense in respect of which a final judgment acquitting or convicting that person has been previously pronounced under the same law and judicial procedure;

(i) Anyone prosecuted for an offense shall have the right to have the judgment pronounced publicly; and

(j) A convicted person shall be advised on conviction of his judicial and other remedies and of the time limits within which they may be exercised.

5. Women whose liberty has been restricted for reasons related to the armed conflict shall be held in quarters separated from men's quarters. They shall be under the immediate supervision of women. Nevertheless, in cases where families are detained or interned, they shall, whenever possible be held in the same place and accommodated as family units.

6. *Persons who are arrested, detained or interned for reasons related to the armed conflict shall enjoy the protection provided by this Article until their final release, repatriation or re-establishment, even after the end of the armed conflict.* (emphasis added)

7. In order to avoid any doubt concerning the prosecution and trial of person accused of war crimes or crimes against humanity, the following principles shall apply:

(a) Persons who are accused of such crimes should be submitted for the purpose of prosecution and trial in accordance with the applicable rules of international law; and

(b) Any such persons who do not benefit from more favorable treatment under the Conventions or this Protocol shall be accorded the treatment provided by this Article, whether or not the crimes of which they are accused constitute grave breaches of the Conventions or of this Protocol.

8. No provisions of this Article may be construed as limiting or infringing any other more favorable provision granting greater protection under any applicable rules of international law, to persons covered by paragraph 1.

The Geneva Convention does not provide for counsel merely because of detention. The Convention only affords a prisoner of war the right to counsel when he has been charged with a crime. Article 105 of the Convention relative to the Treatment of Prisoners of War of August 12, 1949 (GPW) states:

> The prisoner of war shall be entitled to assistance by one of his prisoner comrades to defense by a qualified advocate or counsel of his own choice, to the calling of witnesses and if he deems necessary, to the services of a competent interpreter. He shall be advised of these rights by the Detaining Power in due time before the trial.[32]

As the plain language of Article 105 makes clear, it only applies when the prisoner of war is subject to trial. Therefore it is implicit that the right to counsel only exists when the prisoner of war is charged with a crime.[33]

Since neither the Third Geneva Convention nor Article 75 of the Protocol addresses the quality of evidence that may be used against a defendant, for example the use of hearsay testimony, there is no protection for defendants in these documents. This leaves Rules and Instructions unconstrained by international law when it comes to hearsay evidence.

* * * * * * * * * *

United States military officials have developed a list of alleged al-Qaida operatives who are currently being detained and whom they believe should stand trial before military commissions. Decisions as to who to try have been based, in part, on the interrogations of detainees at Guantanano, Bagram, and other unidentified locations overseas, seized terrorist documents and intercepted communications, among other sources. Under the established Rules, President Bush must designate some or all of those on the list for military trial. Then the commission's appointing authority would decide which individuals would actually stand trial.

In February 2004, for the first time, the Pentagon formally brought charges against two detainees identified as Ali Hamza Ahmed Sulayman al-Bahlul of Yemen and Ibrahim Ahmed Mahmoud al-Qosi of Sudan for conspiracy to commit terrorism and war crimes against civilians. They were both considered senior members of al-Qaida who had served in a variety of capacities for Osama bin Laden.[34] According to the charge sheets the two men were part of a criminal conspiracy that committed the offenses of attacking civilians, attacking civilian objectors and other acts. It was not clear whether the defendants were willing to plead guilty to any of the charges, although neither of them would face the death penalty for their actions.[35] In June 2004 a third detainee, David Hicks of Australia, was formally accused of conspiracy to commit war crimes, attempted murder by an unprivileged belligerent, and aiding the enemy, according to a statement issued by the Pentagon.[36] In July 2004 a fourth detainee, Salim Ahmed Hamdan of Yemen, was formerly accused of attacking civilians, murder by an unprivileged belligerent, and terrorism.[37]

A five-member military tribunal was formed to try the four terrorism suspects. The presiding officer was identified as Retired Army Colonel Peter E. Brownback III who was recalled to active duty. He had 22 years of experience as a judge advocate and 10 years of experience as a military judge. The remaining panel members were two U.S. Marine Corps colonels, an Air Force Colonel and a Air Force Lieutenant Colonel.[38] As a direct result of the U.S. Supreme Court decision in *Rasul and Al-Odah,* Lt. Col. Sharon Schaeffer, the military lawyer representing Ibrahim Ahmed Mahmoud al-Qosi, challenged the jurisdiction of the military tribunal because the Court ruled that foreign nationals held as suspected terrorists in military custody were entitled to challenge their detentions in U.S. courts.

Secretary of Defense Donald Rumsfeld had originally delegated his role as appointing authority for military commissions to his Deputy Defense Secretary Paul Wolfowitz, who would exercise key powers in the commission process. After the chief prosecutor drafts charges against the detainee, Wolfowitz would have the authority to approve the charges and send the detainee to trial. As appointing authority he also was to select military officers to sit in on the commissions. Because of additional responsibilities delegated to him by Defense Secretary Rumsfeld arising from the war in Iraq, a new appointing authority, retired Army. Major General John Altenburg Jr., a career military lawyer, was selected to oversee all the prosecutions, including approving charges and plea agreements as well as naming commission members.

The Chief Prosecutor and Chief Defense counsel originally named were both well respected and highly regarded career judge advocates. Army Colonel Frederic L. Borch III was the lead prosecutor. He served as deputy chairman of the international law department at the Naval War College in Newport, Rhode Island prior to his immediate appointment and previously served as senior legal advisor at the Army Signal Center in Fort Gordon in Georgia. From 1994 to 1998 he worked in the criminal section of the Army Judge Advocate General's Office. In that role, he supervised the high profile prosecutions related to sexual misconduct at Aberdeen Proving Ground in Maryland. From 1990 to 1993, Borch taught criminal law at the Judge Advocate General's School in Charlottesville, Virginia. He received his law degree from the University of North Carolina and his advanced law degrees in military law from the Judge Advocate General's School and in international law from the University of Brussels in Belgium. In April of 2004 Colonel Borch was reassigned to take up the post at the Army Judge Advocates General School. He was replaced by Army Lt. Colonel Robert Swann who has twenty-six years of experience as an Army judge advocate and more than twenty years of litigation experience as a government trial attorney, defense counsel, appellate attorney and judge. Colonel Swann entered active duty in 1978, after receiving his Bachelor of Arts Degree from the University of Tennessee in 1974 and Jurist Doctorate from the University of Memphis Law School in 1977. Prior to selection as Chief Prosecutor, Colonel Swann was assigned as a Circuit Judge in the Army's 2nd Judicial Circuit at Fort Campbell, Kentucky becoming the Chief Circuit Judge in 2001.[39]

Air Force Colonel William Gunn, chief defense counsel, most recently served as executive assistant to the Air Force judge advocate general at the Pentagon. From 1999 to 2001, Gunn supervised all Air Force defense counsel for the central United States. Gunn previously served as chief legal advisor for Pope

Air Force Base in North Carolina, taught environmental law at the Judge Advocate General's School, and worked as a trial lawyer representing the Army in civil litigation. In 1990 Gunn was selected as a White House Fellow. He began his career as the military equivalent of a public defender representing Air Force members in criminal matters. Gunn earned his J.D. at Harvard Law School and an advanced degree in environmental law from the Judge Advocate General's School.

Some may challenge the fairness of military commissions because they are exclusively comprised of commissioned and experienced officer judges who must try terrorist cases. Historical experience does not support such a concern. In the Nuremberg war crimes trials, three of the twenty-two major defendants were acquitted, four were sentenced to twenty years in prison or less, and three received life sentences. The outcome of the military tribunal proceedings against the Germans in China for passing intelligence information to the Japanese even after Germany surrendered produced six defendants who were acquitted by U.S. Army Judges. It is significant that the International Military Tribunal spared the lives of almost half of the principal architects of the Nazi party that led to the Holocaust, World War II and other infamous war crimes during the period of World War II.[40]

The same was true in trials by United States military commissions after World War II where more than 3,000 individuals were tried with a conviction rate of approximately 85 percent, which is lower than the conviction rate in most civilian federal courts. During fiscal year 2001, the conviction rate including guilty pleas and dispositions at trial for civilians tried on criminal charges in our federal court system was 91 percent, and in the Southern District of New York it was 97.2 percent.[41] There has been a long and well-established reputation for command noninterference in military justice issues that ensures independent decision-making by these bodies.

76

Summary

Almost two years after President Bush issued his Military Order authorizing the use of military commissions for trial of terrorist war crimes, the Secretary of Defense issued a finalized set of Instructions to supplement and refine Rules and Procedures for implementing military commissions in law.

Military commissions will resemble conventional courts-martial and war crimes tribunals utilized Post-World War II, and more recently in the former Yugoslavia and Rwanda. The Instructions provide for the qualifications and responsibilities of Prosecution and Defense Counsel, a listing of special crimes for trial, procedures for the conduct of trials, and sentencing procedure among other things.

The commissions will comprise three to seven professional military officer judges, at least one of whom, the chief of the panel, must be a military lawyer. The Office of Chief Defense Counsel will serve as the public defenders for the accused terrorists, and they will be Judge Advocate General officers in the United States Military, but the defendant has the opportunity to supplement their services with a civilian counsel hired at their own expense.

Civilian lawyers must be United States citizens admitted to the practice of law in an American jurisdiction, and they must be provided with a security clearance of secret or higher to have access to sensitive trial materials. They have to work in partnership with military defense counsel assigned to the case and may be denied presence at closed military commission proceedings if evidence to be considered at trial is too sensitive in the context of national security policy. The civilian lawyer must agree to a gag order that extends after trial completion. The military commission proceedings must be the primary duty of the civilian lawyer for the duration of the proceedings, and no delays or continuances of the proceedings that relate to other legal or professional duties are permitted. Lastly, the civilian counsel must agree to monitoring, review and oversight of attorney-client discussions to protect intelligence and national security concerns. The

Pentagon insists that these requirements are essential and totally appropriate in light of our continuing global war on terrorism.

Consistent with elements of our criminal justice system, the Instructions include the feature of plea-bargaining. The way it operates is that once there has been a determination that the plea was voluntary and informed, the military judges must be bound to accept the agreement approved by the Secretary of Defense, and sentence the defendant accordingly. This is distinct from the civilian system where judicial discretion is available to reject a plea-bargain and require the defendant to plead guilty or go to trial and accept the consequences of the trial outcome for sentencing purposes.[42]

The practical effect of this plea-bargaining rule is to place in the hands of the prosecution a very useful lever of control over the defendant getting information and cooperation in exchange for a lighter sentence.

The rules of evidence are essentially the same as those used Post-World War II and at the tribunal in the Hague adjudicating war crimes in the former Yugoslavia and Rwanda. The rules make evidence admissible predicated upon its value as proof and whether the commission determines the evidence to be credible.

The Instructions call for an Appellate Review Panel appeal process after trial completion. In the regular military justice system a case proceeds through three separate levels of appellate review: The Court(s) of Military review in each service, The United States Court of Military Appeals, and in some instances the United States Supreme Court. The three-member review panel covered in the Instructions is solely responsible for appellate jurisdiction subject to any final action taken by the President or Secretary of Defense.

All military commissions are potentially subject to the danger of command influence because of the fact that prosecutors, judges, and in most cases, defense counsel are part of the military structure. The concern is all the more true with respect to the President's Military Order because the President as Commander-in-Chief chooses the individuals to be tried before military commissions.

A principal protection against command influence in military commissions is the existence of independent civilian appeal agencies. The President's Order bars appellate review by any state or federal court. The review panel consists only of military officers or civilians who are commissioned as military officers. Furthermore, the panel lacks the authority of an appellate court. While it can make recommendations to the Secretary of Defense or call for further proceedings, it does not have the power to dismiss charges against the accused. The availability of an appeal to an independent civilian body which is part of American court martial proceedings is crucial to ensure the integrity and impartiality of the commission process as well as providing venues of relief by defense counsels seeking to maximally protect the interests of their accused clients.

Regardless of how the appellate review process is ultimately resolved, the most critical focus of justice continues to be the trial where the center of gravity in the search for truth and justice is the trier of fact. The fairness of the judicial system is predicated upon the same standard of proof that exists in both federal courts and military courts-martial: guilt beyond a reasonable doubt. Commissions will execute their function in such a way as to provide for a trial that is at least as full and fair as that found in any civilian judicial system.

The appointed chief prosecutor and head defense counsel who were assigned to handle the trials of alleged terrorists expected no-holds-barred legal combat between the two sides and that fair trials would be the result. Air Force Colonel William Gunn, chief defense attorney said: "We're going to be able to provide a zealous defense for all detainees brought to trial. . . ."[43] While the chief prosecutor Army Colonel Frederic L. Borch III, commented, "We have been very careful in this process to do everything to guarantee a full and fair trial."[44]

To date, the Pentagon has announced that it will prosecute four Guantanamo detainees filing charges of conspiracy to commit war crimes against civilians and conspiracy to commit terrorism. None will face the death penalty for their actions.

It is highly misleading to conclude that because military commissions are comprised exclusively of commissioned and experienced officer judges who must try terrorist cases that they will automatically be unfair. Historical experience demonstrates to the contrary. At Nuremberg and the thousands of trials convened by military commissions at the close of World War II the conviction rates clearly demonstrate a well-established reputation for command noninterference in military justice issues that ensure independent decisions made by these bodies.

Notes

[1] *See* Department of Defense Military Commission Order No. 1, March 21, 2002 [MCO #1], Appendix C1.

[2] Manual for Court-Martial [MCM], US (1988).

[3] *See* Appendix C for the full set of Military Commission Instructions promulgated pursuant to the President's Military Order of November 13, 2001, and Military Commission Order No. 1, March 21, 2002. The Department of Defense Fact Sheet provides an overview of Military Commission Procedures and a chart which illustrates the Commission Process.

[4] *See* Military Commission Instructions No. 2, Appendix C6 for a complete list of crimes.

[5] G.A. res. 2200A (XXI), 21 U.N. GAOR Supp. (No. 16) at 52, U.N. Doc. A/6316, 999 U.N.T.S. 171. The United States, when it entered the Covenant, declared that in its view, Articles 1 through 27 of the treaty are not self-executing. The United States' position is that these protections are, generally, in the United States Constitution and require no further implementation, and that the Covenant does not provide a basis for individuals to claim relief in United States Courts. Since the United States joined the Covenant, it has not departed from its provisions.

[6] Article 14 provides:
1. All persons shall be equal before the courts and tribunals. In the determination of any criminal charge against him, or of his rights and obligations in a suit at law, everyone shall be entitled to a fair and public hearing by a competent, independent and impartial tribunal established by law. The press and public may be excluded from all or part of a trial for reasons of morals, public order (ordre public) or national security in a democratic society, or when the interest of the private lives of the parties so requires, or to the extent strictly necessary in the opinion of the court in special circumstances where publicity would prejudice the interests of justice; but any judgment rendered in a criminal case or in a suit at law shall be made public except where interest of juvenile persons otherwise requires or the proceedings concern matrimonial disputes or the guardianship of children.
2. Everyone charged with a criminal offense shall have the right to be presumed innocent until proven guilty according to law.
3. In the determination of any criminal charge against him, everyone shall be entitled to the following minimum guarantees, in full equality:
    - To be informed promptly and in detail in a language which he understands of the nature and cause of the charge against him;
    - To have adequate time and facilities for the preparation of his defense and to communicate with counsel of his own choosing;
    - To be tried without undue delay;
    - To be tried in his presence, and to defend himself in person or through legal assistance of his own choosing; to be informed, if he does not have legal assistance, of this right; and to have legal assistance assigned to him, in any case where the interests of the justice so require, and without payment by him in any such case if he does not have sufficient means to pay for it;
    - To examine, or have examined, the witnesses on his behalf under the same conditions as witnesses against him;
    - To have the free assistance of an interpreter if he cannot understand or speak the language used in court;
    - Not to be compelled to testify against himself or to confess guilt.

4. In the case of juvenile persons, the procedure shall be such as will take account of their age and the desirability of promoting their rehabilitation.

5. Everyone convicted of a crime shall have the right to have his conviction and sentence being reviewed by a higher tribunal according to law.

6. When a person has by final decision been convicted of a criminal offense and when subsequently his conviction has been reversed or he has been pardoned on the ground that a new or newly discovered fact shows conclusively that there has been a miscarriage of justice, the person who has suffered punishment as a result of such conviction shall be compensated according to law, unless it is proven that the non-disclosure of the unknown fact in time is wholly or partly attributable to him.

7. No one shall be liable to be tried or punished again for an offense for which he has already been finally convicted or acquitted in accordance with the law and penal procedure of each country.

See Exec. Order No. 13, 107, 63 Fed. Reg. 68,991, (December 15, 1998).

[7] The Human Rights Committee, established under Part IV, Articles 28-45, of the ICCPR has stated, in General Comment Number 13, that it "notes the existence, in many countries, of military or special courts which try civilians," and that "[w]hile the Covenant does not prohibit such categories of courts, nevertheless the conditions which it lays down clearly indicate that the trying of civilians by such courts should be very exceptional and take place under conditions which genuinely afford the full guarantees of Article 14." The ICCPR also includes, in Article 4, a provision permitting parties to derogate from their obligations, "In time of public emergency which threatens the life of the nation and the existence of which is officially proclaimed."

[8] See Chapter I, n.33 supra and accompanying text discussion.

[9] Rules Established by the Military Commission Appointed by Order of the President of July 2, 1942 at 3-4; McCoy Papers.

[10] Military Trial at 991.

[11] In re Yamashita, 327 U.S. 1 (1946).

[12] Id. at 20.

[13] U.S. Constitution, Article I, § 9, cl. 2.

[14] See Chapter I, n.32 supra and accompanying text discussion.

[15] Ex Parte Quirin, 317 U.S. at 24-25. In his Military Order of January 11, 1945, President Roosevelt reissued the authorization for military commissions without the language denying offenders access to the courts. See Military Order of January 11, 1945, 10 Fed. Reg. 549 (January 16, 1945) See also, In re Yamashita, 327 U.S. 1, 8 (1946).

[16] See Johnson v. Eisentrager, 339 U.S. 763 (1950) in Chapter II, supra n.36 at 52 and accompanying text discussion. It is of interest to note that the court pointed out in Yamashita, that Yamashita's offenses and trial occurred in the Philippines, which were at the time possessions of the United States.

[17] See Military Commission Instruction No. 5, Affidavit and Agreement by Civilian Defense Counsel, Annex B, Section II I, Appendix C9.

[18] *Id*. Section II E (2).

[19] *See* Military Commission Order 1, Section 4 (c) (3) (b), Appendix C1.

[20] Military Commission Instruction No. 5, Affidavit and Agreement by Civilian Defense Counsel, Annex B, Section II B, Appendix C9.

[21] *Id*. Annex B, Section II E (1), Appendix C9.

[22] *Id*. Annex B, Section II B, Appendix C9.

[23] *See* Vanessa Blum, "Tribunals Put Defense Bar in a Bind," *Legal Times*, July 15, 2003 where it is reported that the costs of procuring the security clearance, roughly $300 for a basic clearance and $2600 for a top-secret clearance, must be covered by the attorney; Vanessa Blum, "Guantanamo Commissions: The Outlines of Justice," *Legal Times*, May 28, 2003; Pamela Hess, "Pentagon: Tribunals to include gag rule," *UPI, Pentagon Desk*, May 2, 2003; Mary Cocco, "Fair Trial Will Be a Travesty in Terror Cases," *Newsday*, June 3, 2003.

[24] 10 U.S.C. § 867a, 28 U.S.C. § 1259.

[25] *See* David E. Rovella, "Tribunal Rules Don't End Debate on Fairness," *National Law Journal*, March 25, 2002. In a highly unusual filing, five uniformed military lawyers assigned to defend detainees at Guantanamo submitted a brief to the United States Supreme Court challenging the basis of President Bush's plan to use military commissions without civilian review to try some of the prisoners detained there.

In their brief, the lawyers asserted that President Bush worked to create a "legal black hole" and overstepped his constitutional authority as Commander-in-Chief in the way he set up the program for military commissions. They stated that "under this monarchical regime those who fall into the black hole may not contest the jurisdiction, competency, or even the constitutionality of military tribunals." They argued that once the President put them before a commission as the government has established, he moved outside his role as Commander-in-Chief.

They suggest that the government's argument in the case has no stopping point because . . . "if there exists no right to civilian review, the government is essentially free to conduct sham trials and condemn to death those who do nothing more than pray to Allah. . . ."

The defense lawyers state that . . . "permitting those targeted by military commissions to file habeas petitions would not threaten the President's responsibility to protect the nation because the President would always retain the detention power. It is only the far broader step, sought by Petitioners, to permit Article III courts to become forums for en masse Bill-of-Rights challenges to detentions that may conceivably do so. This Court can reject that broad step, but still permit the filing of habeas petitions that challenge the jurisdiction and lawfulness of a military commission, without restricting the President's defense responsibilities at all." *See* Neil A. Lewis, "Bush's Power to Plan Trial of Detainees is Challenged," *N.Y. Times*, January 15, 2004. In a separate court filing one of the military defense lawyers representing a Yemeni laborer, one of the fifteen detainees at Guantanamo designated by President Bush to face a military commission, asserted that the Constitution guaranteed civilian court review of the military justice system. Navy Lt. Commander Charles Swift argued that the commissions unconstitutionally target only aliens and not United States citizens, that President Bush lacks the congressional approval required to permit the special trials to proceed, and that the Constitution grants Congress, not the President, the power to convene tribunals inferior to the Supreme Court, (art. 1, Section 8, cl. 9). John Mintz, "Yemeni's Attorney Tries to Halt Tribunal," *Washington Post*, April 8, 2004 at A15, and Jonathan Mahler, "Commander Swift Objects," *New York Times Magazine*, http://www.nytimes.com/2004/06/ /13/magazine/13MILITARY.html, June 13, 2004.

[26] *See* DoD News Briefing on Military Commissions, March 21, 2002 at 21. While House Counsel Alberto Gonzales has said that the Order preserves judicial review in civilian courts. Under the Order, anyone arrested, detained or tried in the United States by a military commission would be able to challenge the lawfulness of the commission's jurisdiction through habeas corpus proceedings in a federal court. *See* Alberto Gonzales, "Martial Justice, Full and Fair," *N.Y. Times*, Nov. 30, 2001 at A 25. The rule from *Eisentrager* provided guidance with respect to both habeas and appellate review. Any enemy combatant who was tried outside of the United States had no access to American courts for relief, while those who were detained and tried in the United States had a right to habeas review. *See Johnson v. Eisentrager* 339 U.S. 763, at 765-66, and *Rasul v. Bush*, 215 F. Supp. 2d 55 at 68-69 (D.D.C. 2002) ruling that Guantanamo Bay is not part of the sovereign territory of the United States and that *Eisentrager* applied to the aliens held there as detainees. However, the United States Supreme Court in *Rasul et al. v. Bush* and *al-Odah et al. v. United States*, 542 U.S. __ (2004) Nos. 03-334 & 03-343, ruled that since the Guantanamo detainees were held for over two years in territory subject to the long term jurisdiction of control of the United States, they were entitled to habeas corpus challenges in United States federal courts. *See* Chapter V discussion at 160-161.

[27] Military Commission Order No. I § (6) (D) (1). In *Yamashita*, Justice Murphy argued in dissent that section 16 of the evidentiary rules "permits reception of documents, reports, affidavits, depositions, diaries, letters, copies of documents, or other secondary evidence of their contents, *hearsay*, opinion evidence and conclusions, in fact of anything which in the commission's opinion 'would be of assistance in proving or disproving the charge,' without any of the usual modes of authentication. A more complete abrogation of customary safeguards relating to the proof, whether in the usual rules of evidence or any reasonable substitute and whether for use in the trial of crime in the civil courts, or military tribunals, hardly could have been made. So far as the admissibility and probative value of evidence was concerned, the directive made the commission a law unto itself." He concluded that the defendant was rushed to trial under an improper charge, given insufficient time to prepare an adequate defense, deprived of the benefits of some of the most elementary rules of evidence and sentenced to be hanged. Justice Rutledge, who joined in dissent suggested that hearsay evidence of all types . . . affidavits, newspaper articles, propaganda film . . . was admitted which would have been excluded in a U.S. court. *See, In re Yamashita* 327 U.S. at 49-53.

[28] *See* Evan J. Wallach, "The Procedural and Evidentiary Rules of the Post-World War II War Crimes Trials: Did They Provide an Outline for International Legal Procedure?" 37 *Colum. J. Transnat'l L.* 851, 854, 871-72 (1999).

[29] *See* Rule of Procedure and Evidence 89 (c) International Criminal Tribunal for the former Yugoslavia, IT/32/REV. 21 (2001) ("A chamber may admit any relevant evidence which it deems to have probative value").

[30] See *Paquete Habana* 175 U.S. 677 (1900) holding that the United States is obliged to respect customary international law.

[31] President Bush and Secretary of Defense Rumsfeld have consistently maintained that the United States planned, for the most part, to treat the enemy combatants in a manner that is reasonably consistent with the Geneva Conventions. *See* Office of White House Press Secretary, Fact Sheet, Status of Detainees at Guantanamo 1 (Feb. 7, 2002). It has recently been revealed that Alberto Gonzales in a memo to the President in early 2002 laid out broad arguments as to why it was essential not to strictly apply the Geneva Conventions to the Taliban or al-Qaida. He argued that dropping Geneva would allow the President to preserve his flexibility and by "your policy of

providing humane treatment to enemy detainees gives us the credibility to insist on like treatment for our soldiers." *See* Alberto R. Gonzales, Memorandum For the President Decision Re: "Application of the Geneva Convention of War to the Conflict with Al Qaeda and the Taliban," January 25, 2002, and John Barry, Michael Hirsh and Michael Isikoff, "The Roots of Torture," *Newsweek* May 24, 2004, *World News* at 2.

In a separate memorandum written by John Yoo, Deputy Assistant Attorney General to William J. Haynes, General Counsel, Department of Defense in early January 2002, the argument is made that the Geneva Conventions do not protect members of al-Qaida "which is merely a violent political movement or organization and not a nation state. As a result, it is ineligible to be a signatory to any treaty, . . . and these treaties do not protect members of the . . . organization. We further conclude that these treaties do not apply to the Taliban militias." *See* John Yoo, Memorandum for William J. Haynes II, General Counsel, Department of Defense Re: "Application of the Treaties and Laws to al Qaeda and Taliban Detainees," January 9, 2002.

Because of the "enemy combatant" designation for Taliban and al-Qaida detainees at Guantanamo several military officers in Cuba grew concerned that they were operating without clear rules and the judge advocate at the base, Lt. Col. Dwaine Beaver, sought formal clarification from the Pentagon as to what were acceptable interrogation methods.

The request prompted a broad legal review and upon its completion in February 2003, 24 approved techniques were developed which included an individual matrix that indicated whether the method posed problems under United States and international laws, and at what hierarchical level of the Pentagon was approval required. A formal document spelling out the approval interrogation guidelines was sent to Guantanamo in March 2003. *See* Tim Golden and Eric Schmitt, "General Took Guantanamo Rules to Iraq for Handling of Prisoners." *N.Y. Times*, A1, May 13, 2004. In a directive from Secretary of Defense Rumsfeld, Navy Inspector General Vice Admiral Albert Church III was ordered to broaden an earlier review of detention and interrogation procedures at the military prisons at Guantanamo and at Charleston, South Carolina to Army detention and interrogation operations in Afghanistan and Abu Ghraib prison and other detention sites in Iraq. *See*, "Navy Admiral in Charge of Abuse Probe," *Chicago Tribune*, http://www.military.com/NewsContent/0,13319,FL_probe_061004,00.html, June 10, 2004.

In a recent law review article William H. Taft IV, Legal Advisor, United States Department of State commented: "While the United States has major objections to Additional Protocol I, it does regard the provisions of Article 75 as an articulation of safeguards to which all persons in the hands of the enemy are entitled." See William H. Taft IV, "Current Pressures on International Humanitarian Law: The Law of Armed Conflict After 9/11: Some Salient Features," 28 *Yale J. Int'l Law* 319, Summer 2003.

[32] 6 U.S.T. 3316, Article 105.

[33] *Id.*

[34] *See* "U.S. Charges Two at Guantanamo with Conspiracy," *N.Y. Times*, February 24, 2004 at A1.

[35] *Id.*

[36] *See*, United States Department of Defense, News Release 564-04, Guantanamo Detainee Charged, June 10, 2004.

[37] *See* United States Department of Defense, News Release 678-04, July 14, 2004.

[38] United States Department of Defense, News Release 620-04, "Military Commission Charges Referred," June 29, 2004. In October 2004, the appointing authority in charge of all Military Commissions, Gen. John D. Altenburg Jr. ruled that two officers on the panel Col. R. Thomas

Bright of the Marines, and Lt. Col. Timothy Tooney of the Air Force were unsuitable to continue to serve as commission members because they could not judge the cases impartially. A third officer, Lt. Col. Curt Cooper of the Army, who served as an alternate member of the panel was also dismissed on the same grounds. Defense lawyers for the defendants were highly critical of General Altenburg's actions because "they were illogical, inconsistent, and only made the situation more unfair for their clients." With only three officers remaining on the panel and with a two-thirds vote needed to convict a defendant, the prosecution now needs two members to win. With five members they needed four to convict. *See*, Neil A. Lewis, "General Takes Three Officers Off Tribunal at Cuba Base," *N.Y. Times*, October 23, 2004, at A7.

[39] In documents filed September 7, 2004, Colonel Swann urged the commission's presiding officer, Colonel Brownback, to "closely evaluate his own suitability to serve" and to "determine whether good cause exists for his removal." Objections were raised because of Colonel Brownback's ties to the appointing authority John Altenburg who chose the panel and oversees its operation. *See*, Toni Lacy, "U.S. Tribunal Could Lose Members," http://www.usatoday.com/news /washington/ 2004-09-14-tribunals_X.htm?POE=NEWISVA.

[40] *See* Spencer J. Crona and Neal A. Richardson, "Justice for War Criminals of Invisible Armies: A New Legal and Military Approach to Terrorism." 21 *Okla. City U.L. Rev.* 349 n.132, and *Johnson v. Eisentrager,* 339 U.S. 763 (1950).

[41] *See* John P. Elwood, "Prosecuting the War on Terrorism," *Criminal Justice Magazine*, Volume 17 Issue 2, Summer 2002.

[42] *See* Spencer J. Crona and Neal A. Richardson, "Military Tribunals: Commission smooths way for new criminal justice system" http://www.denverpost.com, May 18, 2003, Perspective, article ID 1152540.

[43] *See* John Mintz, "Both Sides Say Tribunal Will be Fair Trials," *Washington Post*, May 23, 2003 at 3.

[44] *Id.*

CHAPTER IV

Enemy Combatants and the Rule of Law Post 9/11

The Military Order of November 13, 2001 establishing military commissions to detain and try alleged terrorists identified with the September 11 attacks applied only to non-citizens in the custody of the United States.[1] The order appears to leave open the possibility that violators of the law who do not fall into the category of persons defined in Section 2 may be nevertheless detained and prosecuted by military commissions.[2]

In a defacto war, can the President unilaterally act to detain enemy combatants without specific congressional authorization? If the President is required to have congressional authorization, has such authorization been provided to him post 9/11? Is it legally appropriate for the President to classify as enemy combatants United States citizens who are suspected of terrorist activity and would that effectively permit the government to detain them indefinitely and deny them access to legal counsel and the judicial system?

The focus of this section of the study is an examination of the cases of Jose Padilla, the dirty bomb suspect, and Yaser Esam Hamdi, the Cajun Taliban, both of whom are United States citizens who have been designated enemy combatants, and Zacarias Moussaoui, the twentieth hijacker, a French national of Moroccan descent, who is the lone defendant charged in an American Court with conspiracy in the September 11 attacks. Padilla and Hamdi have been denied access to lawyers, have had their rights to a hearing before a judge restricted, and have been imprisoned indefinitely without a formal charge being presented against either of them. Moussaoui is defending himself with the aid of court-appointed lawyers in the federal criminal court system.

* * * * * * * * * *

Jose Padilla (Abdullah al-Muhajir)

Jose Padilla was born in Brooklyn, New York and raised in Chicago, Illinois. He was prosecuted and convicted for murder and weapons possession and had served jail time for both crimes before he left the country.[3] He converted to Islam in prison and took the name Abdullah al-Muhajir when he lived in Egypt in the 1990's. He traveled to Saudi Arabia, Pakistan, and Afghanistan. On several occasions in 2001, he met with senior al-Qaida officials.

While in Afghanistan and Pakistan, Padilla trained with al-Qaida operatives and studied how to wire explosive devises and researched radiological dispersion devices. Al-Qaida officials knew that as a citizen of the United States holding a valid passport, Padilla would be able to travel freely in the country without drawing unnecessary attention to himself. He was instructed by senior al-Qaida officials to return to the United States to conduct reconnaissance and/or other attacks on behalf of the terrorist organization.

The United States government was tracking Padilla when on May 8, 2002 he flew from Pakistan into Chicago O'Hare International Airport, where he was placed in the custody of federal law enforcement authorities and held first as a material witness in a federal detention center.

On June 9, 2002 President Bush, acting as Commander-in-Chief, and after consultation with the Secretary of Defense, Attorney General, and other senior officials of the administration, designated Padilla an enemy combatant who posed a serious and continuing threat to the American people and national security, whereupon he was transferred from the custody of the Justice Department to the custody of the Defense Department and placed in a naval brig in South Carolina where he was held incommunicado. Padilla is the first and only United States citizen not captured on a foreign battlefield to be subjected to indefinite detention by the Bush Administration.

Lawyers for Padilla immediately filed a petition in federal district court seeking a writ of habeas corpus asserting that in holding him in military custody, the government violated his constitutional rights as a citizen, including his right to due process, his right to be free from unreasonable seizure, his right to counsel and his right to appear before a grand jury.

Federal District Court Ruling on Padilla

On December 4, 2002 Chief Judge Michael B. Mukasey of the Southern District of New York issued an opinion and an order which held that Jose Padilla would be permitted to consult with counsel in aid of his petition and in particular in aid of responding to the Mobbs Declaration (authored by Michael N. Mobbs, a special advisor in the U.S. Department of Defense) which lays out the President's authority to designate enemy combatants, and why Padilla was so designated.[4]

The opinion directed Secretary of Defense Rumsfeld to let Padilla meet with counsel for the purpose of submitting to the court facts bearing on his petition, "under such conditions as the parties may agree to, or, absent agreement, such conditions as the court may direct to foreclose as far as possible, the danger that Padilla will use his attorneys for the purpose of conveying information to others."[5] The ruling was limited in the sense that no general right to counsel in connection to questioning was assumed to exist, however specific access to counsel was required to permit Padilla to present necessary facts to the court.[6]

In his order Judge Mukasey also made it clear that the President had the power to detain unlawful combatants and it didn't matter that Padilla was a United States citizen captured on United States soil because the President was operating at maximum authority under the United States Constitution and the Joint Resolution of Congress. That did not mean however, that the Commander-in-Chief's broad power to designate enemy combatants was immune from judicial review.[7]

The judge added that detention for the duration of hostilities was supportable logically and legally on the same ground that the detention of prisoners was supportable, namely, to prevent them from rejoining the enemy. The standard to justify the detention was merely whether there was *some evidence* to support the President's conclusion that Padilla was engaged in a mission against the United States on behalf of an enemy with whom we were at war.[8]

The judge gave the parties until December 20, 2002 to work out by agreement the conditions for compliance with his order. If they could not agree then the court would impose conditions for them.[9] The government filed a motion requesting a reconsideration of the court's holding arguing that the consultation would jeopardize the principal purposes for detaining enemy combatants in the first place, and "[t]hat is the gathering of intelligence information about the enemy and preventing the detainee from helping in any further threats to our national security interests. The access to counsel would present a potential opportunity for Padilla to use her to send messages to others."[10]

On January 8, 2003 the United States Court of Appeals for the Fourth Circuit issued an opinion in *Hamdi v. Rumsfeld*.[11] In that case, the Fourth Circuit treated a question certified for appeal by the district court where Yaser Hamdi, an American citizen, had filed a habeas corpus petition: "Whether a declaration by a Special Advisor to the Under Secretary of Defense for Policy[12] setting forth what the government contends were the circumstances of Hamdi's capture was sufficient by itself to justify his detention."[13]

The Fourth Circuit was careful to limit its decision to the issues presented by the facts before it, and specifically disavowed any intention to speak to the circumstances presented in *Padilla's* case:

> Given the concerns discussed in the preceding sections, any broad or categorical holdings on enemy combatant designations would be especially inappropriate. We have no occasion, for example, to address the designation as an enemy combatant of an American citizen captured on American soil or the role that counsel might play in such a proceeding. See, e.g., Padilla v. Bush, No. 02 Civ. 445 (MBM), 2002 WL 31718308 (S.D.N.Y. Dec. 4, 2002). We shall, in fact, go no further in this case than the specific context before us—that of the undisputed detention of a citizen during a combat operation undertaken in a foreign country and a determination by the executive that the citizen was allied with enemy forces.[14]

On January 9, the government offered its written submission in Padilla relying in principal part on a declaration from Vice Admiral Lowell E. Jacoby, Director of the Defense Intelligence Agency (Jacoby Declaration).

The Jacoby Declaration sets forth the factual predicate for one of the two government arguments advanced in support of the motion for reconsideration. Those two arguments are (i) permitting Padilla to consult with counsel could set back by months the government's efforts to bring psychological pressure to bear upon Padilla in a effort to interrogate him, and could compromise the government's interrogation techniques; and (ii) in any event, consultation with counsel is unnecessary in view of the level of proof fixed by the court in the opinion as the standard for deciding whether the government may continue to hold Padilla without formal charges—*some evidence* to justify the conclusion that he is an enemy combatant.[15]

Judge Mukasey suggested that the government had hoped that the Fourth Circuit opinion in *Hamdi* would buttress its position in the *Padilla* case and that it attempted to slow the progress on Padilla until that (Hamdi) opinion was issued.[16]

The principal relevance of the Jacoby Declaration to whether Padilla should be permitted to consult with counsel was its description of the interrogation techniques used by the Defense Intelligence Agency (DIA), and its assessment of the danger of interrupting such interrogation to permit Padilla to consult with counsel. The Jacoby Declaration described the DIA's interrogation technique:

> DIA's approach to interrogation is largely dependent upon creating an atmosphere of dependency and trust between the subject and the interrogator. Developing the kind of relationship of trust and dependency necessary for effective interrogations is a process that can take a significant amount of time. There are numerous examples of situations where interrogators have been unable to obtain valuable intelligence from a subject until months, or even years, after the interrogation process began.
> Anything that threatens the perceived dependency and trust between the subject and interrogator directly threatens the value of interrogation as an intelligence-gathering tool. Even seemingly minor interruptions can have profound psychological impacts on

the delicate subject-interrogator relationship. Any insertion of counsel into the subject-interrogator relationship, for example—even if only for a limited duration or for a specific purpose—can undo months of work and may permanently shut down the interrogation process. Therefore, it is critical to minimize external influences on the interrogation process.[17]

The Jacoby Declaration also stressed the need for ongoing intelligence, as new information was learned that could suggest new lines of inquiry to those already in custody.[18] Padilla "could potentially provide information" on about a dozen subjects, including not only the so-called "dirty bomb" plot in which he was alleged to have been involved, but also more general subjects such as al-Qaida training, planning, recruitment methods, and operations in several countries, including the United States.[19] In addition, Admiral Jacoby stated that the information Padilla "may be able to provide is time-sensitive and perishable."[20]

The Jacoby Declaration contained the following assessment of the "Potential Impact of Granting Padilla Access to Counsel":

> Permitting Padilla any access to counsel may substantially harm our national security interests. As with most detainees, Padilla is unlikely to cooperate if he believes that an attorney will intercede in his detention. DIA's assessment is that Padilla is even more inclined to resist interrogation than most detainees. DIA is aware that Padilla has had extensive experience in the United States criminal justice system and had access to counsel when he was being held as a material witness. These experiences have likely heightened his expectations that counsel will assist him in the interrogation process. Only after such time as Padilla has perceived that help is not on the way can the United States reasonably expect to obtain all possible intelligence information from Padilla.
>
> Because Padilla is likely more attuned to the possibility of counsel intervention than most detainees, I believe that any potential sign of counsel involvement would disrupt our ability to gather intelligence from Padilla. Padilla has been detained without counsel for seven months—since the [Department of Defense] took control of him on 9 June 2002. Providing him access to counsel now would create expectations by Padilla that his ultimate release may be obtained through an adversarial civil litigation process.

This would break—probably irreparably—the sense of dependency and trust interrogators are attempting to create.

At a minimum, Padilla might delay providing information until he believes that his judicial avenues have been exhausted. Given the nature of his case, his prior experience in the criminal system, and the length of time that has already elapsed since his detention, Padilla might reasonably expect that his judicial avenues of relief may not be exhausted for many months or years. Moreover, Padilla might harbor the belief that his counsel would be available to assist him at any point and that seven months is not an unprecedented time for him to be without access to counsel.

Any such delay in Padilla's case risks that plans for future attacks will go undetected during that period, and that whatever information Padilla may eventually provide will be outdated and more difficult to corroborate.

Additionally, permitting Padilla's counsel to learn what information Padilla may have provided to interrogators, and what information the interrogators may have provided Padilla, unnecessarily risks disclosure of the intelligence sources and methods being employed in the War on Terrorism.[21]

Judge Mukasey in response to the serious potential consequences raised in the Jacoby Declaration expressed his concern that the document was silent on two issues: (i) the particulars of Padilla's actual interrogation and what they suggested about the prospect of obtaining additional information from him, and (ii) when, if at all, intelligence personnel had ever experienced effects of an interruption in interrogation like the effects predicted in both of the excerpts from the Jacoby Declaration.

Government counsel disclosed that information from interrogations was purposely excluded in order to maintain separation between national security interrogation and the litigation.[22] Since the information was not there, there was a certain "lack of concreteness"[23] in the Jacoby Declaration. Judge Mukasey ruled that Admiral Jacoby may be expert in intelligence related matters, however the Declaration focused on a matter of human nature—Padilla's in particular—with respect to his reactions in interruptions of interrogation—matters in which there were no true experts, including intelligence experts.

In refusing to reverse his original decision Judge Mukasey insisted that the only way he could properly examine whether Padilla's detention was consistent with due process was to allow limited access to counsel. The judge was confident that given such an opportunity the most likely outcome would be a confirmation that Padilla's detention was not arbitrary and that the President was properly fulfilling his responsibilities and duties as Commander-in-Chief provided to him in the Constitution. Judge Mukasey was of the view that, like *Quirin,* the Padilla case dealt with isolated events and had limited application.

Relevance of *Quirin* Case to *Padilla*

Jose Padilla's case is distinct from that of *Quirin* in several respects. In the period of the *Quirin* decision, as previously noted, the United States was in a formally declared war.[24] However, it is well established that in the past the United States has been involved in partial wars and non-declared wars pursuing military objectives under the law of war.[25]

A second distinction comes from the definition of unlawful combatant in the *Quirin* decision. An unlawful combatant is one who is associated with the military arm of an enemy government, directed by that government to enter the country secretly to perform hostile acts and to act on its behalf.[26] The discarded uniforms, explosives and other incendiary devices provided sufficient evidence that the saboteurs in *Quirin* belonged to the enemy nation and were intending to carry out acts of sabotage, espionage, or other hostile or war like acts. The saboteurs in *Quirin* came into the country secretly on a submarine, and had a mission to blow up rail centers, bridges, water supply systems and industrial plants.[27]

In both a factual and legal sense, Padilla cannot be deemed a combatant in Operation Enduring Freedom in Afghanistan between the military forces of the Taliban and the United States (and other allied nations) because he did not participate in any battle or serve as a member of any organized armed forces, groups and units under the command responsible to the Taliban Government.

Padilla received training from al-Qaida operatives, and studied the wiring of explosive devices. Padilla was directed by al-Qaida members to return to the United States from Pakistan in 2002 to explore and advance plans for further attacks against the United States. The Declaration of Michael Mobbs,[28] Special Advisor to the Under Secretary of Defense for Policy, set forth the evidentiary basis for the President's determination to declare Padilla an enemy combatant, although it did not provide any details about the alleged threats posed by Padilla in conjunction with specific al-Qaida terrorist plots. The Declaration did not establish that Padilla took any steps to launch an attack; indeed, it stated the attack was "still in the initial planning stages, and there was no specified time set for the operation to occur."[29] Furthermore, there was no evidence to suggest that Padilla had the means to develop a radioactive bomb.[30]

The *Quirin* court relied extensively on President Roosevelt's authority conferred on him by Congress to issue the Military Orders and to act as he did under the prevailing circumstances of that period.[31] President Bush's Military Order cites the Joint Resolution adopted by the Congress post September 11, and Sections 821 and 836 of Title 10 of the U.S. Code which authorized President Roosevelt to use the military tribunals in *Quirin*, although it specifically excludes United States citizens from its jurisdiction.[32]

In *Quirin*, those persons who aided and abetted in the plot in the United States, but who were not themselves members of the German army were not held as enemy combatants but were tried in ordinary civilian courts for crimes such as treason.[33] In the *Padilla* case the government claims that he was associated with al-Qaida, which is similar to the Haupt and Cramer associations with the German saboteurs in *Quirin*.

Relevance of *Hamdi* Case to *Padilla*

The government relied upon the *Hamdi* decision in which the Fourth Circuit found that Yaser Hamdi was not entitled to challenge the facts presented in the Mobbs Declaration.[34] In *Hamdi*, the Fourth Circuit held that when "a habeas petitioner has been designated an enemy combatant and it is undisputed that he was captured in a zone of active combat operations abroad, further judicial inquiry is unwarranted when the government has responded to the petition by setting forth factual assertions which would establish a legally valid basis for the petitioner's detention."[35] That is, if Hamdi did not dispute that he was captured in a zone of active combat operations abroad and the government adequately alleged that he was an unlawful combatant, than he had no right to present facts in connection with his habeas petition. His petition failed as a matter of law.

Because Hamdi did not dispute that he was captured "in Afghanistan during a time of active military hostilities,"[36] and the government set forth factual assertions establishing a valid basis for Hamdi's detention, the Fourth Circuit concluded that Hamdi was lawfully detained.[37] In reaching that conclusion, the Court did not have to decide what standard to apply if Hamdi were to deny that he was captured in a zone of active combat operations abroad.[38]

The Court in *Hamdi* took pains to point out that its holding was limited to "the specific context before us—that of the undisputed detention of a citizen during a combat operation undertaken in a foreign country and a determination by the executive that the citizen was allied with enemy forces."[39] Padilla was detained in the United States initially by law enforcement officers pursuant to a material witness warrant. Soldiers in combat did not capture him on a foreign battlefield.

In his concluding comments Judge Mukasey offered a few choice words in response to the Chicken Little, the sky is falling, warnings articulated by several parties to the case. The Jacoby Declaration, at one point, suggested that permitting Padilla to consult with a lawyer "risked that plans for future attacks will go undetected."[40] In amicus submissions the hue and cry raised the specter of revisiting the ignominious history of "American concentration camps of WWII reminiscent of *Korematsu*,[41] as well as considering the detention of Padilla as a repudiation of the Magna Carta."[42] It was suggested that if Padilla were not provided the full panoply of protections afforded defendants in criminal cases we

- the enemy combatant must be represented by an assigned defense counsel, but is permitted to hire a civilian defense lawyer at his own expense;
- a presumption of innocence exists for the accused;
- hearsay evidence can be admissible;
- the government must establish proof beyond any reasonable doubt;
- decisions are based on a two-thirds majority of commission members, except in death penalty cases where a unanimous verdict is required;
- cases are reviewed by a military review panel, but there is no appeal to a civilian court; and
- final review rests with either the Secretary of Defense or the President.

Detention and trial procedures of detainee enemy combatants under the Combatant Status Review Tribunals, Administrative Review Boards, and Military Commissions permit the Executive to act as a unilateral lawmaker, law enforcer and law adjudicator. No one branch in a constitutional system of government has a total monopoly of authority, nor should it. Congress should exercise its legitimate constitutional role in assuring that the Executive is effectively protecting our national security interest while sufficiently assuring our civil liberties.

While Congress has authorized the President to use all necessary and appropriate force it has yet to expressly authorize the use of detention or military commissions. Spelling out in detail the requirements for detention and military commissions and the procedural protections afforded to detainee enemy combatants would ensure that decisions when handed down survive judicial scrutiny.

Under our Constitution, there are certain indispensable safeguards to civil liberty that must be preserved even during periods of national crisis and military emergency. Military Tribunals, Boards, and Commissions cannot deny detained

would be a "sea change in the constitutional life of this country and . . .
unprecedented in civil society."[43] Judge Rosemary Pooler said the President must
go to Congress because it has the power to let the President make a United States
citizen captured on American soil an enemy combatant.[44] "As terrible as 9/11 was,
it didn't repeal the Constitution."[45] The third panel member, Judge Richard
Wesley, suggested the case shouldn't have been brought to the Second Circuit.
"This should be litigated in South Carolina."[46]

Second Circuit Court of Appeals Ruling on *Padilla*

On December 18, 2003, Judges Barrington Parker and Rosemary Pooler
issued a majority panel opinion from the Second Circuit Court of Appeals which
concluded:

- Secretary of Defense Rumsfeld was the proper respondent in
  the case and the District Court had jurisdiction;

- Padilla's detention was not authorized by Congress, and absent
  such authorization, the President did not have the power under
  Article II of the Constitution to detain as an enemy combatant
  an American citizen seized on American soil outside a zone of
  combat;

- Clear congressional authorization is required for detention of
  American citizens on American soil because 18 U.S.C. §
  4001(a) (2000) (the Non-Detention Act) prohibited such
  detentions absent specific congressional authorization;

- Congress's Authorization for Use of Military Force Joint
  Resolution Pub L. No. 107-40, 115 Stat. 224 (2001) (*Joint
  Resolution*) was not such an authorization and no exception to
  section 4001(a) existed;

- The government did not show that Padilla's detention could be
  grounded in the President's inherent constitutional powers.[47]

The panel did not address the detention of an American citizen seized
within a zone of combat in Afghanistan, such as the court confronted in *Hamdi*.[48]
The court remanded to the District Court with instructions to issue a writ of
habeas corpus directing Secretary Rumsfeld to release Padilla from military

custody within 30 days, at which point the government could act within its legislatively conferred authority to take further action. Options included: transferring Padilla to civilian authorities who could bring criminal charges against him and if appropriate he could be held as a material witness in connection with grand jury proceedings.[49] The court reached no conclusion as to Padilla's guilt or innocence. The White House sought an immediate stay of the *Padilla* decision and appealed the ruling to the United States Supreme Court.

In reaching its decision the panel provided several telling observations. In determining that Secretary of Defense Rumsfeld was the proper respondent in this case, the majority commented that the legal reality of control was vested only with Secretary Rumsfeld, since he alone could inform the President that further restraint of Padilla as an enemy combatant was no longer required. Such an "extraordinary and pervasive role that he [the Secretary] played in this matter was virtually unique."[50] Such a degree of cabinet–level involvement was unprecedented in our nation's history.[51]

The power to detain Padilla was said by the government to derive from the President's authority, settled by *Ex Parte Quirin*[52] to detain enemy combatants in wartime—authority that was argued to encompass the detention of United States citizens seized on United States soil.[53] The majority panel did not agree that *Quirin* controlled in the *Padilla* case because *Quirin* did not address to what degree the President could impose military authority upon United States citizens domestically without a clear congressional mandate. Since the *Quirin* court did not determine to what extent the President as Commander-in-Chief had constitutional power to create military commissions without the support of congressional legislation,[54] the Second Circuit majority did not want to read into *Quirin* a principle the *Quirin* Court itself declined to promulgate.[55]

The majority in Padilla were not persuaded by the factual parallels between the *Quirin* saboteurs and Padilla because the *Quirin* Court relied on congressional authorization to justify the detention and military trial of the *Quirin* saboteurs, an authorization that the panel believed did not exist in the *Padilla* case.[56] Furthermore, there were other important distinctions between *Quirin* and Padilla. When *Quirin* was decided in 1942, the Non-Detention Act had not yet been enacted and the *Quirin* Court therefore had no occasion to consider the effects of legislation prohibiting the detention of American citizens without statutory authorization.[57]

In *Quirin* the saboteurs admitted that they were soldiers in the armed forces of a nation against whom the United States had formally declared war. Padilla disputed his designation as an enemy combatant and pointed to the fact that the civilian accomplices of the *Quirin* saboteurs, citizens who advanced the sabotage plots, but were not members of the German armed forces, were charged and tried as civilians in civilian courts, not as enemy combatants subject to military authority.[58]

Quirin, in the majority's view, rested upon the principle that primary authority for imposing military jurisdiction upon American citizens lies with Congress. At a minimum, an Act of Congress was required to expand military jurisdiction.[59]

The panel agreed that great deference should be afforded the President's exercise of his authority as Commander-in-Chief, and they also agreed that "whether a state of armed conflict exists against an enemy to which the laws of war apply is a political question for the President, not the courts."[60] However they reasoned that the President could not, even in times of grave national security threats of war, whether declared or undeclared, lay claim to any powers that expressly or implicitly belonged to the Congress.

"Separation of Powers concerns are further heightened when the Commander-in-Chief's powers are exercised in the domestic sphere."[61] In the *Padilla* case the government insisted that the Constitution authorized the President to detain an enemy combatant as an exercise of inherent executive authority. Padilla contended that the President, by his order denominating him an enemy combatant, engaged in the "lawmaking" function entrusted by the Constitution to Congress in violation of the separation of powers. He also argued that there had been no legislative articulation of what constitutes an "enemy combatant," what circumstances triggered the designation, or when it ended.[62] The panel agreed with Padilla that the Constitution lodged such power with the Congress and not the President. Without express congressional authorization the President's Commander-in-Chief power did not support Padilla's confinement. Congress then had the power to authorize the detention of United States citizens under the circumstances of *Padilla's* case, the President, acting alone, did not.[63]

The panel disagreed with the District Court with respect to the Joint Resolution providing the necessary statutory authorization to uphold Padilla's detention. The plain language of the Joint Resolution contained nothing authorizing the detention of American citizens captured on United States soil. "While it may be possible to infer a power of detention from the Joint Resolution in the battlefield context where detentions are necessary to carry out the war, there is no reason to suspect from the language of the Joint Resolution that Congress believed it would be authorizing the detention of an American citizen already held in a federal correctional institution and not 'arrayed against our troops' in the field of battle"[64]

The majority also opined that it was highly unlikely, if not inconceivable, that Congress would leave unstated and to inference in the Joint Resolution something so significant and unprecedented as authorization to detain American citizens under the Non-Detention Act.[65]

The dissenting opinion of Judge Richard Wesley argued that the President as Commander-in-Chief "has the inherent authority to thwart the acts of belligerency on U.S. soil that would cause harm to U.S. citizens and, in this case, Congress through the Joint Resolution specifically and directly authorized the President to take the actions contested."[66]

Judge Wesley suggested that both common sense and the Constitution permitted the Commander-in-Chief to protect the nation when we were confronted with belligerency and that the President should determine what degree of responsive force was appropriate.[67] Citing the *Prize Cases*[68] Judge Wesley argued that congressional authorization was not necessary for the Executive to have exercised his constitutional authority to prosecute armed conflicts when, as on September 11, 2001, the United States was attacked,[69] and courts may not review the level of force selected.[70]

Judge Wesley viewed the Joint Resolution passed by Congress as impliedly authorizing the President to detain Padilla and that such action was necessary to prevent future terrorist attacks against the United States. Padilla's citizenship in this case was irrelevant to Judge Wesley and the fact that he was captured on U.S. soil was a "distinction without a difference."[71]

As to the significance of the Non-Detention Act, Section 4001(a), Judge Wesley assumed that Congress was aware of its existence when it adopted the Joint Resolution, and furthermore "Congress had to know the President might detain someone who fell within the categories of identified belligerents in carrying out his charge."[72] In Judge Wesley's view, "if Section 4001(a) was an impenetrable barrier to the President detaining a U.S. citizen who was alleged to have ties to the belligerent and who was part of a plan for belligerency on U.S. soil, then Section 4001(a) was unconstitutional."[73]

Finally, Judge Wesley expressed his concern with respect to right to counsel: "No one has suspended the Great Writ."[74] Padilla's right to prove a remedy through the writ would be meaningless if he had to do so alone. I therefore would extend to him the right to counsel as Chief Judge Mukasey did.[75]

Yaser Esam Hamdi

Yaser Esam Hamdi was born in Louisiana but left for Saudi Arabia when he was a young child. As determined by the Pentagon, Hamdi traveled to Afghanistan in approximately July or August of 2001 and proceeded to affiliate with a Taliban military unit and receive weapons training. While serving with the Taliban in the aftermath of September 11, he was captured when his unit surrendered to the Northern Alliance forces with which it had been engaged in battle. He was in possession of an AK-47 rifle at the time of his surrender.

Hamdi was transported with his unit from Konduz, Afghanistan to the Northern Alliance prison in Majar-e-Sharif, Afghanistan and after a prison uprising there to a prison at Sheberghan, Afghanistan. Hamdi was next transported to the U.S. short-term detention facility in Kandahar, and then transferred to the Norfolk Naval Station Brig after it was discovered that he had not renounced his U.S. citizenship. He began his detention in Norfolk in April 2002. On July 30, 2003 Hamdi was transferred to the same naval brig in Charleston, South Carolina where Jose Padilla had been detained.

In June 2002, Hamdi's father filed a petition for a writ of habeas corpus alleging that Hamdi was a citizen of the United States who was residing in Afghanistan when he was seized by the United States government. Although acknowledging that Hamdi was seized in Afghanistan during a period of active military hostilities, the petition alleged that as an American citizen Hamdi was entitled to the full panoply of constitutional protections and that the government's detention of him in this country without charges, access to a judicial tribunal, or the right to counsel, violated the United States Constitution.

The district court appointed counsel for Hamdi and the Fourth Circuit Court of Appeals reversed that order in July 2002.[76] It did so because Hamdi's petition involved highly complex and sensitive national security issues and the district court had not shown proper deference to the government's legitimate security and intelligence interests.[77] The Court of Appeals sanctioned a limited and deferential inquiry into Hamdi's status, noting that if "Hamdi is indeed an 'enemy combatant' who was captured during hostilities in Afghanistan the government's present detention of him is a lawful one."[78]

On July 25, the government filed a response and motion to dismiss the petition for a writ of habeas corpus. An affidavit from Special Advisor Michael Mobbs to Under Secretary of Defense for Policy was attached which confirmed that Hamdi was captured in Afghanistan during armed hostilities and that the executive branch classified him an enemy combatant.

The district court on August 16 filed an opinion finding that the Mobbs Declaration fell short of supporting Hamdi's detention. The Court ordered the government to turn over, among other things, statements, notes, names and addresses of interrogators of Hamdi, statements by members of the Northern Alliance relative to Hamdi's surrender, and dates and locations of his detention.

Fourth Circuit Court of Appeals Rulings on *Hamdi*

The government petitioned for interlocutory review on appeal with the principal question certified by District Judge Robert Doumar: whether the Mobbs Declaration, standing alone, was sufficient as a matter of law to allow judicial review of Yaser Esam Hamdi's classification as an enemy combatant. The Fourth Circuit granted the government petition, noting that "this court may address any issue fairly included within the certified order because it is the order that is applicable and not the controlling question identified by the district court."[79] The court considered the dual status of Hamdi—that of American citizen and that of alleged enemy combatant—as important questions about the role of courts in times of war.

The court reasoned that the provisions of Article II Section 2 war powers investing the President as Commander-in-Chief with the power to wage war also included the authority to detain those captured in armed struggle.[80] On past occasions the Supreme Court had shown great deference to the political branches when called upon to decide cases implicating sensitive matters of foreign policy, national security, or military affairs and that was not difficult to discern.[81]

Chief Judge J. Harvie Wilkinson writing for a three-judge panel explained that it is the political branches that are organized to conduct overseas conflicts and they are accountable to the people for their actions. The courts are not in a position to comprehend the implications and ramifications of global conflicts and wars.

Measured against this understanding Judge Wilkinson observed, was the awareness of the fact that judicial deference to executive decisions made in the name of war was not unlimited. The Bill of Rights, and due process of law for American citizens are matters that no court should take lightly, and any detention of United States citizens must be subject to judicial review.[82]

Judge Wilkinson reasoned that the court approached this case with sensitivity to both the fundamental liberty interest asserted by Hamdi and the extraordinary breadth of war-making authority of the executive branch.

Hamdi presented two legal grounds for relief: 18 U.S.C. Section 4001 regulates the detention of United States citizens. It states in part:

> (a) No citizen shall be imprisoned or otherwise detained by the United States except pursuant to an Act of Congress.

Hamdi argued that there was no congressional sanction for his incarceration under this section and therefore he could not be further detained.

The panel responded that the President was authorized by Congress in the wake of September 11 terrorist attacks to "use all necessary and appropriate force . . . against . . . persons he determined planned, authorized, committed, or ordered the terrorist attacks."[83] The necessary and appropriate force in the resolution meant the capture and detention of any and all hostile forces arrayed against the United States troops. Furthermore, Congress authorized funds for "maintenance... of persons in the custody of the military whose status is determined . . . to be similar to prisoners of war."[84] Judge Wilkinson suggested that it would be difficult if not impossible to understand how Congress could appropriate for detaining persons similar to prisoners of war without also authorizing their detention in the first instance, and therefore Hamdi's contention that Section 4001(a) barred his detention was rejected.

Article 5 of the Geneva Convention, argued Hamdi, required a formal determination of his status as an enemy belligerent by a competent tribunal.[85] The panel dismissed this contention because the Geneva Convention is not self-executing and does not create private rights of action in the domestic courts of the signatory countries.[86] It is up to governments and diplomats of nations as disputing parties to invoke the Convention, not individuals.

The court concluded that there was no legal barrier to Hamdi's detention. The Fourth Circuit then turned to the question of whether the order of District Judge Doumar relative to the Mobbs affidavit was proper on its own terms.

The court expressed considerable concern about the order "risking standing the war-making powers of Articles I and II on their heads."[87] The emphasis was again placed on the President's exercise of military judgment in the capture of alleged combatants and the basic facts relied upon to support a legitimate exercise of that authority.[88] In this case "the government had voluntarily submitted—and urged us to review—an affidavit from Michael Mobbs, Special Advisor to the Under Secretary of Defense for Policy, describing what the government contends were the circumstances leading to Hamdi's designation as an enemy combatant under Article II's war power."[89]

The Mobbs affidavit consists of two pages and nine paragraphs in which Mobbs states that he was "substantially involved with matters related to the detention of enemy combatants in the current war against the al-Qaida terrorists and those who support and harbor them." In the affidavit, Mobbs acknowledged that a United States interrogation team in Afghanistan determined that Hamdi met "the criteria for enemy combatants over whom the United States was taking control."[90]

The panel stated that the district court went far beyond any reasonable scope of review of the Mobb's declaration by examining it line by line. Furthermore, they felt that this was not a case involving criminal charges in the exercise of the executive's law enforcement powers, but a case of the executive's power to detain under war powers of Article II. To review executive determinations involving military operations in the panel's view would carry a risk of intruding into the most basic responsibilities of a coordinate branch of government, which was inappropriate for the judiciary.

Therefore, the court reasoned, Hamdi would be entitled to due process normally found in the criminal justice system, including the right to counsel, if he were charged with a crime. But since he was not charged with any crime, he was being held as an enemy combatant pursuant to well-established laws and the customs of war. Hamdi's citizenship might entitle him to file a petition to challenge his detention but the fact that he was a citizen did not affect the legality of his detention as an enemy combatant.[91]

Since Hamdi took up arms against the United States in a foreign theater of war, regardless of the fact that he was a U.S. citizen, he could be properly designated an enemy combatant. His citizenship entitled Hamdi to a limited judicial inquiry about his detention only to the extent that it was legal under the war powers of the political branches. The panel reasoned that courts were not the appropriate bodies to second guess the military as to who should or should not be detained in an arena of combat, and courts were not in the position to overturn the military's decision to detain those persons in one location or another.

Although the panel decision expressed extensive deference to the Executive with respect to military detention of enemy combatants, the court rejected the sweeping proposition that an American citizen alleged to be an enemy combatant could be indefinitely held without charges simply on the government's say so.[92] The fact remained that Hamdi was not just any American citizen; he was captured and detained in a foreign theater of war and he was determined to be allied with enemy forces.

The panel decision was appealed to the full Court of Appeals for the Fourth Circuit and on July 9, 2003, in an 8 to 4 vote the court upheld President Bush's authority to detain as an enemy combatant a United States citizen captured on the battlefield and to deny him access to a lawyer. The court did not issue a majority opinion, just an order denying the petition for rehearing and suggestion for rehearing en banc. Judge Wilkinson and Judge Traxler filed separate concurring opinions in the denial of rehearing and Judge Luttig and Judge Motz filed opinions dissenting from the denial of rehearing.

Judge Wilkinson reminded Judge Motz that the conduct of war was delegated to the coordinate branches of government by provisions of Articles I and II of the Constitution, and that by embarking on a course that permitted litigation of detention in American courts, the judiciary was trespassing upon those powers of the Congress and Executive to the detriment of its own obligation to respect the limits and boundaries of its proper role. To start down such a road placed judges in a position in which they were ill-equipped to serve, namely, as final and ultimate arbiters of the degree to which litigation should be permitted to burden foreign military operations.[93]

"While it is true that the federal judiciary plays a vital role in securing our rights, the other branches of government play their part in securing the blessings of our liberty and in this particular case," Judge Wilkinson concluded, "the paramount right was that citizens of our country have their democracy's most vital life or death decisions made by those whom the Constitution charges with the task."[94]

In his separate concurring opinion Judge Traxler reasoned that during hostilities all persons in an enemy country were deemed to be enemies regardless of nationality pursuant to time-honored rules of law in wartime. That is not to say that all persons residing within the enemy country were in _fact_ enemies or that specifically Hamdi was necessarily an enemy combatant because he was in Afghanistan during a conflict between the United States and the Afghan government.[95] Hamdi's presence in Afghanistan placed his individual rights in tension with the Executive wartime powers under Article II, and the Judiciary was compelled by the nature of war and separation of powers to give deference to the Executive to determine who within a hostile country was friend and who was foe.[96] "Our decision" stated Judge Traxler, "does not sanction indefinite detention but rather contemplates detention for the duration of such hostilities.[97] This determination is just like other non-citizen detainees captured in an enemy country by our military forces making a battlefield determination that the person detained was there to take up arms against our soldiers."[98]

Judge Luttig in dissent argued the case should be reopened because the panel decision had not gone far enough in granting the appropriate power to the administration. The panel opinion was unpersuasive and beyond that it refused to rest decision on the proffer made by the President of the United States, and "its insistence instead upon resting decision on a putative concession by the detainee, had yielded reasoning that all but eviscerates the President's Article II power to determine who are and who are not enemies of the United States during times of war."[99]

Judge Luttig found it most troubling that the panel promised the Executive that the Judiciary would not sit in full review of his judgment as to who was an enemy combatant of the United States, but it adopted a rule that would henceforth do just that, "casting the Judiciary as ultimate arbiter in each and every instance of whether the Executive has properly so classified a detainee."[100]

He would most likely conclude that the facts recited in special Advisor Mobbs' affidavit were sufficient to satisfy the constitutionally appropriate standard for the President's designation of an enemy of the United States and he believed that the President was entitled to "receive from the Judiciary the deference when he exercised his Article II powers in designating a person an enemy combatant against the United States."[101]

Judge Motz in a separate dissent expressed her concern that the panel decision by the court held that a "short hearsay" declaration by Michael Mobbs, an un-elected and otherwise unknown government advisor, was sufficient as a matter of law to allow meaningful judicial review and approval of the Executive's designation of Hamdi as an enemy combatant.[102] In her view, to forfeit a United States citizen's constitutional rights the Executive must establish enemy combatant status with far more than hearsay.

In Judge Motz's view this case marked an historical precedent since a federal court, for the first time in history, approved denial of due process rights afforded a citizen exclusively based upon the President's designation of Hamdi as an enemy combatant, without testing the accuracy of the designation. *Ex Parte Quirin* was distinguishable since the Court in that case determined the citizen could be treated as an enemy combatant because the "citizen after consultation with legal counsel stipulated to the facts supporting the enemy combatant designation."[103]

Judge Motz argued that the Supreme Court had never suggested that an enemy combatant is without recourse to challenge that designation in court.[104] Rather the Court has held that a resident alien who has far less status than Hamdi, who enjoyed the high privilege of citizenship, can challenge the Executive's designation of him as an enemy.[105] Since Hamdi had not stipulated to anything, and having been denied the most basic of procedural protections, he could not possibly mount a challenge to the President's designation of him as an enemy combatant.

The slippery slope of indefinite detention . . . without access to a lawyer or the courts for any American citizen, even one captured on American soil, who the Executive designates an enemy combatant, was of grave concern to Judge Motz. However, she quickly added that the inadequacy of the President's action in this case did not provide license for a searching inquiry into the factual circumstances of every detainee's capture because such an approach could hamper the Executive's ability to wage war.[106] According to Judge Motz, there must be credible evidence that "the citizen is an enemy combatant and the courts should be striking a balance between ensuring the Executive's ability to wage war effectively and protecting the individual rights guaranteed to all American citizens."[107]

Judge Motz accepted the fact that President Bush acted in good faith when he designated Hamdi an enemy combatant. However she argued that it was the judge's responsibility to ensure due process of law regardless of individual judge's beliefs about the deference due the President because under our doctrine of separation of powers, the Executive branch must be subjected to checks on its power if individual liberties were to be preserved.

The treatment of Hamdi by the Pentagon was, in Judge Motz's view, a threat to freedoms that every American deserved and the panel's opinion supporting the President constituted an even greater and more subtle blow to liberty.[108] Recalling the darkest days of World War II after the devastating attack on Pearl Harbor Judge Motz observed that the Supreme Court recognized a greater role for the courts in safeguarding individual liberties than the panel was providing Hamdi in its majority opinion. She regretted that in the name of deference to the political branches' preeminence in matters of war, the panel permitted the subversion of the very liberties that made defense of this country worthwhile.[109]

Setting up a potential showdown with the Bush Administration, the Supreme Court announced that it would review both the *Hamdi* and *Padilla* cases and decide by the end of its 2004 term whether their detention as enemy combatants by the government was constitutional.[110] In agreeing to hear both appeals the justices rejected the administration's request to stay out of the cases because of their grave danger to national security.

Issues Related to the *Padilla* and *Hamdi* Cases

Jose Padilla and Yaser Hamdi have been detained indefinitely at the behest of the Commander-in-Chief based upon the following determinations.

First, the government maintains that the President's war powers provide him with plenary authority because we are in a defacto war. Second, in response to the argument that the President does not have exclusive authority to define the parameters of the war, or to make unilateral decisions about detentions without congressional authorization, the government insists that the Joint Resolution of Congress from September 18, 2001, Authorizing the Use of Force, provides ample justification for the President to make decisions impacting upon the conduct of the war, including the decision to detain American citizens in the interest of national security.

The law regarding the issue of enemy combatants is devoid of extensive statutory or Constitutional standing. Rather it is developed from case law, specifically *Quirin* from the period of World War II. The principal position taken by the Supreme Court in *Quirin* and accepted in the *Hamdi* decision by the Fourth

Circuit is that the President can constitutionally classify someone as an enemy combatant given some degree of congressional authorization.[111] Although the courts are entitled to review such classifications, they must demonstrate sensitivity and deference to the Executive's decision. Neither the Joint Resolution nor any laws enacted in response to the September 11 attacks have specifically addressed the detention of United States citizens as enemy combatants.

Title 18, § 4001(a) U.S. Code

Title 18, § 4001(a) U.S. Code provides that "[n]o citizen shall be imprisoned or otherwise detained by the United States except pursuant to an Act of Congress." This language makes it very clear that the Executive cannot detain American citizens without specific legislative approval for such detention. That includes the cases of Jose Padilla and Yaser Hamdi.

The legislative history of 4001(a) reinforces the need for legislative authorization for the detention of American citizens. The House report declared that the "purpose of [§ 4001(a)] is (1) to restrict the imprisonment or other detention of citizens by the United States to *situations in which statutory authority for their incarceration exists.*"[112] The Judiciary Committee Report further stated, "The Committee believes that imprisonment *or other detention* of citizens should be limited to situations in which statutory authorization, an Act of Congress, exists."[113]

Attorney General John Ashcroft maintains that the President's authority to detain enemy combatants, including U.S. citizens is based on his Commander-in-Chief responsibilities under the Constitution, not provisions of the criminal code. He argues: first, Section 4001(a) does not interfere with the President's constitutional power as Commander-in-Chief. Secondly, even if Section 4001 were susceptible to a different interpretation, "[a] Court's duty would be to adopt the facially reasonable—if not textually compelled—interpretation that Section 4001 is addressed to civilian, rather than military detentions."[114]

A second purpose of the amended bill was "to repeal the Emergency Detention Act of 1950 (EDA), Title II of the Internal Security Act of 1950, which both authorized the establishment of detention camps and imposed certain conditions on their use."[115] The Detention Act was a relic of the Cold War period when it was considered essential for the President to have the necessary powers to act upon the communist threat to our national security interests: "The mere continued existence" of the act had "aroused much concern among American citizens, lest the Detention Act become an instrumentality for apprehending and detaining citizens who hold unpopular beliefs and views."[116]

The House Report added that the Act was "subject to grave challenge" because it permitted detention based upon a "reasonable ground to believe that such person will probably engage in, or probably will conspire with others to engage in, acts of espionage or sabotage and allowed the government to refuse to divulge information essential to a defense which made the provisions . . . for judicial review inadequate."[117] When Congress concluded that the Emergency Detention Act had to be repealed it determined to go further. "Repeal alone," the Committee stated, "might leave citizens subject to arbitrary executive action, with no clear demarcation of the limits of executive authority."[118]

In *Howe v. Smith*,[119] the only case to date that addressed the statute to come before the United States Supreme Court, Chief Justice Burger, writing for the Court reaffirmed the significance of the text and legislative history: "The plain language at Section 4001(a) proscrib[es] detention *of any kind* by the United States, absent congressional grant of authority to detain."[120] The Second Circuit in the *Padilla* decision ruled that the plain language of Section 4001(a) prohibited all detentions of citizens, and the legislative history of the Non-Detention Act was fully consistent with their reading of it.[121] That meant that it would limit detentions in times of war and peace and that the Act meant what it said, no American citizen could be detained without a congressional act specifically authorizing such detention.[122] It is therefore clear that absent such a congressional

114

grant of authority to detain, Padilla and Hamdi's ongoing detention must be strictly proscribed by law.

Joint Congressional Resolution Authorizing the Use of Force and 10 U.S.C. § 956

To justify its action under Section 4001(a) the executive relies principally upon the Joint Resolution Authorization for the Use of Military Force.[123] The text explicitly authorizes all "necessary and appropriate force" which essentially invokes the law of war permitting capture incident to the use of military force.

Hamdi was seized in a zone of active hostilities, because he was captured in Afghanistan as part of our military operations against the Taliban. Padilla was seized in the United States, on American soil, which was not a zone of active hostilities. He was already subject to criminal process pursuant to statutory law.

There is no provision in the Joint Congressional Resolution Authorizing the Use of Force providing for the power to detain, much less the power to specifically detain a United States citizen seized on American soil in a civilian setting (Padilla).

The Fourth Circuit panel in the *Hamdi* decision ruled that the Joint Congressional Resolution, authorizing necessary and appropriate force meant that the capture of Hamdi included his detention as a member of a hostile force arrayed against United States troops.[124] The Second Circuit panel in the *Padilla* decision ruled that the language in the Joint Resolution authorizing necessary and appropriate force did not include the authority to detain American citizens seized on American soil and not actively engaged in combat.[125] The Second Circuit conceded that "it might be possible to infer a power of detention from the Joint Resolution in the battlefield context where detentions were essential for the conduct of war but there was no reason to suspect from the plain language of the Joint Resolution that Congress believed it would authorize the detention of an American citizen (Padilla) already held in a federal correctional institution and not 'arrayed against our troops' in the field of battle."[126] Next, the Secretary of

Defense argued that Hamdi and Padilla's detention was authorized by 10 U.S.C. § 956 (5), which allowed the use of appropriated funds for "expenses incident to the maintenance, pay, and allowances of prisoners of war, other persons in the custody of the Army, Navy or Air Force whose status was determined by the Secretary concerned to be similar to prisoners of war and persons detained in the custody of [the Armed Services] pursuant to Presidential Proclamation."[127] The Fourth Circuit found that 956 (5) along with the Joint Resolution was sufficient to authorize Hamdi's detention,[128] stating that "[I]t is difficult . . . to understand how Congress could make appropriations for the detention of persons 'similar to prisoners of war' without also authorizing the detention of American citizens deemed to be enemy combatants."[129]

The Second Circuit in *Padilla* disagreed with that reading of Section 956 (5) at least as it relates to "American citizens seized off the battlefield."[130] Since there was no language in the appropriation Act to "clearly and unmistakably" authorize the detention of American citizens then allocated funds could not be earmarked for such a detention.[131] The Supreme Court has said that for Congress to use an appropriations act to authorize Executive action it must plainly show a purpose to bestow the precise authority which is claimed.[132] The Defense appropriations bill[133] made no reference to enemy combatants or the ability of the President to detain American citizens without any charge on American soil.

Writ of Habeas Corpus

Under United States law, the validity of the detention of citizen detainees may be challenged by filing a writ of habeas corpus. Article I Section 9, cl.2 of the Constitution makes it clear that the President does not have the authority to detain citizens without charge. Since the authority exists in Article I, the Framers, proscribed the power to authorize detentions without charge to the Legislature— not the Executive.

The President cannot rely upon his power as Commander-in-Chief to detain because such power is limited to the detention of persons seized in a zone of active hostilities and members of the armed forces of an enemy nation. Congress may suspend the writ of habeas corpus in Cases of Rebellion or Invasion, which means that the right to detain on American soil exists exclusively with the Congress, and the President cannot unilaterally detain American *citizens* without charge. If and when Congress determines that "Rebellion or Invasion" threatens national security it may vest the Executive with the authority to detain individuals without charge. The Supreme Court has held, "If at any time the public safety should require the suspension of [habeas] . . . it is for the legislature to say so." [134]

The Fourth Circuit decision in *Hamdi* disavowed any intention of suspending the writ of habeas corpus, which requires judicial review of detentions. In practicality however the decision did suspend habeas corpus review during the indeterminate pendency of war. The Mobbs Declaration from the Department of Defense provided information about Hamdi's capture and designation as an enemy combatant. The District Judge found that general hearsay information proferred inadequate to allow him to conduct the "searching review" required of a court in a habeas case. The Fourth Circuit did not require a searching review, accepting the Mobbs Declaration to be sufficient.

The Second Circuit in *Padilla* ruled that the Constitution explicitly provides for suspension of the writ of habeas corpus "when in Cases of Rebellion or Invasion the public safety may require it."[135] This power however lies exclusively with the Congress,[136] and "any further determinations about the scope of the writ belong with the Congress for Congress to determine."[137]

The Right to Counsel

The United States Supreme Court's decision in *Hamdi* is truly historic because it provides the first opportunity to determine whether a citizen who the government detains indefinitely without charging a crime has the right to counsel on a habeas petition to challenge that detention. There are several legal justifications for a citizen designated an enemy combatant to seek right to counsel on a habeas petition.

The most fundamental due process approach is found in the Sixth Amendment which specifically provides the accused the right to counsel: "The accused shall enjoy the right to ... have the Assistance of Counsel for his defense."[138] The due process provisions of the Fifth and Fourteenth Amendments also assure right to Counsel.[139] The Sixth Amendment would appear to provide the most concrete and protective basis for a citizen detained as an enemy combatant to be granted counsel for a habeas petition.

Chief Judge Michael Mukasey of the Southern District held in the *Padilla* case that the Sixth Amendment right to counsel did not apply to him because he had not been charged with a crime and was not an accused and the Fourth Circuit in *Hamdi* ruled similarly.[140] The Supreme Court has ruled that an accused need not be formally accused or indicted for the right to counsel to attach.[141] The accused enjoys the right to counsel at any critical stage in the proceedings against him. However, in pre-charge proceedings, a court must undertake a very fact intensive inquiry to determine whether the right to counsel has attached.[142]

Since Yaser Hamdi and Jose Padilla must both be accused under Sixth Amendment requirements to have a right to counsel in their habeas corpus proceedings, and since neither case has produced formal accusations by the government, until such time as that occurs neither Padilla or Hamdi can rely upon the Sixth Amendment for right to counsel.

Judge Mukasey granted Padilla's right to counsel in his habeas petition on the basis of habeas corpus statutes, which allow a court's appointment of counsel if "the interests of justice so require."[143] The Court maintained that Padilla should have access to counsel for the limited purpose of challenging his classification as an enemy combatant through his habeas petition. The court rejected the government's contentions that permitting Padilla access to counsel might negatively impact national security and public safety. Although the court left open the question of whether the evidence provided by the U.S. government was sufficient to justify the detention of Padilla, it signaled that merely "some evidence of Padilla's hostile status" would be sufficient.[144] Nevertheless since Padilla had the right to present evidence challenging his classification as an enemy combatant, and since the most useful way of his doing so was through counsel, the district court determined that Padilla must be permitted to consult with counsel in aid of prosecuting his petition.[145] This access to counsel was based on the discretionary power of the court in hearing habeas corpus petitions.[146]

Second Circuit Judge Richard Wesley in dissent in the *Padilla* case argued that since no one suspended the Great Writ, Padilla's right to pursue a remedy through the writ would be meaningless if he had to do so alone. "I therefore would extend to him the right to counsel as Chief Judge Mukasey did."[147]

Hamdi was distinguishable because the lower court never did evaluate whether permitting Hamdi access to counsel would have national security implications. The Fourth Circuit in *Hamdi* declined to even adopt the "some evidence" factual standard that the government had proposed.[148] The undisputed facts that the military captured Hamdi in Afghanistan with a weapon and that he was affiliated with the Taliban were sufficient for the Fourth Circuit to determine that he was an enemy combatant subject to denial of due process constitutional rights.[149]

Even though the *Hamdi* court admitted that habeas corpus review was possible[150] it imposed another restriction that virtually made the review meaningless: according to the Court, once the government classified an individual as an enemy combatant, he had no right to access to counsel to assist him in challenging that classification. The Executive is granted tremendous power over citizens allowing it virtual unilateral authority to define the charges against the detainee, arrest him, and try him. The Fourth Circuit instructed the district court to determine whether or not Hamdi was an enemy combatant before determining whether he should have access to counsel. Hamdi was assumed to be an enemy combatant until he could prove otherwise, and without counsel to argue that he was not an enemy combatant on habeas review and that the charges against him were not violations of the law of war, this citizen had a very heavy burden to overcome in disproving his enemy combatant status.[151] The only protection the *Hamdi* court gave the accused citizen enemy combatant was the right to have a court review the charges against him on a habeas petition, with great deference to the Executive, without a lawyer to argue the case.

The *Padilla* ruling, in contrast to *Hamdi*, found a right for the citizen detained as an enemy combatant to have access to counsel to challenge the classification through a habeas petition. The *Padilla* decision also provided the courts with flexibility in permitting that right to counsel. Rather than relying upon the Sixth Amendment or Due Process clauses of the Constitution, the court turned to a statutory basis for the right. This means that an accused enemy combatant's right to counsel is not immutable, and courts have the flexibility to restrict the right under given circumstances, as the *Padilla* court demonstrated, restricting it to representation for the habeas petition and not allowing representation of counsel for other interrogations of Padilla.[152]

On December 2, 2003 the Department of Defense announced that Yaser Hamdi would be allowed access to a lawyer subject to appropriate security restrictions. DoD decided to allow Hamdi access to counsel because "Hamdi is a U.S. citizen detained by DoD in the United States, because DoD has completed its intelligence collection with Hamdi, and because DoD has determined that the access will not compromise the national security of the United States."[153] Two months later, the Department of Defense announced that Padilla would be allowed access to a lawyer subject to appropriate security restrictions. DoD decided to allow Padilla access to counsel for the very same reasons determined in the *Hamdi* case, namely that such access will not compromise national security of the United States.[154]

Viet Dinh, a former assistant attorney general who was instrumental in drafting the government's anti-terror policies, was quoted as suggesting that the decision to give Mr. Hamdi access to counsel was a significant development in the case, one that moves the government to a more sustainable position before the court.[155]

A second senior former official in the Justice Department, Judge Michael Chertoff, has also called for new methods of dealing with enemy combatants' rights of due process. Judge Chertoff formerly served as assistant attorney general in charge of the criminal division, and currently is on the United States Court of Appeals for the Third Circuit.[156]

Zacarias Moussaoui (Abu Khahl al-Suhrawi)

Zacarias Moussaoui was born in France of Moroccan descent. Before 2001 he was a resident of the United Kingdom where he held a master's degree from Southbank University. From 1989 until August of 2001 Moussaoui along with other members and associates of al-Qaida, were allegedly conspiring to undertake terrorist activities against the United States including plots to kill Americans, and damage structures and property of the United States.

In the early spring of 2001 Moussaoui attended Airman Flight School in Norman, Oklahoma and made inquiries about starting a crop dusting company. He provided flight deck videos for Boeing 747 Model 400 and Model 200 from the Ohio Pilot Store in June 2001, and in the middle of August 2001, he attended Pan Am International Flight Academy in Minneapolis, Minnesota for simulator training on the Boeing 747 Model 400. On or about August 17, 2001 Zacarias Moussaoui was interviewed by federal agents in Minneapolis and attempted to explain his presence in the United States by falsely stating that he was simply interested in learning how to fly.

Moussaoui was arrested and indicted in December of 2001 on charges of conspiring to commit acts of terrorism transcending national boundaries,[157] conspiring to commit aircraft piracy,[158] conspiring to destroy an aircraft,[159] conspiracy to use weapons of mass destruction,[160] conspiracy to murder United States employees,[161] and conspiring to destroy property.[162] The government sought the death penalty for Moussaoui on the first four counts of the indictment.

Zacarias Moussaoui is the lone defendant charged in an American court with conspiring in the September 11 attack.

Zacarias Moussaoui has acknowledged his role as an al-Qaida loyalist but he contends that he was never the twentieth hijacker in the September 11 terrorist attack. Rather he suggests that he was part of another operation to occur outside the United States involving different members of al-Qaida some time after September 11. As part of his defense, Moussaoui argued that a critical witness had information that would be useful to his case. That witness is Ranzi Bin al-Shibh who the government contends coordinated the attacks of September 11. Bin al-Shibh allegedly had a role in the USS Cole bombing and was a member of the al-Qaida cell in Hamburg, Germany where the planning for the September 11 attacks occurred.

According to the government as well as the defense there is no case precedent for seeking access to a non-citizen witness being held as an enemy combatant in military custody outside the United States. The government's position on Bin al-Shibh was consistent with respect to all enemy combatant detainees currently held by the United States outside our borders, and that is they are not available in a court of law as a witness or otherwise. To permit Moussaoui's lawyers to depose an enemy combatant would interfere with ongoing military operations, creating a clear conflict between the executive and judicial branches over national security issues. Therefore the Sixth Amendment of the United States Constitution was not applicable.[163] To support its argument the United States relied heavily on *United States v. Valenzuela-Bernal*[164] finding no Fifth or Sixth Amendment violation when the United States deported an alien witness who was determined by the government not to possess material evidence relevant to the prosecution or the defense.

In response, Moussaoui's counsel contended the government's reliance on *Valenzuela-Bernal* was misplaced because it concerned lost evidence. Rather the defense argued that Moussaoui's Sixth Amendment right to secure the trial testimony of favorable witnesses outweighed the national security concerns of the United States.

On March 10, 2003 U.S. District Judge Leonie Brinkema of the Eastern District of Virginia ruled for Moussaoui citing in part *Hamdi v. Rumsfeld* in her decision:

> Despite the clear allocation of war powers to the political branches, judicial deference to executive decisions made in the name of war is not unlimited. The duty of the judicial branch to protect [individual rights] does not simply cease whenever our military forces are committed by the political branches to armed conflict. Rather certain protections guaranteed by the Bill of Rights are triggered when an individual is charged with a crime.[165]

The Government's good faith interest in protecting national security did not categorically override the defendant's right to a fair trial, and this right included the Sixth Amendment right to compulsory process for favorable witnesses. Judge Brinkema made it clear that this process is not absolute. The defendant (Moussaoui) would have to make a plausible showing that the testimony of the witness would be both material and favorable to his defense, and as the government argued in this case such testimony may be tempered by the United States' good faith exercise of legitimate executive functions including the right to remove illegal aliens.[166]

The court did not question the good faith of the United States in prosecuting its war against terrorism, however a determination must be made whether the government could categorically refuse to produce witnesses on the ground that such production would interfere with its war on terrorism. The court maintained that consistent with well-established principles of due process, the government could not suppress evidence favorable to an accused that was material either to guilt or punishment. In this case the defense made a significant showing that Bin al-Shibh would be able to provide favorable testimony on Moussaoui's behalf as to his guilt and potential punishment. The ultimate determination as to the value of such testimony was for the jury, not the prosecution to produce, in the context of the other evidence introduced at trial.

The government's position was absolute and intractable. There were no adequate substitutes or alternatives for trial testimony in a case of this nature because anything concerning a detainee (Bin al-Shibh) remained classified. Any attempt to produce information from the witness, in any form, would amount to improper judicial interference in the conduct of the war and seriously compromise national security interests.

Judge Brinkema refused to accept this position. She argued that both the defendant and the public were denied a fair trial if Moussaoui was deprived of the opportunity to present Bin al-Shibh's testimony. Aware of the national security sensitivity of unfettered access to such a witness, Judge Brinkema crafted her own resolution to the government's concerns while satisfying the due process needs of the defense. Rather than grant counsel unmonitored pretrial access to Bin al-Shibh, Judge Brinkema required the government to make him available for video deposition. She found the suggestion that any defense access to Bin al-Shibh as diverting the military's attention from its offensive efforts abroad as unpersuasive. She concluded her opinion by suggesting that the government might want to reconsider whether the civilian criminal courts were the appropriate place in which to prosecute alleged terrorists in the context of an ongoing war.

The Justice Department appealed the district court decision to the United States Court of Appeals for the Fourth Circuit. A three-judge panel of the court dismissed the appeal on June 26, 2003 stating that the lower court's order to permit Moussaoui's lawyers to interview a captured key witness had not yet reached the stage at which it was reviewable. The order of the district court would not become final unless and until the government refused to comply and the district court imposed a sanction and the government had not notified the district court of its refusal to comply.[167]

On August 2, 2003, in a similar ruling to the Bin al-Shibh decision, Judge Brinkema ordered that Zacarias Moussaoui be granted access to Khalil Sharik Mohammed, a principal mastermind of the September 11 plot, and Mustafa Ahmed Hawsawi, an alleged paymaster for the September 11 hijackers. Judge

Brinkema stated that the pre-trial testimony and possibly trial testimony from these two witnesses may well support Moussaoui's contention that he was never contacted to participate in the terror attack.

Mohammed, a Pakistani, had been wanted since 1995 on federal charges that he conspired with his nephew, Ramzi Yousef, the leader of the 1993 World Trade Center bombing, in a Philippines-based plot to blow up eleven airliners simultaneously in the Far East. A joint team of Pakistani and FBI agents captured Mohammed and Hawsawi, a Saudi who was accused in the Moussaoui indictment of transferring thousands of dollars from accounts he controlled in Dubai, UAE to the hijackers' accounts in the United States. They were both hiding at an al-Qaida safe house when they were captured on March 1, 2003 in Rawalpindi, Pakistan, and subsequently placed in detention at undisclosed military locations.

The government objected to Mohammed or Hawsawi becoming trial witnesses on national security grounds, contending that the court could not order the executive branch to produce an enemy combatant detained on foreign soil and to do so would disrupt the war on terrorism.

To further weaken the government's case in prosecuting Zacarias Moussaoui, Judge Leonie Brinkema, on October 2, 2003 ruled that prosecutors could not seek the death penalty because of the government's refusal to allow Moussaoui to question al-Qaida captives. The judge also banned the government from presenting evidence or argument that the defendant was involved in, or had knowledge of, the planning or execution of the attacks of September 11, 2001.[168] Brinkema stayed her order pending an appeals court review.

The Justice Department had several options in light of this ruling. It could appeal the decision to the Fourth U.S. Circuit Court of Appeals with the expectation that the court would reinstate the prosecution's case; it could proceed in a more limited conspiracy prosecution in light of Judge Brinkema's ruling that would allow pursuit of life imprisonment; or it could seek a new grand jury indictment of Moussaoui that would attempt to address the major fair-trial concerns raised by Judge Brinkema. An additional option raised by Judge

Brinkema in an earlier ruling was to abandon the civil prosecution and turn Moussaoui over to the Defense Department for a military commission proceeding where procedures are distinct from the civilian justice system.

Five days later the Justice Department, in a two-paragraph filing, appealed Judge Brinkema's ruling to the Fourth Circuit Court of Appeals. The government served notice that its appeal was based upon the Classified Information Procedures Act since the questioning of the al-Qaida captives could jeopardize national security by disclosing classified information.[169]

At a hearing before a three-judge panel of the United States Court of Appeals for the Fourth Circuit, Paul Clement, Deputy Solicitor General argued that Mr. Moussaoui had no right to profit from the windfall created when the government captured an enemy combatant abroad. "An alien held abroad is not subject to the courts' compulsory process and the Sixth Amendment offers no absolute right to secure live testimony from potential witnesses."[170]

Judge Roger Gregory, who appeared openly skeptical of the government's position asked: "We want the government to engage in war powers to protect the nation and our liberties, but at what point is national security concerns so great that a person can't get a fair trial?"[171]

Judge Karen Williams suggested that although she was sympathetic to some of the Justice Department's arguments, "Mr. Moussaoui is an alien in the United States trying to vindicate his rights under the Constitution. Is there no right for Mr. Moussaoui to reach the witnesses and use their favorable testimony?"[172]

On April 22, 2004 a three-judge panel of the United States Court of Appeals for the Fourth Circuit ruled that Moussaoui could not be denied access to information from the three al-Qaida prisoners who might be able to exonerate him, however the majority said that he could only receive written statements from the prisoners in a form that crafts adequate substitutions as determined by the trial judge rather than by remote video hookup as ordered by the trial court. Furthermore, the panel restored the government's ability to seek the death penalty as well as present evidence to a jury that might link Moussaoui to the September 11 terrorist attacks.

Chief Judge William W. Wilkins stated: "We are presented with questions of grave significance . . . questions that test the commitment of this nation to an independent judiciary, to the constitutional guarantee of a fair trial even to one accused of the most heinous crimes, and to the protection of our citizens against additional terrorist attacks. These questions do not admit of easy answers."[173]

The court rejected the view that ordering the production of witnesses infringed on the Executive's war-making authority in violation of the separation of power principles.[174] The court stated that separation of powers does not mean that each branch is prohibited from any activity that might have an impact on another.[175] This was not a case involving the arrogation of powers, or duties of another branch. The district court ordered production of the enemy combatant witnesses that involved the resolution of questions . . . exclusively reserved to the judiciary.[176]

The panel accepted as true that the al-Qaida witnesses were invaluable as intelligence sources "in our effort to combat terrorism and that interruption of the detention process will have devastating effects on the ability to gather information from them."[177] Therefore the burdens placed on the government to produce the enemy combatant witnesses would be substantial because it could adversely impact its grave responsibility of protecting the lives of our nation's citizenry.[178]

The solution for the panel majority was to reject the ruling of the district court that any substitution for the witnesses' testimony was inadequate even though the "particular proposals submitted by the government were inadequate in their current form."[179] Since the district court had greater familiarity with the facts of the case the "crafting of substitutions is a task best suited to the district court."[180]

Judge Williams in part dissented stating that the separation of power principles placed the enemy combatant witnesses beyond the reach of the district court.[181] Requiring the Government to "produce for depositions enemy combatants detained abroad would prevent the Executive from exercising its war and foreign relations powers"[182] and produce such risks to national security that it "cannot be justified by the need to promote objectives within the constitutional authority of the Judiciary.[183] Judge Williams also opined that the Fifth Amendment's guarantee of a fundamentally fair trial gave Moussaoui the right to introduce at least some material and favorable information at trial[184] and that the district court should aid the parties in crafting acceptable substitutions.[185]

Judge Gregory dissented in part based upon his belief that by forcing the district court to construct substitutions, "we are asking the court to do something it has stated cannot be done. It will be difficult—perhaps impossible—for the district court to credibly prepare substitutions."[186] Additionally, Judge Gregory argued that the death penalty should be removed from consideration as a possible sentence because Moussaoui "will not have access to the witnesses who could answer the questions of his involvement and he is undeniably and irretrievably handicapped in his ability to defend himself from a sentence of death."[187]

Attorney General John Ashcroft reacted favorably to the ruling. In a written statement he said: "The government can provide Zacarias Moussaoui with a fair trial while still protecting national security interests. This ruling allows us to seek the death penalty and to present evidence regarding the conspiracy of the September 11 terrorist attacks"[188]

The panel opinion of the fourth circuit is clearly not a victory for either Moussaoui or the government. The court was divided in the sense that we have two partial concurrences and two partial dissents which on the one hand permit Moussaoui's right to have access, in some written form, to witness testimony, and on the other hand demonstrate a recognizable deference to national security concerns expressed by the government. What is unique about this case is that it presents a charge of conspiracy to commit a specific act (the 9/11 attacks), presumably supported by little evidence, and the defendant able to credibly identity other suspects who are in a position to refute the charge. Given the significance of the issues involving the testimony of captured terrorists abroad to the September 11 attacks, the Moussaoui case will eventually work its way to the United States Supreme Court.

Summary

Although the Military Order of November 13, 2001 establishing military commissions to detain and try alleged terrorists identified with the September 11 attacks exclusively applied to non-citizens in the custody of the United States, the President has designated as enemy combatants two Americans who are suspected of terrorist activity. Jose Padilla, the dirty bomb suspect, and Yaser Esam Hamdi, the Cajun Taliban, both of whom are United States citizens, have been denied access to lawyers, have had their rights to a hearing before a judge restricted, and have been imprisoned indefinitely without a formal charge being presented against either of them.

Jose Padilla was born in Brooklyn, New York and was captured by federal law enforcement authorities in Chicago in May 2002 pursuant to a material witness warrant. The government charged that Padilla is an enemy combatant because while he was in Afghanistan and Pakistan he trained with al-Qaida operatives, studied how to wire explosive devices, and researched radiological dispersion devices. It is alleged that he was instructed by senior al-Qaida officials to return to the United States to detonate a radioactive "dirty bomb" in this country.

Padilla, through his counsel, filed a habeas corpus petition challenging his detention and sought an order that he be permitted to consult with counsel. The District Court, in December 2002, ordered that Padilla be permitted to consult with counsel in aid of his petition even though the government had the power to detain unlawful combatants, regardless of the fact that they were United States citizens captured on United States soil. The court determined that this authority for the President was derived from the Commander-in-Chief Clause of the Constitution and the Joint Resolution of Congress.

The court recognized that Padilla's right to counsel in his habeas petition was not a Sixth Amendment right, or a due process right, which did not apply to him. Rather, it was derived from habeas corpus statutes, which permit a court's appointment of counsel "if the interests of justice so require."[189] The *Padilla* Court also permitted Padilla, through counsel, to present his own facts and evidence to counter the government's contention that he was an enemy combatant.[190] The court also established a standard that was highly deferential to the government that would justify the detention which required *some evidence* to support the President's conclusion that Padilla was engaged in a mission against the United States on behalf of the enemy with whom we were at war.[191]

The government appealed the district court decision to the Second Circuit Court of Appeals and in December of 2003 a majority panel issued its ruling which concluded:

- Padilla's detention was not authorized by Congress, and absent such authorization, the President did not have the power under Article II of the Constitution to detain an enemy combatant an American citizen seized on American soil outside a zone of combat;

- Clear congressional authorization was required to detain American citizens on American soil because the Non-Detention Act prohibited such detentions without specific congressional authorization;

- Congress's Authorization for Use of Military Force Joint Resolution was not such an authorization and no exception existed in the Non-Detention Act;

- The government did not show that Padilla's detention was grounded in the President's inherent constitutional powers.[192]

In its sixty-five page decision the appeals court distinguished *Padilla* from the case of Yaser Hamdi, a U.S. citizen accused of fighting with the Taliban who was arrested in Afghanistan on a foreign battlefield engaged in armed conflict against the United States and who when captured was in the possession of an AK-47, in a "zone of active combat in a foreign theater of conflict."[193]

The government had also argued that the President's authority to detain Padilla as an enemy combatant stemmed from the *Quirin* case of Nazi saboteurs arrested on United States soil during World War II. The judges disagreed. "We do not agree that *Quirin* controls," they wrote, "because *Quirin* does not speak to whether or to what degree, the President may impose military authority upon United States citizens domestically without clear congressional authorization . . . petitioners for Quirin admitted that they were soldiers in the armed forces of a nation against whom the United States had formally declared war . . . Padilla makes no such concession."[194]

The panel also noted that when the Congress passed the Non-Detention Act which repealed the Emergency Detention Act of 1950 it curtailed the powers of the President and the executive branch of government. The Circuit noted that it would be highly unlikely, if not unconceivable, that Congress would leave unstated as to inference in the Joint Resolution something so significant and unprecedented as authorization to detain American citizens under the Non-Detention Act.

The dissenting opinion argued that the President did possess the inherent authority as Commander-in-Chief to act against any belligerency on United States soil and that Congress directly authorized the President in the Joint Resolution, to act accordingly. The President could detain Padilla because such action was necessary to prevent future terrorist attacks against the United States and Padilla's citizenship was irrelevant as was the fact that he was captured on United States soil.

Yaser Esam Hamdi, the "Cajun Taliban," was born in Lousiana and is a United States citizen. Hamdi was captured by the United States military in the fall of 2001 while he was fighting in Afghanistan with the Taliban. Initially he was held in a short term detention facility in Kandahar, and then transferred to the Norfolk Naval Station Brig after it was discovered that he had not renounced his U.S. citizenship. He was subsequently transferred to the naval brig in Charleston, South Carolina where Jose Padilla had been detained.

In June 2002 Hamdi's father filed a petition for a writ of habeas corpus alleging that Hamdi was a citizen of the United States and as an American citizen Hamdi was entitled to full constitutional protection, including access to counsel, and access to the judicial system. The district court agreed, ordering that "Hamdi be allowed to meet with his attorney because of fundamental justice requirements under the Constitution."[195]

The government in July appealed the decision to the Fourth Circuit arguing that Hamdi was an enemy combatant, and as such he could be detained for the duration of hostilities, and that "enemy combatants who are captured and detained on the battlefield in foreign land have no general right under the law, and customs of war, or the Constitution to meet with counsel concerning their detention, much less to meet with counsel in private."[196] The Fourth Circuit reversed the district court's order and remanded the case for further proceedings to determine whether Hamdi could be properly classified an enemy combatant.[197]

The district court ordered the government to produce further evidence pertaining to Hamdi's capture including "copies of Hamdi's statements, notes taken from interviews with him, names and addresses of interrogators, and circumstances related to his surrender."[198]

The government petitioned for interlocutory review on appeal with the principal question being whether an affidavit from Special Advisor Michael Mobbs to Under Secretary of Defense for Policy which confirmed that Hamdi was captured in Afghanistan during armed hostilities and that the executive branch classified him as enemy combatant was sufficient as a matter of law to allow judicial review of Hamdi's classification as an enemy combatant.

The Fourth Circuit granted the government's petition and a three-judge panel upheld the President's authority as Commander-in-Chief to detain those captured in armed struggle.[199] The panel explained that it is the political branches that are organized to conduct overseas conflicts and are accountable to the people for their actions, and not the courts who are not in a proper position to comprehend the implications and ramifications of global conflicts and wars.

The Fourth Circuit further held that the disclosure information sought by the district court was improper and "given the great deference due to the Executive by nature of his war powers, a further factual inquiry into Hamdi's activities in Afghanistan would be inappropriate and violate the separation of powers."[200] The court, however, also indicated that the President's discretion to make decisions in wartime was not unlimited and could, in some cases, be reviewed by the judiciary.[201] The court rejected any "broader categorical holdings on enemy combatant detentions,"[202] and disclaimed "placing our imprimatur upon a new day of executive detentions."[203]

The panel decision was appealed to the full Court of Appeals for the Fourth Circuit and on July 9, 2003 in an 8-4 vote the court upheld President Bush's authority to detain Hamdi as an enemy combatant captured on the battlefield and to deny him access to counsel.

In December the Department of Defense announced that Hamdi would be allowed access to a lawyer because intelligence collection had been completed and Hamdi would not compromise the national security interests of the United States. Hamdi appealed his detention to the Supreme Court which heard his case and Padilla's and announced its decisions at the end of the 2004 term.

Zacarias Moussaoui was born in France of Moroccan descent. From 1984 until August of 2001 Moussaoui along with other members and associates of al-Qaida conspired to undertake terrorist activities against the United States including plots to kill American citizens.

In December of 2001 Moussaoui was arrested and indicted on charges of conspiring to commit acts of terrorism in the September 11 attack and the government sought the death penalty for him. Although Moussaoui acknowledged his role as an al-Qaida loyalist, he consistently contended that he was never part of the September 11 terrorist attack.

As part of his defense, Moussaoui argued that a critical witness had information that was vital to his case; however, that witness was a non-citizen being held as an enemy combatant in military custody outside the United States.

The government insisted that enemy combatant detainees currently held by the United States outside our borders could not be deposed because it would interfere with ongoing military operations, and compromise vital national security operations that belong exclusively in the domain of the executive branch of government. The judiciary should therefore demonstrate deference to the executive and deny any Sixth Amendment application from the United States Constitution for Moussaoui.

In March of 2003 the district court of the Eastern District of Virginia ruled for Moussaoui, citing in part *Hamdi* in its reasoning that "certain substantive due process rights guaranteed by the Bill of Rights are triggered when an individual is charged with a crime."[204] The government's interest in protecting national security did not override Moussaoui's right to a fair trial which included his Sixth Amendment right to a compulsory process for producing favorable witnesses. The court maintained that consistent with well-established principles of due process, the government could not suppress evidence favorable to an accused that was material either to guilt or punishment.

The government's position was absolute and unyielding. Any attempt to produce information for the witness, in any form, would amount to improper judicial interference in the conduct of the war and seriously compromise national security interests.

The district court crafted its own resolution to the government's concerns about national security sensitivity by requiring the government to make the witness available for a video deposition rather than unmonitored pre-trial accessibility. The Justice Department appealed the district court decision to the United States Court of Appeals for the Fourth Circuit.

In June of 2003 a three-judge panel of the court dismissed the appeal because the case had not yet reached the stage at which it was reviewable and in August of 2003 the district court ordered that Moussaoui be granted access to two additional witnesses who may be able to support his contention that he was never contacted to participate in the terror attack. In October of 2003, to further weaken the government's case, the district court ruled that the government's prosecutors could not seek the death penalty for Moussaoui because of its refusal to permit Moussaoui to question any of the al-Qaida captives. The court also banned the government from presenting evidence or argument that the defendant had any knowledge of the planning or execution of the September 11 attacks.

In December the Justice Department appealed the district court ruling to the Fourth U.S. Circuit Court of Appeals arguing that "an alien held abroad is not subject to the courts' compulsory process" and that "the Sixth Amendment offered no absolute right to secure live testimony from potential witnesses."[205] In late April 2004 a Fourth U.S. Circuit Court of Appeals panel issued a ruling permitting Moussaoui to receive written statements from the enemy combatant witnesses in a compromise form that crafts adequate substitutions rather than by remote video hookup. The panel also tossed out the two-part penalty imposed by the district court on the government for its refusal to arrange video questioning.

What is unique about the Moussaoui case is that it presents a charge of conspiring to commit a specific act (the 9/11 attacks), presumably supported by little evidence, and the defendant able to credibly identify other suspects who are in a position to refute the charge. Given the significance of the issues involving the testimony of captured terrorists abroad to the September 11 attacks, this case will eventually work its way to the United States Supreme Court for resolution.

Notes

[1] *See* Military Order on the Detention, Treatment, and Trial of Certain Non-Citizens in the War Against Terrorism (November 13, 2001) § 1(a), 66 Fed. Reg. 57 833 (November 16, 2001), Appendix A.

[2] See § 7 (3) which states that nothing in the order is to be construed as limiting the authority of the Secretary of Defense, military commander or officer of the United States to detain or try any person not an individual subject to this order. It should be recalled that in *Ex Parte Quirin*, the Supreme Court upheld the trial during World War II, by military commissions for war crimes of a person presumed to be a U.S. citizen because the citizen was a belligerent in a declared war. *See* Chapter I n.39 *supra* and accompanying text.

[3] *Padilla ex rel. Newman v. Bush*, 233 F. Supp. 2d 564 at 572.

[4] *Id.* at 603.

[5] *Id.* at 605.

[6] *Id.* at 603.

[7] *Id.* at 593.

[8] *Id.* at 593-96.

[9] *Id.* at 605, 610.

[10] *Id.* at 603.

[11] *Hamdi v. Rumsfeld*, 316 F.3d 450 (4th Cir. 2003) (*Hamdi III*).

[12] That declarant was Michael Mobbs, the same declarant as in *Padilla. See Padilla*, 233 F. Supp. 2d at 572.

[13] *Id.* at 459.

[14] *Id.* at 465.

[15] *Padilla* 233 F. Supp. 2d at 608.

[16] *Padilla v. Rumsfeld*, 02 Civ. 4445 (MBM) at 13.

[17] Jacoby Declaration at 4-5.

[18] *Id.* at 5-6.

[19] *Id.* at 7-8.

[20] *Id.* at 8.

[21] Jacoby Declaration at 8-9; sealed Jacoby Declaration at 12-13.

136

[22] Respondents Opposition to Motion to Strike n.6 at 14.

[23] *Id.*

[24] *See Ex Parte Quirin,* 317 U.S. 1 at 20 (1942), and Chapter I infra n.32-40 and accompanying text.

[25] *See Talbot v. Seeman,* 5 U.S. 1 at 28 (1801); and Chapter II infra n.14, and accompanying text.

[26] *See Ex Parte Quirin,* 317 U.S. 1 at 31 (1942).

[27] *Id.* at 20-22, and Chapter I infra n.32-33 and accompanying text.

[28] *See Padilla ex rel. Newman v. Bush* 233 F. Supp. 2d 564 at 603.

[29] *Id.* at 605.

[30] *See* Samantha A. Pitts-Kiefer, *Jose Padilla: Enemy Combatant or Common Criminal?,* 48 *Vill. L. Rev.* 875 at 909 (2003).

[31] *See Ex Parte Quirin,* 317 U.S. 1 at 21-22 (1942), and Chapter I infra n.34-35 and accompanying text.

[32] *See* Military Order of November 13, 2001, Title 3, Detention, Treatment, and Trial of Certain Non-Citizens in the War Against Terrorism, 66 Fed. Reg. 57, 833 (Nov. 16, 2001). *See also,* Chapter IV infra n.1-2 and accompanying text.

[33] *See Cramer v. United States,* 325 U.S. 1 (1945), *United States v. Haupt,* 136 F.2d 661 (7th Cir. 1943).

[34] *See, Hamdi v. Rumsfeld,* 316 F.3d 450 (4th Cir. 2003) (*Hamdi III*) at 476.

[35] *Id.*

[36] *Id.* at 463.

[37] *Id.* at 476.

[38] *Id.* at 474.

[39] *Id.* at 465.

[40] Jacoby Declaration at 9.

[41] *Korematsu v. United States,* 323 U.S. 214 (1944). Supplemental brief of New York State Association of Criminal Defense Lawyers at 825.

[42] *Id.*

[43] Phil Hirschkorn and Deborah Feyerick, *Court Weighs 'Dirty Bomb' Suspect's Detention,* CNN Law Center, www.cnn.com/2003/LAW/11/17/padilla.appeal/index.html, November 18, 2003.

[44] *Id.*

[45] *Id.*

[46] *Id.*

[47]*Padilla ex rel. Newman v. Rumsfeld,* 352 F.3d 695 (No. 03-2235) at 4-5 (2d Cir. 2003).

[48] *See Hamdi v. Rumsfeld,* 316 F.3d 450 (4th Cir. 2003) (*Hamdi III*).

[49] *Id. See United States v. Awadallah,* 349 F.3d 42 (2d Cir. 2003).

[50] *Padilla ex rel. Newman v. Rumsfeld,* 352 F.3d 695 (No. 03-2235) (2d Cir. 2003*). See also, Henderson v. INS* 157 F.3d 106, 126 (2d Cir. 1998).

[51] *Id.*

[52] *See Ex Parte Quirin,* 317 U.S. 1 (1942).

[53] *Padilla ex rel. Newman v. Rumsfeld,* 352 F.3d 695 (No. 03-2235) at 24 (2d Cir. 2003).

[54] *See Ex Parte Quirin,* 317 U.S. 1 at 29 (1942).

[55] *Id.*

[56] *Padilla ex rel. Newman v. Rumsfeld,* 352 F.3d 695 (No. 03-2235) at 33 (2d Cir. 2003).

[57] *Id. at 34.*

[58] *Haupt v. United States,* 330 U.S. 631 (1947), *Cramer v. United States,* 325 U.S. 1 (1945).

[59]*Padilla ex rel. Newman v. Rumsfeld,* 352 F.3d 695 (No. 03-2235) at 35 (2d Cir. 2003).

[60] *See Johnson v. Eisentrager,* 339 U.S. 763, 789 (1950).

[61] *See Youngstown Sheet and Tube v. Sawyer,* 343 U.S. 579 at 644-50 (1952).

[62] *Padilla ex rel. Newman v. Rumsfeld,* 352 F.3d 695 (No. 03-2235) at 29-30 (2d. Cir. 2003).

[63] *See Youngstown Sheet and Tube v. Sawyer,* 343 U.S. 579 at 631-32 (1952) (Douglas, J. concurring).

[64] *Padilla ex rel. Newman v. Rumsfeld,* 352 F.3d 695 at 46 (2d Cir. 2003) quoting *Hamdi III,* 316 F.3d at 467.

[65] *See* 18 U.S.C. § 4001(a).

[66] *Padilla ex rel. Newman v. Rumsfeld,* 352 F.3d 695 (No. 03-2235) at 54 (2d Cir. 2003).

[67] *Id. at 57.*

[68] 2 Black 635 (1863).

[69] *Padilla ex rel. Newman v. Rumsfeld,* 352 F.3d 695 (No. 03-2235) at 51 (2d Cir. 2001).

138

[70] *See Campbell v. Clinton*, 203 F.3d 19, 27 (D.C. Cir. 2000) (Silberman, J. concurring).

[71] *Padilla ex rel. Newman v. Rumsfeld*, 352 F.3d 695 (No. 03-2235) at 64 (2d Cir. 2003).

[72] *Id.*

[73] *Id. at 65.*

[74] *See* U.S. Const. art. I, § 9, cl. 2.

[75] *Padilla ex rel. Newman v. Rumsfeld*, 352 F.3d 695 (No. 03-2236) at 65 (2d. Cir. 2003).

[76] *Hamdi v. Rumsfeld*, 296 F.3d 278, at 279 (4th Cir. 2002) (*Hamdi II*).

[77] *Id.*

[78] *Id.* at 283.

[79] *Hamdi v. Rumsfeld*, No. 02-7338 (4th Cir. 2002) (order granting petition for interlocutory review).

[80] *Hamdi II*, 296 F.3d at 281-82. Persons captured during wartime are often referred to as enemy combatants . . . a designation provided Hamdi.

[81] *Id.* at 281.

[82] *See Hamdi II*, 296 F.3d at 283.

[83] Authorization for Use of Military Force, Pub. L. No. 107-40, 115 Stat. 224 (Sept 18, 2001) *See* Appendix B.

[84] 10 U.S.C. § 965 (5) 2002.

[85] *See* Geneva Convention Relative to Treatment of Prisoners of War, Aug 12, 1949 art. 5, 6 U.S.T. 3316, 75 U.N.T.S. 135.

[86] *See Huynh Thi Anh v. Levi*, 586 F.2d 625, 629 (6th Cir. 1978); *See also, Holmes v. Laird*, 459 F.2d 1211, 1222 (D.C. Cir. 1972).

[87] *Hamdi II*, 296 F.3d at 284.

[88] *Id.* at 283.

[89] *Id.*

[90] *Id.* at 284.

[91] The same issue arose in *Quirin*, 317 U.S. at 37 where the court noted that "citizenship in the United States of an enemy belligerent does not relieve him from the consequences of belligerency which is unlawful." *See* Chapter I n.39 *supra* and discussion.

[92] *Hamdi II*, 296 F.3d at 283.

[93] *Hamdi v. Rumsfeld*, No. 02-7338 at 8 (4th Cir. 2003).

[94] *Id.* at 10.

[95] *Id.* at 33.

[96] *Id.* at 34.

[97] *Id.* at 36.

[98] *Id.*

[99] *Id.* at 52.

[100] *Id.* at 56.

[101] *Id.* at 82.

[102] *Id.* at 85. *See Hamdi v. Rumsfeld*, 316 F.3d 450 (4th Cir. 2003) (*Hamdi III*).

[103] *Ex Parte Quirin*, 317 U.S. 1 (1942) (emphasis added).

[104] *See Hamdi v. Rumsfeld*, No. 02-7338 at 90.

[105] *Id.* at 91 and *Johnson v. Eisentrager*, 339 U.S. 763, 770, 775 (1950).

[106] *Id.* at 101.

[107] *Id.*

[108] *Id.* at 106.

[109] *Id.* at 108. *See e.g., Quirin*, 317 U.S. at 46.

[110] *Hamdi v. Rumsfeld (Hamdi III)*, 316 F.3d 450 (4th Cir. 2003) cert. Granted 124 S. Ct. 981 (2004) (No. 03-6696); *Padilla v. Rumsfeld*, 352 F.3d 695 (2d Cir. 2003) cert. granted 124 S. Ct. 1353 (2004) (No. 03-1027).

[111] *Ex Parte Quirin*, 317 U.S. 1, 47 (1942). *Quirin* did not address whether the President could act unilaterally as Commander-in-Chief if Congress were to restrict or withdraw statutorily for the President the authority to act as he did under the circumstances. *See* Chapter I at 12 for additional discussion.

[112] H.R. Rep. No. 92-116 at 1, *reprinted in* 1971 U.S.C.C.A.N. 1435,1435 (*"Judiciary Committee Report"*) (emphasis added).

[113] *Id.* at 1438 (emphasis added): The point is not that Congress meant to preclude the detention of U.S. citizens as enemy combatants; the point is that such detentions cannot be based on a unilateral decision by the executive branch. In that regard, 4001(a) is a manifestation of the most foundational—and most fundamental separation of powers principles. *See* Stephen I. Vladeck, *A Small Problem of Precedent: 18 U.S.C. § 4001(a) and the Detention of U.S. Enemy Combatants*, 112 *Yale L. J.* 961 (January 2003).

140

[114] Oversight of the Department of Justice: Hearing before the Senate Committee on the Judiciary, 107th Cong. 2002 WL 1722725 (2002). In a letter dated November 26, 2002, the Justice Department stated, in part, the following to the chairman of the Senate Judiciary Committee's Subcommittee on the Constitution:

> The term enemy combatant describes those persons who are part of or associated with enemy forces who may lawfully be held during an armed conflict under the laws of war. . . .
>
> . . . there is no requirement imposed by the Constitution or laws of the United States that the President personally make a determination each time a United States citizen is taken into control of the military as an enemy combatant . . .
>
> A United States citizen detained as an enemy combatant can challenge his detention solely by seeking a writ of habeas corpus in the appropriate Federal district court. An enemy combatant has no right to counsel under the Constitution. The rights the Constitution affords persons in the criminal justice system simply do not apply in the context of detention of enemy combatants. Daniel J. Bryant, Assistant Attorney General at A-1 to A-5 (Nov. 26, 2002).

[115] Id. at 1435.

[116] Id. at 1436.

[117] Id. See American Bar Association Task Force on Treatment of Enemy Combatants, Preliminary Report, at 11 August 8, 2002.

[118] Id. at 1438.

[119] Howe v. Smith, 452 U.S. 473 (1981).

[120] Howe, 452 U.S. n.3 at 479. The Court set an unequivocal standard for 4001(a): it applies to any detention of a U.S. citizen by the government, and such detentions are impermissible unless legislatively mandated.

[121] See Padilla ex rel. Newman v. Rumsfeld, 352 F.3d 695 (No. 03-2235) at 38 (2d Cir. 2003).

[122] Id.

[123] Pub. L. No. 107-40, 115 Stat. 224 (2001).

[124] See Hamdi v. Rumsfeld, 316 F.3d at 465 (4th Cir. 2002) (Hamdi III).

[125] See Padilla ex rel. Newman v. Rumsfeld, 352 F.3d 695 (No. 03-2235) at 46 (2d Cir. 2003).

[126] Id. see Hamdi III, 316 F.3d at 467.

[127] 10 U.S.C § 956 (5).

[128] See Hamdi III, 316 F.3d at 467-68.

[129] Id.

[130] See Padilla ex rel. Newman v. Rumsfeld, 352 F.3d 695 (No. 03-2235) at 47 (2d Cir. 2003).

[131] *Id.*

[132] *Ex Parte Endo*, 323 U.S. 283 (1944) n.24 at 304.

[133] 10 U.S.C. § 956.

[134] *Ex Parte Bollman*. 8 U.S. (4 Cranch) 75, 101(1807). Early in the Civil War, Chief Justice Taney, sitting as Circuit Justice in *Ex Parte Merryman*, 17 F. Cas. 144 (C.C. Md. 1861) (No. 9, 487), ruled that Congress has the exclusive authority to suspend the writ. The Chief Justice, relying on the English history of habeas corpus, Blackstone's Commentaries, the language in the Constitution in Article I, and *Ex Parte Bollman*, stated that there was "no ground whatever for supposing that the President in any emergency, or in any state of things, can authorize the suspension of the privileges of habeas corpus. . . ." *Id.* at 149. In *Harris v. Nelson,* the Supreme Court stated that "There is no higher duty of a court, under our constitutional system, than the careful processing and adjudication of petitions for writs of habeas corpus, for it is in such proceedings that a person in custody charges that error, neglect, or evil purpose has resulted in his unlawful confinement and that he is deprived of his freedom contrary to law." *Harris*, 394 U.S. 286 at 291 (1969).

[135] U.S. Const. art. I, § 9, cl. 2.

[136] *See Ex Parte Bollman*, 8 U.S.(4 Cranch) 75, 101 (1807).

[137] *See Lonchar v. Thomas*, 517 U.S. 314, 323 (1996).

[138] U.S. Constitution amendment VI.

[139] U.S. Constitution amendments V, XIV.

[140] *Padilla*, 233 F. Supp. 2d at 600, *Hamdi* 296 F.3d at 283.

[141] *See White v. Maryland*, 373 U.S. 59, 60 (1963).

[142] *Kirby v. Illinois*, 406 U.S. 682 at 689-91 (1972).

[143] *Padilla*, 233 F. Supp. 2d at 600, [quoting 18 U.S.C. 3006 A (2) (B) (2002)].

[144] *Padilla ex rel. Newman v. Bush* 233 F. Supp. at 593-96 (2002).

[145] *Id.* at 603.

[146] *See* All Writs Act, 28 U.S.C. § 1651a (2000), reasoning that the habeas statutes contemplate an opportunity for a detainee to present facts in support of the petition.

[147] *See Padilla ex rel. Newman v. Rumsfeld*, 352 F.3d 695 (No. 03-2235) at 65 (2d Cir. 2003).

[148] *See Hamdi v. Rumsfeld*, No. 02-7338 at 38 (2003).

[149] *Id.* at 41.

[150] *Yamashita* and *Quirin* rule that enemy combatants may challenge their status through habeas petition. The government argues against this position in *Hamdi.*

[151] The Fourth Circuit in *Hamdi* never recognized any right of Hamdi to a lawyer, and on remand ordered the district court to consider the government's national security arguments with "respect at every step." *Hamdi,* 296 F.3d at 284.

[152] *Padilla,* 233 F. Supp. at 207.

[153] *See* United States Department of Defense News Release, DoD Announces, Detainee Allowed Access to Lawyer, No. 908-03, December 2, 2003.

[154] *See* United States Department of Defense News Release, Padilla Allowed Access to Lawyer, No. 097.04, February 11, 2004. To date, at the government's invitation, there has been one informational meeting for Hamdi and Padilla with their attorneys. Each session was video taped and military personnel looked on from an adjoining room.

[155] *See* Neil A. Lewis, "Sudden Shift on Detainee," *N Y. Times,* December 2, 2003, A36. In this same article, Mr. Dinh said the administration needed to provide better form of due process to make its case bulletproof.

[156] *Id.*

[157] *See* 18 U.S.C.A. § 2332 b (a) (2).

[158] *See* 49 U.S.C.A. § 46502 (a) (1)(A) (a).

[159] *See* 18 U.S.C.A. § 32 (a) (7).

[160] *See* 18 U.S.C.A. § 2332 a.

[161] *See* 18 U.S.C.A. § 1114, 1117.

[162] *See* 18 U.S.C.A. § 844 (f) (i).

[163] *See* 18 U.S.C.A. 3 § 5 (a), referring to procedures set forth in the Classified Information Procedures Act (CIPA).

[164] 458 U.S. 858 (1992).

[165] *See Hamdi v. Rumsfeld,* 316 F.3d 450 at 464 (4th Cir. 2003) (*Hamdi III*).

[166] *See Valenzuela-Bernal,* 458 U.S. 858.

[167] *See United States v. Moussaoui* 336 F.3d 279, 282 (4th Cir. 2003) (Wilkins, C. J. concurring in denial of rehearing en banc) ("Siding with the government in all cases where national security concerns are asserted would entail surrender of the independence of the judicial branch and abandon our sworn commitment to the rule of law.")

[168] *United States of America v. Moussaoui* No. 01-455-A (United States District Court, Eastern District of Virginia) October 2, 2003.

[169] *See* Classified Information Procedures Act, 18 U.S.C. App. 3 § 7(a), Title 18 United States Code, Section 3731, and Title 28, United States Code, Section 1291.

[170] *See* Philip Shenon, "Judges Hear U.S. Appeal in Terror Case," *N.Y. Times*, December 3, 2003, A36.

[171] *Id.*

[172] *Id.*

[173] *United States v. Moussaoui*, (No. 03-4792) at 3 (4th Cir. 2004).

[174] *Id.* at 13.

[175] *Id.* at 17.

[176] *Id.* at 18.

[177] *Id.* at 20.

[178] *Id.* at 30.

[179] *Id.* at 32.

[180] *Id.* at 34.

[181] *Id.* at 42.

[182] *Id.* at 48.

[183] *Id.*

[184] *Id.* at 55.

[185] *Id.*

[186] *Id.* at 59.

[187] *Id.* at 62.

[188] *See* U.S. Department of Justice, of Attorney General John Ashcroft on the fourth circuits Ruling in *U.S. v. Moussaoui*, (No. 04-264) (April 22, 2004).

[189] *Padilla ex rel. Newman v. Bush*, 233 F. Supp. 2d 564, at 600 (S.D. N.Y. 2002).

[190] *Id.* at 607.

[191] *Id.* at 593-96.

[192] *Padilla ex rel. Newman v. Rumsfeld*, 352 F. 3d 695 (No. 03-2235) at 4-5 (2d Cir. 2003).

[193] *Hamdi v. Rumsfeld*, 316 F.3d 450 at 476 (4th Cir. 2003) *(Hamdi III)*.

[194] *See Ex Parte Quirin*, 317 US1 at 20, 31 (1946).

[195] *Hamdi v. Rumsfeld*, 296 F.3d 278, at 280 (4th Cir. 2002) *(Hamdi II)*.

[196] *Id.* at 282.

[197] *Id.* at 284.

[198] *Id.*

[199] *Id.* at 281-82.

[200] *Id.* at 283.

[201] *Hamdi III*, 316 F.3d 450, 463 (4th Cir. 2003). The court focused on the significance of the Bill of Rights and the Fourteenth Amendment to the United States Constitution and reasoned that it was the responsibility of the judicial branch to protect individual freedoms, even when military forces are involved in armed conflicts.

[202] *Id.* at 465.

[203] *Id.* at 476.

[204] *Id.* at 464.

[205] *See* Philip Shenon, "Judges Hear U.S. Appeal in Terror Case," *N.Y. Times*, December 3, 2003, A36.

CHAPTER V

United States Supreme Court Review
of Enemy Combatants Post 9/11

Within a few days of the Supreme Court's announcement that it would review the indeterminate detention of Jose Padilla, White House Counsel Alberto Gonzales appeared before the American Bar Association's Standing Committee on Law and National Security to describe the decision-making process in designating American citizens as enemy combatants.[1] The principal governmental actors in that determination include the Central Intelligence Agency, the Department of Defense, and the Department of Justice.

According to Mr. Gonzales the process begins with a preliminary assessment by the Justice Department's Office of Legal Counsel. Applying the standards from *Ex Parte Quirin*[2] "citizens who associate themselves with the military arm of the enemy government, and with its aid, guidance and direction enter this country bent on hostile acts are enemy belligerents."[3] Given this legal threshold the respective agencies evaluate the detainee's threat potential, his ability to provide intelligence, and the potential that criminal prosecution might compromise sensitive national security interests of the nation. These assessments are made by professionals including behavioral psychologists, intelligence officers and law enforcement officers. A written evaluation is presented to the White House, and the President makes a final determination based on the written assessments and recommendations from all the agencies.

The intent of Mr. Gonzales in providing this elaborate and lengthy review procedure was to demonstrate to his immediate audience, the members of the ABA, and more importantly to potential critics of the Administration, and the United States Supreme Court, that the President's Commander-in-Chief authority is exercised in a rational, reasoned, deliberate and constitutional manner in detaining and interrogating enemy combatants with or without charges until the war with al-Qaida and Taliban fighters has ended.[4] Critics of the Administration found little comfort in Mr. Gonzales' assurance that United States citizens held as enemy combatants were to be provided with legal counsel when Defense Department officials determined that such actions no longer interfered with national security concerns for our nation. To them the legal "black hole"[5] continued to exist because enemy combatants could not contest the jurisdiction, competency or constitutionality of their detention.

It is evident that the Bush Administration was concerned about the United States Supreme Court hearing three potential landmark national security cases that could well test the very foundation of the balance of power in American government and establish precedence which could have significant impact on future litigation contests in the modern era of terrorism. The focus of this section of the study is on the Court's role in determining the Administration's power:

1. to declare American citizens as "enemy combatants" and detain them indefinitely without trial (*Hamdi,*[6] *Padilla*[7]), and

2. to hold noncitizen enemy combatants at the American military base at Guantanamo Bay, Cuba, without the opportunity to challenge the basis for their detention in any court of the United States (*Rasul* and *Al-Odah*[8]).

****

Inter Arma Silent Leges and the Canons of *Youngstown*

The Supreme Court sailed into uncharted waters with limited aids to maneuver these cases since precedents have addressed war in the traditional sense of armed conflict between nation states. During the presidency of Abraham Lincoln a wide range of extraordinary powers were assumed by the Commander-in-Chief as a matter of necessity to insure the survival of the state. The Court deferred to President Lincoln in military matters and thereby legitimized a change in the Constitution. The decision in the *Prize Cases*[9] is a classic example of the living Constitution meeting emergency circumstances, and the President taking action to defend our nation. The case illustrates court deference and *inter arma silent leges,* but even more, the law is not merely silent, it is instrumental, which means a wide range of Presidential actions are made lawful by Supreme Court decisions.[10]

Early in World War II President Roosevelt issued an executive order[11] that authorized the Secretary of War to establish "military areas" from which military personnel could restrict, exclude, or expel dangerous persons. This executive and legislative action resulted in the forced evacuation and relocation of more than 112,000 Japanese-Americans from the West Coast, more than two-thirds of whom were native-born citizens, to the interior portion of the Western United States. In *Korematsu*[12] the Court was faced with a direct challenge to the constitutionality of this blatantly discriminatory procedure exercised by the President as Commander-in-Chief. The Court, in what has been considered a "total judicial surrender to an outrage against individual liberties committed under the claim of executive direction to meet military necessities"[13] deferred to the military perspective that the Japanese posed a potentially dangerous threat to our national security, that efforts to determine their loyalty were impractical, and that the actions were therefore constitutional. Three Justices dissented. Justice Murphy took the majority to task by suggesting that it was deep seated racial prejudice against Japanese-Americans which motivated the forced evacuation and prison camps, not any public necessity related to national security. Justices Jackson and Roberts argued that the Court should not give constitutional approval to "a military expedient which has no place in law under the Constitution."[14]

There is no denying the fact that the decisions and impacts of these decisions have raised considerable concern for those with interest in civil liberties, and the threat of war or quasi war to those liberties. American citizens were deprived of their liberty and property because the nation was confronting a sudden and devastating attack which required extreme responses that war dictates. In clear cut issues of national security, as these cases demonstrate, the Supreme Court has had a recognized tendency to yield to military necessity and has been generally unwilling to interfere with the powers of the President.

Even when the Court held that Congress had not intended the Hawaii Organic Act to authorize the supplanting of courts by military tribunals in *Duncan v. Kahanamoku,*[15] it did so long after the hostilities had ceased, and after the Court postponed decision in the case until February 1946. As in *Milligan,*[16] the judiciary flexed its muscles once the "rumble of guns were silenced."[17]

The Supreme Court post-September 11 was called upon to address the President's policy and actions in an emergency setting that juxtaposed individual rights with national security interests. The Court could no longer maintain its traditional passive role with respect to the executive branch in its conflicts with other elements of the constitutional system because the war on terror is ongoing.

The Court in deciding the "enemy combatant" cases could have sought guidance from Justice Jackson's concurring opinion in *Youngstown Sheet and Tube Company v. Sawyer*[18] which "outlined the three now-canonical categories that guide modern analysis of separation of powers."[19]

First, when the President acts pursuant to an express or implied authorization of Congress, his authority is at a maximum, for it includes all he possesses in his own right plus all that Congress can delegate. If his act is held unconstitutional under these circumstances, it usually means that the Federal Government as an undivided whole lacks power.[20]

Jackson's second category is the so called "zone of twilight" which argues that when the President acts in absence of either a congressional grant or denial of authority, he can only rely upon his own independent powers, but there is a zone of twilight in which he and Congress may have concurrent authority, or in which its distribution is uncertain. Therefore, congressional inertia, indifference or quiescence may sometimes, at least as a practical matter, enable, if not invite, measures on independent presidential responsibility. In this area, any actual test of power is likely to depend on the imperatives of events and contemporary imponderables rather than on abstract theories of law.[21]

Finally, Jackson's third category addresses presidential power "at its lowest ebb:" When the President takes measures incompatible with the expressed or implied will of Congress, his power is at its lowest ebb, for then he can rely only upon his own constitutional powers minus any constitutional powers of Congress over the matter. Courts can sustain exclusive presidential control in such a case only by disabling the Congress from acting upon the subject. Presidential claim to a power at once so conclusive and preclusive must be scrutinized with caution, for what is at stake is the equilibrium established by our constitutional system.[22]

Youngstown, it has been suggested, is "perhaps the Court's most important attempt to fit the needs of executive branch decision-making at times of crisis within our constitutional tradition."[23] It has proven to be an important landmark for subsequent judicial decision-making as it relates to executive power.[24]

In its Supreme Court brief in the Jose Padilla case, the administration argued that the President's constitutional powers and the post-September 11 congressional authorization to use military force permit Padilla's continued detention. As Solicitor General Theodore Olson wrote: "The authority of the Commander-in-Chief to engage and defeat the enemy encompasses the capture and detention of enemy combatants wherever found, including within the nation's boundary. That is particularly true in the current conflict in view of the nature of the September 11 attacks, which were perpetrated by combatants who had assimilated into the civilian population and launched their attack from within the United States.... The enemy is composed of combatants who operate in secret and aim to launch surprise, sporadic, and large-scale attacks against the civilian population."[25] The President's power is "not limited to alien or foreign battlefields or conditioned on an act of Congress."[26]

The position of the Administration was that Article III Courts could not second guess or micromanage the Executive's enemy combatant determination even in habeas corpus petitions properly filed on behalf of American citizens. Olson argued that judicial review would "superintend the executive's conduct of an armed conflict."[27]

In a landmark series of decisions handed down one day prior to the end of its 2004 term, the United States Supreme Court provided mixed signals to the

150

Administration with respect to its detention of citizen and alien enemy combatants in the United States and at Guantanamo Bay in Cuba. The three separate opinions, although characterized by fractionalism and unusual alliances among the justices, are consistent in one respect, and that is the executive branch does not have a blank check to impose indeterminate detention on citizens and non-citizens in undertaking its war on terror. Each of the cases will be discussed in detail below.

Hamdi v. Rumsfeld[28]

Justice Sandra Day O'Connor delivered the opinion in which she was joined by Chief Justice Rehnquist, and Associate Justices Kennedy and Breyer. The plurality ruling held that although Congress authorized the detention of combatants in the narrow circumstance of being part of, or supporting forces hostile to the United States or coalition partners in Afghanistan and who engaged in an armed conflict against the United States there, due process demands that a citizen held in the United States as an enemy combatant be given a meaningful opportunity to contest the factual basis for that detention before a neutral decisionmaker.[29]

The Court did not address the question as to whether the provisions of Article II authorized the President to detain enemy combatant citizens of the United States because a majority of the justices agreed with the Government's position that Congress had authorized Hamdi's detention through the Joint Congressional Resolution Authorizing the Use of Military Force (AUMF).[30] Therefore the AUMF satisfied Title 18 § 4001(a)'s requirement that a detention be pursuant to an Act of Congress.[31] Justice O'Connor expressed the view that although the AUMF did not provide any explicit language referring to detention it should have been inferred as "incidental to waging war and using necessary and appropriate force."[32]

A legitimate concern recognized by the plurality and raised by Hamdi was that his detention could conceivably last for the rest of his life. Congress did not authorize indefinite detention which he was potentially facing since the "war on terror" was unconventional and was "unlikely to end with a formal cease-fire agreement."[33] Justice O'Connor reasoned that as long as active combatant operations against the Taliban in Afghanistan were on-going then the United States "may detain for the duration of these hostilities."[34]

Justice O'Connor called for a proper balancing of interests in detaining those who pose a threat to the national security and the legitimate interest in preserving the rights of those who have been wrongfully detained and who do not present that sort of threat.[35] The way to protect the citizen's right to be free from illegitimate involuntary confinement by his government is to ensure due process of law. She ruled that a citizen-detainee seeking to challenge his classification as an enemy combatant must "receive notice of the factual basis for that classification, and a fair opportunity to rebut the Government's factual assertion before a neutral decision maker."[36]

Recognizing the existing circumstances of on-going conflict, Justice O'Connor reasoned that such a proceeding "may be tailored to alleviate the uncommon potential burden"[37] the Executive is confronting. Hearsay could be accepted as reliable available evidence, as well as a "presumption in favor of the Government's evidence, provided that presumption was a rebuttable one and fair opportunity for rebuttal were provided."[38]

In the proceeding the Government puts forth its evidence that the detainee meets the enemy combatant criteria, and then the onus would shift to the detainee to rebut that evidence with more convincing evidence that he does not meet that criteria. Such a process, in Justice O'Connor's view, would not have dire impact on the Government's war-making capability, and the process would only be employed once a determination is made to *continue* to hold those who have been seized, and not for initial captures on the battlefield. (emphasis added)

Justice O'Connor emphasized the need for great respect and consideration for military authorities in their ability to effectively prosecute a war, however "it does not infringe on the core role of the military for the courts to exercise their own time honored and constitutionally maintained roles of reviewing and resolving cases like this one."[39] The Court therefore rejected the position of Solicitor General Olson that separation of powers principles mandate a heavily circumscribed role for the courts in such circumstances,..."[b]ecause such an approach serves only to condense power into a single branch of government. We have long since made clear that a state of war is not a blank check for the President when it comes to the rights of the Nation's citizens."[40]

Justice O'Connor reinforced the basis of separation of governmental powers into the three coordinate branches of government where checks and balances would turn on its head if a citizen could not make his way to court to challenge his detention by the government, simply because the Executive opposed making available such a challenge,[41] and she rejected the "some evidence" standard as inadequate because it permits the Executive's factual assertions to go unchallenged or to be presumed as correct. This position is forcefully articulated by Judge Motz in her Fourth Circuit dissenting opinion in *Hamdi*.[42]

Justice O'Connor concluded with a reference to authorizing a "properly constituted military tribunal" to conduct such proceedings involving enemy detainees.[43] The President's Executive Order establishing Military Commissions post-September 11 specifically exempted United States citizens from their jurisdiction, although a question is raised as to whether American citizens could come under their purview.[44] Given the public position of the President on this issue it would appear that he would either have to revise his Executive Order to reflect Justice O'Connor's position, or seek authorization from the United States Congress to act prospectively.

In a separate concurring and in part dissenting opinion written by Justice Souter, who is joined by Justice Ginsburg, the two justices argue that the government's attempt to limit Hamdi's exercise of habeas jurisdiction was unwarranted. Since Hamdi's detention was authorized by an Act of Congress as required by the Non-Detention Act, Justice Souter reasoned that the government failed to demonstrate that the Force Resolution authorized such detention, and therefore Non-Detention Act § 4001(a) entitled Hamdi to be released.[45]

Justice Souter maintained that the Government failed to make its case for detention of Hamdi on any theory including "authorization to the Department of Defense to pay for 'detaining prisoners of war' and 'similar' persons, under 10 U.S.C. § 956 (5),"[46] the Force Resolution, or even the Commander-in-Chief clause under Article II of the Constitution. Justice Souter called for a broad reading of the Non-Detention Act because the intent of its framers in avoiding another *Korematsu* was to preclude reliance on vague congressional authority and to insure that the § 4001(a) had teeth in its demand for congressional authorization.[47]

Justice Souter raised an additional concern that in a governmental system such as ours which is characterized by separated powers, decisions related to reasonable degrees of guaranteed liberty in peace or war "cannot be effectively entrusted to the Executive Branch of Government,"[48] because its particular responsibility is to maintain security. For Justice Souter, the appropriate branch of government is Congress because it is more likely to reach a reasonable balance of liberty and security interests in our society.[49]

Justice Souter provided one argument for treating the Force Resolution as sufficiently clear to authorize detention of Hamdi consistent with § 4001(a) and that is through the treaties and customs known collectively as the laws of war.[50] Hamdi was taken bearing arms on the Taliban side of the field battle in Afghanistan, and according to Justice Souter he would seem to qualify for treatment as a prisoner of war under the Third Geneva Convention, to which the United States is a party.[51] Since the government held him incommunicado he was not treated as a prisoner of war, and the Government in fact claimed that no Taliban detainee was entitled to prisoner of war status.[52] Justice Souter commented that this appeared to be a violation of the Geneva Convention since captives are "entitled to be treated as prisoners of war until such time as their status has been determined by a competent tribunal."[53] Additionally, according to Justice Souter, Hamdi's treatment was in violation of United States military regulation which required "a competent tribunal of three commissioned officers to determine Hamdi's status."[54] Therefore there was every reason to question whether the United States was acting in accordance with the laws of war.

Justice Souter cited Justice Jackson's observation in *Youngstown* that the "President is not Commander-in-Chief of the country, only the military,"[55] and that Presidential authority is at its lowest ebb where the President acts contrary to congressional will.[56] Justice Souter opined that "in a moment of genuine emergency, when the Government must act with no time for deliberation, the Executive may be able to detain a citizen if there is reason to fear he is an imminent threat to the safety of the Nation,"[57] however that was not the case with Hamdi since he was locked up for over two years.

Justice Souter concluded his opinion by stating that since his position did not command a majority of the Court he "would join with the plurality in ordering a remand on terms closest to those I would impose,"[58] because it would permit Hamdi to offer evidence that he was not an enemy combatant, a benefit he was entitled to as a matter of due process.

Justice Scalia was joined by Justice Stevens in dissent arguing that Hamdi was entitled to a habeas decree requiring his release unless (1) criminal proceedings were promptly brought, or (2) Congress suspended the writ of habeas corpus.[59] Justice Scalia rejected the view that the AUMF authorized detention of a citizen with the "clarity necessary to satisfy the interpretive canon that statutes should be construed so as to avoid grave constitutional concerns,"[60] and even if it did he wouldn't permit it to overcome Hamdi's entitlement to habeas corpus relief.

He attacked the plurality for finding congressional authorization for detention of citizens where none clearly existed, and coming up with "an unheard of system in which the citizen bears the burden of proof, testimony is by hearsay rather than live witnesses, and the presiding officer may well be a 'neutral' military officer rather than judge or jury."[61] Such a remedy of "executive default is unheard of, . . . and this approach reflects what might be called a Mr. Fix-it Mentality."[62] Justice Scalia chided the plurality for its mission to "Make

Everything Come Out Right, rather than merely decreeing the consequences, as far as individual rights are concerned of the other two branches' actions and omissions."[63] Justice Scalia concluded his dissent by stating that "many think . . . it entirely proper that liberty give way to security in time of national crisis, *inter arma silent leges,*"[64] but that view "has no place in the interpretation and application of a Constitution designed precisely to confront war and, in a manner that accords with democratic principles, to accommodate it."[65]

Justice Thomas is the lone dissenter who fully supported the actions of the government stating that Hamdi's detention fell squarely within the Federal Government's war powers, and "we (the courts) lack the expertise and capacity to second-guess that decision."[66] He argued that the Federal Government's War powers "cannot be balanced away by this court, ... and the plurality utterly fails to account for the Government's compelling interest and for our own institutional ability to weigh competing concerns correctly."[67] This position coincides directly with the opinion of Chief Judge Wilkinson of the Fourth Circuit in *Hamdi*.[68]

Citing the *Prize Cases*, Justice Thomas held that the President had the authority to protect national security with broad discretion and "although Congress has a substantial and essential role to play in foreign affairs and national security, the principal responsibility belongs to a Unitary Executive."[69] Any question as to whether Hamdi's executive detention was lawful was a question that Justice Thomas suggested was to be properly resolved by the Judicial Branch, but the question "comes to the Court with the strongest presumptions in favor of the Government."[70] The question of whether Hamdi was an enemy combatant is "of a kind for which the Judiciary has neither the aptitude, facilities nor responsibility and belongs in the domain of political power not subject to judicial intrusion or inquiry."[71] Although Justice Thomas agreed with the plurality that the Congress authorized the President to detain Hamdi with reliance upon AUMF, he expressed concern that "it (the plurality) appears to limit the President's authority to detain by requiring that the record establish that United States troops are still involved in active combat in Afghanistan, because in that case, detention would be part of the exercise of necessary and appropriate force."[72]

Justice Thomas strongly criticized the plurality for undertaking "judicial second-guessing of the Executive in enemy-combatant determinations that could defeat the unity, secrecy and dispatch that the Founders believed so important to the war making function."[73]   He concluded his opinion by reasserting the legitimate role of the President in detaining Hamdi, and since the President acted well within his authority, "Hamdi thereby received all the process to which he was due under the circumstances, and ... this is no occasion to balance the competing interests, as the plurality unconvincingly attempts to do."[74]

What we can determine from the *Hamdi* decision is the following:

- Eight justices agreed that the indefinite detention of Hamdi by the Government was invalid based upon provisions of the Constitution and/or statutory law;

- Only Justice Clarence Thomas supported the role of the Government to indefinitely detain Hamdi based upon Article II authority and the AUMF;

- A four-justice plurality of the Court (O'Connor, Rehnquist, Kennedy, Breyer) acknowledged that the President did have the authority to designate citizens as enemy combatants relying upon the AUMF and *Quirin* as precedent;

- A five-member majority of the Court (the plurality plus Thomas) stood for the proposition that U.S. citizens could be held as enemy combatants;

- A six-member majority of the Court (the plurality plus Breyer and Ginsburg) supported the part of the plurality opinion that outlined a hearing for Hamdi;

- Three justices (Scalia, Stevens and Thomas) refused to accept a balanced hearing process for Hamdi;

- The plurality opinion recommended that the government be permitted to introduce hearsay evidence and that there could be a "presumption in favor of the government's evidence" as long as the detainee had a "fair opportunity for rebuttal;"

- The plurality opinion suggested that a detainee's case, based upon the standards articulated, could be met by a properly constituted military tribunal.

Justice O'Connor's opinion in Hamdi did not provide a time frame for how long detainees were to be held before they were provided a fact finding process that is both "prudent and incremental." Nor is the decision specific about what kind of hearing Hamdi should get. Those matters were left to the lower courts and the government to resolve.

Rumsfeld v. Padilla[75]

Chief Justice Rehnquist delivered the opinion of the Court, in which the majority considered who was the proper respondent to the habeas petition, and whether the Southern District had jurisdiction over him or her.

Relying upon statutory language[76] and precedence involving the immediate custodian rule[77] the Court concluded that the proper respondent was Melanie Marr, Commander of the Consolidated Naval Brig in Charleston, South Carolina where Padilla was being held and not Secretary of Defense Rumsfeld as had been decided by the Second Circuit Court of Appeals in *Padilla ex rel. Newman v. Rumsfeld.*[78]

The Court of Appeals conclusion that Secretary Rumsfeld was the proper respondent because he exercised the "legal reality of control over Padilla"[79] only came into play when there was no immediate physical custodian with respect to the challenged custody. In this case, according to Chief Justice Rehnquist, there was an immediate custodian, namely, Commander Marr. Furthermore, Padilla's detention was not unique in any way that would provide an arguable basis for a departure from the immediate custodian rule.

As to the second question, Justice Rehnquist commented that District Courts are limited to granting habeas relief "within their respective jurisdictions,"[80] which means that "jurisdiction over Padilla's habeas petition lies in the Southern District only if it has jurisdiction over Commander Marr. We conclude it does not."[81]

Chief Justice Rehnquist cited action taken by the United States Congress in 1867 to add the limiting clause "within their respective jurisdictions" to the habeas statute to "avert the inconvenient [and] potentially embarrassing possibility that every judge anywhere [could] issue the Great Writ on behalf of applicants far distantly removed from the courts whereon they sat."[82] "The plain language of the habeas statute confirmed the rule that for core habeas petitions challenging present physical confinement, jurisdiction was in only one district: the district of confinement."[83]

This rule, derived from the terms of the habeas statute, according to the Chief Justice, "serves the important purpose of preventing forum shopping by habeas petitioners. Without it, a prisoner could name a high level supervisory official and then sue that person wherever he is amenable to long-arm jurisdiction. The result would be rampant forum shopping."[84]

In response to Justice Stevens's plea, in dissent, that the "jurisdictional rules be bent because the merits of this case are of profound importance,"[85] Chief Justice Rehnquist replied that "it is surely just as necessary in important cases as in unimportant ones that courts take care not to exceed their respective jurisdictions established by Congress."[86] The habeas petition should have been brought by Padilla in the District of South Carolina and not the Southern District of New York.[87]

Justice Stevens wrote an impassioned dissenting opinion, which was joined by Justices Souter, Ginsburg and Breyer. Although he conceded that all members of the Court agreed "that the immediate custodian rule should control in the ordinary case and that habeas petitioners should not be permitted to engage in forum shopping, they also all agreed that special circumstances can justify exceptions from the general rule."[88] He challenged the majority opinion for seeking to enforce a "bright line rule" and then acknowledging the "numerous exceptions that we have made to the immediate custodian rule."[89] In recognizing "exception upon exception and corollaries to corollaries, the Court itself persuasively demonstrates the rule is far from iron clad."[90]

Justice Stevens challenged the majority view as disingenuous at best to classify Padilla's petition as part of a group of "run-of-the-mill collateral attacks"[91] on federal criminal convictions. Padilla's case is singular because it calls into question "those decisions that have created a vague and unprecedented threat to the freedom of every American citizen."[92]

Justice Stevens agreed with the Second Circuit's opinion that the Non-Detention Act prohibited, and the AUMF failed to authorize the protracted incommunicado detention of American citizens arrested in the United States.[93] He compared unconstrained Executive detention for the purpose of investigating and preventing subversive activity as the hallmark of the infamous Star Chamber.[94] Incommunicado detention, in his view, could never be justified by the "naked interest in using unlawful procedures to extract information."[95] He concluded his opinion with the following observation ... if this Nation is to remain true to the ideals symbolized by its flag, it must not wield the tools of tyrants to resist an assault by the forces of tyranny.[96]

What we get from the *Padilla* decision is the following:

- Five Justices in the majority (Chief Justice Rehnquist joined by Justices Kennedy, O'Connor, Scalia, and Thomas) dismissed Padilla's case on jurisdictional grounds ruling that his attorney incorrectly went to a New York Court in search of an order releasing him when she should have sought review in South Carolina;

- Four Justices dissented in this ruling, (Justices Stevens, Breyer, Ginsburg and Souter) and unless the Government decides to charge Padilla, it would appear that there will be five votes to release him once his case comes back up. Justice Scalia is on record in the *Hamdi*

decision as being opposed to the Executive's approach to the detention
of enemy combatants.

Rasul et al. v. Bush and Al-Odah et al. v. United States

Justice Stevens delivered the opinion of the Court in these two cases
which were consolidated into a single court opinion. The question considered was
whether United States courts lack jurisdiction to consider challenges to the
legality of the detention of foreign nationals captured abroad in connection with
hostilities, and incarcerated at the Guantanamo Bay Naval Base in Cuba. The
narrow but important issue did not extend beyond the question of jurisdiction.[97]
The petitioners in these cases included two Australian citizens and 12 Kuwaiti
citizens[98] who were captured during the hostilities between the United States and
the Taliban.

Justice Stevens examined the historical roots and application of the
authority of federal district courts "within their respective jurisdictions" to hear
applications for habeas corpus by any person who claims to be held "in custody in
violation of the Constitution or laws or treaties of the United States."[99]

The Court has recognized the federal courts' power to review applications
for habeas relief in a broad context of Executive detention in wartime and in
peace and Justice Stevens specifically cited Ex parte Milligan,[100] Ex parte
Quirin,[101] and In re Yamashita[102] as precedence for the case "before us which is
whether the habeas statute confers judicial review … of aliens in a territory over
which the United States exercises plenary and exclusive jurisdiction but not
ultimate sovereignty."[103] The Government argued that the answer to the
jurisdictional question is controlled by the Court's decision in Eisentrager.[104]
Justice Stevens suggested that the circumstances in the current cases differed
markedly from the Eisentrager detainees in several respects including: "They are
not nationals of countries at war with the United States, and they deny that they
have engaged in or plotted acts of aggression against the United States; they have
never been afforded access to any tribunal, much less charged with or convicted

of wrongdoing; and for more than two years they have been imprisoned in territory over which the United States exercises exclusive jurisdiction and control."[105]

The majority reasoned that the application of the habeas statute to persons detained at Guantanamo is consistent with the historical reach of the writ of habeas corpus extending back "to common law when courts exercised habeas jurisdiction over the claims of aliens detained within sovereign territory of the realm."[106] As Lord Mansfield wrote in 1759, "even if territory was no part of the realm, there was no doubt as to the Court's power to issue writs of habeas corpus if the territory was under the subjection of the Crown."[107]

The Court held that "§ 2241 confers on the District Court jurisdiction to hear petitioners' habeas corpus challenges to the legality of their detention at the Guantanamo Bay Naval Base in Cuba"[108] since they were detained for over two years in territory subject to the long term jurisdiction and control of the United States without access to counsel and without being charged with any wrongdoing, which unquestionably described custody in violation of the Constitution or laws or treaties of the United States.[109] Justice Stevens concluded the majority opinion by stating that "nothing in *Eisentrager* or any of our other cases categorically excludes aliens detained in military custody outside the United States from the privilege of litigation in U.S. courts, and the courts of the United States have traditionally been open to non-resident aliens."[110]

Justice Kennedy in his brief concurring opinion examined the historical significance of *Eisentrager* and the need for "its faithful application to the circumstances of the current case."[111] That decision recognized and acknowledged the power of the President as Commander-in-Chief, the joint role of the President and the Congress in the conduct of military affairs, and "the realm of political authority over military affairs where the judicial power may not enter."[112] However, he did suggest that there were circumstances in which the courts maintained "the power and the responsibility to protect persons from unlawful detention even where military affairs were implicated."[113]

What was critically distinguishable in the current case from *Eisentrager*, according to Justice Kennedy, was first the nature of the lease agreement between the United States and Cuba for Guantanamo Bay. Its term was "indefinite and at the discretion of the United States."[114] United States' control over that area has gone totally unchallenged, and from a practical perspective "it has produced a place that belongs to the United States."[115]

The second critical set of facts for Justice Kennedy was that the Guantanamo detainees were held without any benefit of any legal proceeding to determine their status while "in *Eisentrager* the prisoners were tried and convicted by a military commission of violating procedures establishing their status and were sentenced to prison terms."[116] Perhaps, he argued, if the detainees were held without proceedings or trial for a matter of weeks it could be justified, however when the period of detention "stretches from months to years, the case for continued detention to meet military exigencies becomes weaker."[117] Justice Kennedy concluded that in light of both the status of Guantanamo Bay, and indefinite pretrial detention, federal-court jurisdiction would be permitted in these cases and "this approach would avoid creating automatic statutory authority to adjudicate claims of persons located outside the United States, and remains consistent with the precedent reasoning in *Eisentrager*."[118]

Justice Scalia filed a dissenting opinion in the case with whom Chief Justice Rehnquist and Justice Thomas joined in. In his opinion, Justice Scalia turned to the plain words of § 2241 which clearly established as a "necessary requirement for issuing the writ that *some* federal district court have territorial jurisdiction over the detainee."[119] (emphasis added) Since the Guantanamo Bay detainees "were not located within the territorial jurisdiction of any federal district court one would think that is the end of the case."[120]

The majority opinion, in Justice Scalia's view, clearly overruled *Eisentrager*, and extended the habeas statute for the first time to aliens held beyond the sovereign territory of the United States and beyond the territorial jurisdiction of its courts.[121] Such a ruling created a trap for the Executive, because it subjected Guantanamo Bay to the oversight of the federal courts and made it a "foolish place to have housed alien wartime detainees."[122] In abandoning the statutory line drawn in *Eisentrager*, the Court, according to Justice Scalia, "extends the scope of the habeas statute to the four corners of the earth."[123]

The consequence of such a ruling is "breathtaking because from this point forward, federal courts will entertain petitions from their prisoners and others like them around the world, challenging actions and events far away, and forcing the courts to oversee one aspect of the Executive's conduct of a foreign war."[124] Relying upon the opinion of Justice Jackson in *Eisentrager*, Justice Scalia wrote that it would be "difficult to devise more effective fettering of a field commander than to allow the very enemies he ordered to reduce to submission to call him to account in his own civil courts and divert his efforts and attention from the military offensive abroad to the legal defensive at home."[125]

What was most troubling to Justice Scalia was how the "complete jurisdiction and control" of Guantanamo Bay without sovereignty caused "an enclave to be part of the United States for purposes of its domestic laws."[126] Employing that logic, Justice Scalia reasoned that parts of "Afghanistan and Iraq should logically be regarded as subject to our domestic laws, . . . and so should the Landsberg Prison in Germany, where the United States held the *Eisentrager* detainees."[127]

The dissent strongly questioned Justice Stevens historical analysis of the writ of habeas corpus and its "extraordinary territorial ambit which extended to exempt jurisdictions, outlying dominions and the like."[128] That extension applied only to British *subjects*, and even Lord Blackstone explained that the writ "run[s] into all parts of the King's dominions," because "the King is at all times entitled to have an account why the liberty of any of his *subjects* is restrained."[129] (emphasis added)

Justice Scalia concluded his opinion by suggesting that the majority's treatment of Guantanamo Bay was, like its treatment of § 2241, "a wrenching departure from precedent."[130] The President as Commander-in-Chief had every reason to believe that internment of enemy combatants at Guantanamo Bay would not have the "cumbersome machinery of our domestic courts,"[131] intruding into military affairs. Since Congress was in session, if it wished to change federal judges' habeas jurisdiction from historic precedence, it could readily amend the law. The practical consequence of this "clumsy, counter textual reinterpretation" of the law, which was judicial adventurism of the worst sort, was that it freed detainees to forum shop in any of the 94 federal judicial districts and created such a monstrous scheme in time of war that it would frustrate military commanders reliance upon clearly stated prior law.[132]

The significance of the Guantanamo case is the following:

- Six Justices (Justice Stevens, joined by Justices O'Connor, Souter, Ginsburg, Kennedy and Breyer) formed a majority that determined federal law permits U.S. Courts to consider petitions for writs of habeas corpus from non-citizen detainees who argue that they are being unlawfully held;

- The majority's analysis suggested that federal courts may have jurisdiction to hear claims of illegal detention from those prisoners being held in other foreign locations, since it did not define the intended scope of its ruling;

- Justice Stevens left it for the lower courts to address whether and what further proceedings may become necessary after the government responded to the merits of the detainees claims;

- Three Justices (Justice Scalia, joined by Chief Justice Rehnquist and Justice Thomas) in dissent complained about the rejection of *Eisentrager* as clear precedence and its intended consequences, namely extending the scope of the habeas statute to the four corners of the earth;

- An agreement was reached by the lawyers for the 13 detainees in the consolidated case and the Justice Department to permit, for the first time, civilian lawyers to visit Guantanamo to consult with their clients.

• United States courts are now opened to the nearly 600 detainees who would otherwise be denied any forum in which to proclaim their innocence as well as protest how they are being treated.

In response to the last point administration officials were considering several alternatives to granting military detainees access to U.S. courts. Since Guantanamo Bay is not within any federal court jurisdiction, prisoners may be moved from Cuba to specifically designated locations in the United States. Possible sites include Fort Leavenworth, Kansas where there is an Army base with a military prison, and Charleston, South Carolina, home of the Charleston Naval Weapons Station, which houses the Navy brig where Hamdi and Padilla are currently held. Another option would be to allow prisoners to file for the writs at a makeshift court at the base in Cuba, and a final option is to ask Congress to designate one federal district court to try the cases in a jurisdiction that includes the Pentagon (Eastern District of Virginia). As Justice Scalia suggested in his dissent, detainees will be permitted, as a result of this decision, to forum shop and seek redress in any of the 94 federal district courts of the United States.

Summary

For the first time in over half a century the United States Supreme Court was called upon to address the President's claimed broad authority post-September 11, 2001 to seize and hold potential terrorists or their protectors for as long as the Executive determined without any interference from the courts or lawyers in the detention and interrogation process.

The position of the Administration was that Article III Courts could not second guess or micromanage the Executive's enemy combatant determination even in habeas corpus petitions filed on behalf of American citizens.

The Court, in deciding the "enemy combatant cases could have been guided by Justice Jackson's concurring opinion in *Youngstown*, which outlined the three categorical analyses of Executive power under the separation of powers in our constitutional system.

First, when the President acts pursuant to an express or implied authorization of Congress, his authority is at its peak; second, when the President acts in absence of either a congressional grant or denial of authority, he is in a zone of twilight, because he and Congress may have concurrent authority, or the distribution of power is uncertain; and finally, when the President takes measures incompatible with the expressed or implied will of Congress, his power is at its lowest ebb.

In a pair of landmark decisions the Court struck a constitutional balance which made it clear that even during the war on terror when the President must be able to exercise his military authority and protect our national security, the government must adhere to the rule of law. The Court also reminded the administration that the Court, and no one else, is the final arbiter between the branches of government. Whether the prisoners will be released, and on what terms, will be decided by the federal courts. Although the resolution of these cases have yet to be determined, it is a fact that the courts have the power to resolve them.

In *Hamdi*, eight of the justices argued that the indefinite detention of Hamdi by the Government was invalid based upon provisions of the Constitution and/or statutory law. Justice Clarence Thomas supported the role of the Government to indefinitely detain Hamdi based upon Article II authority and the AUMF. A four-justice plurality acknowledged that the President had the authority to designate citizens as enemy combatants relying upon the AUMF and *Quirin*. A five-member majority supported the proposition that U.S. citizens could be held as enemy combatants because the Congress in its Joint Resolution impliedly authorized in the AUMF the President to use detention as part of the necessary and appropriate force in defeating terrorists. A six-member majority supported some form of hearing process for Hamdi, although the plurality recommended that the Government be permitted to introduce hearsay evidence and that there be a presumption in favor of the government as long as the detainee had a fair opportunity for rebuttal.

In *Hamdi*, the precise details of what a fair process meant was left to the lower courts to decide, although the basic elements were mandated including the opportunity to contest the government's position before a neutral decision maker.

In the *Rasul* decision, Justice Stevens writing for the majority ruled that practically there was no difference between being held in Guantanamo and being held in the United States. Detainees in both settings were entitled to review by neutral adjudicators, which was a major departure for the Court in its usual wartime deference to the wishes of the Executive. However, Justice Stevens specifically stated that he was offering no opinion as to what type of proceedings were appropriate for the Guantanamo detainees. The Court said that the Cuban base was not beyond the reach of American courts regardless of the fact that it is located outside the territorial boundaries of the United States because Guantanamo is territory over which the United States exercises exclusive jurisdiction and control. Since the majority's analysis did not define the intended scope of its ruling it is conceivable that federal courts may have jurisdiction to hear claims of illegal detention from prisoners being held in other foreign locations.

The Administration is currently considering several alternative options now that the nearly 600 detainees have potential access to 94 federal district courts for habeas relief. They include moving all detainees to specifically designated locations; permitting prisoners to file for writs at a makeshift court at the base in Cuba; or asking Congress to designate one federal district court to try the cases.

In the *Padilla* ruling, the majority sidestepped the issue of whether the government had the authority to indefinitely detain Jose Padilla, a U.S. citizen, seized on American soil. The Court found that Padilla's habeas corpus petition was filed in the wrong court, the Southern District of New York instead of in South Carolina, where Padilla was held in a Naval brig. Now that Padilla has refiled his case in the correct court, it is very difficult to believe that his result will differ from that of Hamdi or the Guantanamo detainees.

The United States Supreme Court in deciding these terrorism cases has demonstrated that our constitutional system is effectively working with the judiciary being prepared to exercise its balanced independent role. The Court was fractious, deliberative, and passionate in addressing issues of law, historical precedence, and the Constitution. It is safe to suggest that *Hamdi* and *Rasul* are merely the tip of the iceberg because a series of court cases on other matters related to the war on terrorism, such as whether Guantanamo prisoners can be exempted from international law and whether military commissions satisfy both constitutional and international law standards, are on the horizon for judicial review.[133]

Notes

[1] Vanessa Blum, "Powers of Designating 'Enemy Combatant' Outlined," *New York Law Journal*, http://www.abanet.org/natsecurity, March 1, 2004.

[2] *Ex Parte Quirin*, 317 U.S. 1 (1942).

[3] *Id.* at 32.

[4] Additionally, the Pentagon announced an administrative review process to reassess the need to continue to detain an enemy combatant in custody at Guantanamo Bay Naval Base at least annually during the course of hostilities. The Secretary of the Navy is the designated civilian official to operate and oversee the annual administrative review process. He is to be assisted by a number of military boards, each with three military officers, who are to determine whether the enemy combatant continues to be a threat to the national security of the United States, and if not, whether it is in the interest of the United States and its allies to release him. The detainee is entitled to appear before the board to explain why he is no longer a threat. He may be provided with written information helpful to his status by the government of which he is a national, as well as his family who can testify on his behalf.

Although the process permits the enemy combatant assistance by an assigned military officer in preparing his presentation to the board, there is no provision for representation by counsel which creates a fatal flaw in the process. Regardless of the fact that there exists reference to appropriate fact gathering, independent judgment based upon review of all reasonably available information, as well as designated civilian official oversight and determination of continued detention release, or transfer of the enemy combatant to another government, the denial of legal representation creates a gap that potentially taints the entire review system. Lawyers are properly trained to help the detainees make the strongest arguments on their behalf. Additionally the standards and burden of proof are not presented clearly enough. The Order does not stipulate which side will have to prove how much of a threat a detainee poses, or for that matter, how minimal a threat is posed. If the threshold is too high a burden for the detainee then it will serve as a carte blanche mechanism for indefinite detention. United States Department of Defense, Order, Administrative Procedures for Enemy Combatants in the Control of the Department of Defense at Guantanamo Bay Naval Base, Cuba May 11, 2004. *See* Appendix D for a discussion of the document.

[5] *See* Chapter III *supra* n.25 at 82. *See also, Abbasi & Anor. v. Sec'y of State for Foreign and Commonwealth Affairs*, (2002) EWCACiv 1598, para. 64 (U.K. Sup. Ct. Judicature, C.A.) Nov. 6, 2002.

[6] *Padilla v. Rumsfeld*, 352 F.3d 695 (2d Cir. 2003) cert. granted 124 S. Ct. 1353 (2004) (No. 03-1027).

[7] *Hamdi v. Rumsfeld (Hamdi III)*, 316 F.3d 450 (4th Cir. 2003) cert. granted 124 S. Ct. 981 (2004) (No. 03-6696).

[8] *Rasul et al. v. Bush* and *Al-Odah et al. v. United States*, 321 F.3d 1134 (D.C. Cir. 2003) Cert. granted 124 S. Ct. 534 (2003).

[9] 67 U.S. 635 (1863). *See* Chapter I *supra* n.56 at 21.

[10] *See* Arthur S. Miller, *Presidential Power* (Minneapolis: West Publishing Company, 1977) at 174.

[11] Executive Order 9066, 7. Fed. Reg. 1407 (1942) as ratified by Congress 56 Stat. 173 (1942).

[12] *Korematsu v. United States* 323 U.S. 214 (1944).

[13] *See* Martin Shapiro and Douglas S. Hobbs, *The Politics of Constitutional Law* (Cambridge, Mass. Winthrop Press, 1974) at 433. *Korematsu* has been widely condemned for its tolerance of racism underlying the Japanese Exclusion Order, and although the Supreme Court has had no occasion to reconsider that decision, the Court's sensitivity to individual rights and liberties is far greater today than it was in 1944. Forty years after Korematsu was decided, federal judges finding that determination of necessity had depended on official's lies, upset the Japanese-Americans' convictions. *Korematsu v. United States*, 584 F. Supp. 1406 (N.D. Cal. 1984); *see also, Hirabayshi v. United States*, 828 F.2d 591 (9th Cir. 1987), Congress asked pardon "on behalf of the Nation" from the 112,000 internees, and made payments of $20,000 each in "restitution." Civil Liberties Act of 1988, 50 U.S.C. 1989 (1988).

[14] *Id.*

[15] 327 U.S. 304 (1946).

[16] *Ex Parte Milligan*, 4 Wall 2 (1866).

[17] Miller, op. cit. at 182.

[18] 343 U.S. 579, 635 (1952).

[19] *See* Neal K. Katyal & Laurence H. Tribe, *Waging War, Deciding Guilt: Trying the Military Tribunals*, 111 *Yale L.J.* 1259 at 1274.

[20] 343 U.S. 579 at 635.

[21] *Id.* at 637.

[22] *Id.* at 637-38.

[23] *See* Kaytal and Tribe, *Waging War, Deciding Guilt: Trying the Military Tribunals, supra* at 1254, 1273 (2002).

[24] *See, Dames and Moore v. Regan*, 453 U.S. 654, 668-69 (1981), and *Padilla v. Rumsfeld*, 352 F.3d 695 (2d Cir.) Drawing extensively on Justice Jackson's *Youngtown* concurrence, the Court held that the detention of a citizen was in violation of a statute, 18 U.S.C. § 4001(a), and therefore involved an exercise of Presidential authority at its lowest ebb. The reason offered is that the President's war power did not support such detention in this case since the Constitution allocated the emergency powers to Congress and Congress specifically had not authorized the detention, distinguishing both *Quirin* and the *Prize Cases* where such authorization was present. *Padilla*, at 710-24. Additionally, the court in Padilla relies upon Justice Jackson's *Youngtown* concurrence when it cites the "Constitution's policy that Congress, not the Executive, should control utilization of the policy." *Padilla*, at 713.

In sharp contrast, in *Hamdi v. Rumsfeld* 316 F.3d 450 (4th Cir. 2003) (*Hamdi III*) the Fourth Circuit relied on the "appropriate force" language from the Joint Resolution enacted by Congress on September 18, 2001 to permit the President to detain an American citizen captured in active combat in Afghanistan. The President's Detention Order which also relied on the Chief

Executive's power as Commander-in-Chief of the Armed forces for authority to detain those involved in the war on terror drew strength from Justice Jackson's first category of Presidential power in which the President acts pursuant to an express or implied congressional authorization. The decision of the *Hamdi* court makes it clear that the application of military commissions referred to in the Detention Order were within the authority that Congress conferred on the President when it authorized him to "use all appropriate force" in prosecuting a war on terrorism. As Justice Jackson emphasized, when Congress has provided the President with express authorization, the President's power is at its apex because the President is acting not only with the authority constitutionally vested in him as Commander-in-Chief, but also with the express authority of Congress as provided in the Joint Resolution.

[25] Phil Hirschkorn, "U.S. Defends Holding 'Enemy Combatant,'" http://www.cnn.com/2004/LAW/03/18/padilla, March 18, 2004.

[26] *Id.*

[27] *See* Brief for Respondents—Appellants at 12, *Hamdi v. Rumsfeld*, 296 F.3d 278 (4th Cir. 2002) (No. D2-6895).

[28] *Hamdi v. Rumsfeld*, 542 U.S. __ (2004), 124 S. Ct. 2633 (2004), No. 03-6696. Yaser Esam Hamdi was released by the United States Government and returned to Saudi Arabia on October 11, 2004. The agreement for Hamdi's freedom was to require him to formally renounce his United States citizenship, and not to sue the United States over his captivity. *See* http://www.msnbc.msn.com/id/6227035.

[29] *Id.* at 1.

[30] *Id.* at 9. *See* discussions in Chapter I relative to the President's authority to act unilaterally in *Ex Parte Quirin* at 11-12.

[31] *Id.* at 10. *See* discussion in Chapter IV, Title 18, § 4001(a) U.S. Code at 112-114.

[32] *Id.* at 12.

[33] *Id.* at 13.

[34] *Id.* at 14.

[35] *Id.* at 23.

[36] *Id.* at 26.

[37] *Id.* at 27.

[38] *Id.*

[39] *Id.* at 28 citing *Korematsu v. United States*, 323 U.S. 214, 233-34 (1944). She adds that "courts when faced with these sensitive matters will pay proper heed both to matters of national security and to the constitutional limitations safeguarding essential liberties that remain vibrant in times of security concerns" at 32.

[40] *Id.* at 29.

[41] *Id.* at 30. *See* Chapter IV and the discussion related to Chief Judge Wilkinson's opinion in *Hamdi II* and "risking standing the war-making powers of Articles I and II on their heads," n.87 at 106.

[42] *Id.* at 30 and Chapter IV at 109-111.

[43] *Id.* at 31.

[44] *See* Military Order on the Detention, Treatment, and Trial of Certain Non-Citizens in the War Against Terrorism (November 13, 2001). *See* Appendix A, and Chapter IV, n.1, 2 at 135.

[45] *Hamdi v. Rumsfeld*, 542 U.S. __ (2004), 124 S. Ct. 2633 (2004), (No. 03-6696) Souter opinion at 3.

[46] This argument was raised by Chief Judge Wilkinson in *Hamdi III*, and discussed in Chapter IV at 114-115, and n.127-130.

[47] *See* discussion Chapter IV at 112-114 in passim and n.112-121.

[48] *Hamdi v. Rumsfeld*, 542 U.S. __ (2004), 124 S. Ct. 2633 (2004) (No. 03-6696) Souter opinion at 7.

[49] *Id.*

[50] *Id.* at 10 citing *Ex Parte Quirin*, 317 U.S. 1 (1942).

[51] *Id.* at 11.

[52] *Id., See* Chapter II discussion at 34-35, 39-40.

[53] *Id.* at 12. *See* Chapter II, n.27, 49 and accompanying text.

[54] *Id., See* Enemy Prisoners of War, Retained Personnel, Civilian Detainees and Other Detainees. Army Reg. 190-8, § 1-5, 1-6 (1997) and discussion in Chapter II, n.49 at 52-53.

[55] *See Youngstown Sheet and Tube v. Sawyer*, 343 U.S. 579, 643-44 (1952).

[56] *Id.* at 637-38. *See* discussion in Chapter V, n.18-24 at 148-149.

[57] *Hamdi v. Rumsfeld*, 542 U.S. __ (2004), 124 S. Ct. 2633 (2004), (No. 03-6696) Souter opinion at 14.

[58] *Id.*

[59] *Id.* Scalia dissent at 21.

[60] *Id.* at 22-23.

[61] *Id.* at 23.

[62] *Id.* at 24.

[63] *Id.* at 24-25.

[64] *Id.* at 27. *See* Chapter I discussion, n.41 at 12, and Chapter V, n.10 at 147.

[65] *Id.*

[66] *Id.* Thomas dissent at 1.

[67] *Id.*

[68] *See Hamdi v. Rumsfeld*, No. 02-7338, (4th Cir. 2003), Chapter IV discussion, n.93 at 107-108.

[69] *Id.* at 4. *See* discussion, Chapter I, n.56 at 21.

[70] *Id.* at 7.

[71] *Id.* at 7-8 citing *Chicago & Southern Airlines*, 333 U.S. at 111.

[72] *Id.* at 10.

[73] *Id.* at 14.

[74] *Id.* at 17.

[75] *Rumsfeld v. Padilla*, 542 U.S. __ (2004), 124 S. Ct. 2711 (2004), (No. 03-1027) 352 F.3d 695 (2004) reversed and remanded.

[76] *See* 28 U.S.C. § 2242, 2243; "[T]he person who has custody over the petitioner."

[77] *Wales v. Whitney*, 114 U.S. 564, 575 (1885); "[T]hese provisions contemplate a proceeding against some person who has *immediate custody* of the party detained."

[78] 352 F.3d 645 (No. 03-2235) (2nd Cir. 2003). *See* Chapter IV discussion, n.50, 51 at 99.

[79] *Id.* at 707.

[80] 28 U.S.C.§ 2241(a).

[81] *Rumsfeld v. Padilla* 542 U.S. __ (2004), 124 S. Ct. 2711 (2004), (No. 03-1027) at 5.

[82] *Id.* at. 5-6.

[83] *Id.* at 6.

[84] *Id.* at 8-9.

[85] *Id.*

[86] *Id.*

[87] It is of interest to note that Judge Richard Wesley of the Second Circuit made that very point in the *Padilla* appeal hearing on November 17, 2003. He suggested "[t]his case shouldn't have been brought in Manhattan. This should be litigated in South Carolina."

[88] *Id.* Stevens dissent at 4.

[89] *Id.* at 6.

[90] *Id.*

[91] *Id.*

[92] *Id.* at 7.

[93] *Id.* at 11. *See* Chapter IV discussion, n.64-65 at 101.

[94] *Id.* at 11.

[95] *Id.*

[96] *Id.*

[97] *See Rasul v. Bush* and *Al-Odah v. United States,* 542 U.S. __ (2004), 124 S. Ct. 2686 (2004), Nos. 03-334, 03-343 and Chapter II discussion, n.75 at 43.

[98] *Id.* at 2. When the court originally granted certiorari, the petitioners also included two British citizens who were subsequently released from custody.

[99] *Id.* at 4. *See* 28 U.S.C. § 2241(a), (c) (3).

[100] 4 Wall 2 (1866) discussed in Chapter I, n.20-21 at 5-6.

[101] 317 U.S. 1 (1942) discussed in Chapter I, n.32-40 at 8-12 in passim.

[102] 327 U.S. 1 (1946), discussed in Chapter I, n.28-31 at 7-8.

[103] *Rasul v. Bush* and *Al-Odah v. United States,* 542 U.S. __(2004), 124 S. Ct. 2686 (2004), Nos. 03-334, 03-343 at 6.

[104] *Id.* at 7, citing *Johnson v. Eisentrager,* 339 U.S. 763 (1950). *See* discussion in Chapter II, n.36-45 at 37-39 in passim.

[105] *Id.* at 8, and *see* discussion in Chapter II, n.43-45 at 38-39, in which the D.C. Circuit Court of Appeals discussed how the Guantanamo detainees had much in common with the German prisoners in *Eisentrager.*

[106] *Id.* at 13, citing *King v. Schiever,* 2 Burr. 765, 97 Eng Rep 551 (K.B. 1759); *Sommersett v. Stewart,* 20 How. St. Tr. 1, 79-82 (K.B. 1772); and the *Case of Hottentot Venus,* 13 East 195, 104 Eng Rep 344 (K. B. 1810).

[107] *Id.* at 14, citing *King v. Cowle,* 2 Burr. 834-854, 855, Eng Rep 587, 598-599 (K.B. 1759).

[108] *Id.* at 15.

[109] *See* 28 U.S.C § 2241 (c) (3). *United States v. Verdugo-Urquidez* 494 U.S. 259, 277-278 (1990).

[110] *Id.* at 16.

[111] *Id.* Kennedy concurring opinion at 2.

[112] *Id.*

[113] *Id.* citing *Ex parte Milligan* 4 Wall 2 (1866).

[114] *Id.*

[115] *Id.* and *see* discussion in Chapter II, n.50-62 at 40-42 of the Ninth Circuit Court of Appeals decision in *Gherebi v. Bush*, No. 03-55785 (9th Cir. 2003).

[116] *Id.*

[117] *Id.*

[118] *Id.*

[119] *Id.* Scalia dissent at 2-3.

[120] *Id.*

[121] *Id.* at 10.

[122] *Id.* at 11.

[123] *Id.*

[124] *Id.* at 12.

[125] *Id.* at 13. *See* discussion in Chapter II, n.76 at 44.

[126] *Id.* at 14.

[127] *Id.* at 14-15.

[128] *Id.* at 17.

[129] *Id.* citing 3 Blackstone 131 (emphasis added).

[130] *Id.* at 29.

[131] *Id.*

[132] *Id.* at 20.

176

[133] As a direct result of the Supreme Court decision on the Guantanamo detainees, the Department of Defense established yet another review mechanism to determine whether a detained suspect is properly classified as an enemy combatant. If not, then the detainee would be released to his home country. The Combatant Status Review Tribunal is comprised of three "neutral" military officers who had no role in capturing, interrogating, or determining the status of the detainee before them. It operates with the presumption in favor of the government's evidence and a preponderance of evidence standard for case review purposes. Although detainees who choose to appear before a panel are permitted to call witnesses, it must be deemed a reasonable request by the reviewing authority. Additionally, detainees are permitted a personal representative to assist them, but that individual is appointed by the convening authority and is not a lawyer although at least one panel member is a lawyer. This process is most problematic since it does not permit any of the detainees access to legal counsel, and it excludes the detainee from all proceedings where his presence might compromise national security. Similar criticism was raised with respect to the announced annual review process examined earlier in this chapter. See n.4 at 169. In early August 2004, an Afghan detainee who appeared before a Combatant Status Review Tribunal was denied the right to call witnesses to the hearing because the tribunal president determined that their evidence would be irrelevant. See www.cnn.com/2004/LAW/08/11/gitmo.tribunals.ap/index.html. See also, Appendix E for a discussion of the document.

CHAPTER VI

Military Commissions and Enemy Combatants Post 9/11: Balancing Civil Liberties with National Security Policy

After the unprecedented acts of destructiveness undertaken by al-Qaida against the United States on September 11, 2001 the President indicated that we are facing a new and different type of enemy in the 21st century. "This enemy is nameless, this enemy is faceless, this enemy has no specific borders. This enemy is terrorism whose front is here in America."[1]

Such large scale terrorism directed at the World Trade Center, the symbol of global finance and capitalism, and the Pentagon, the heart of America's national security command, caused a catastrophic loss of human life and an unprecedented threat to our national sense of well being. For the first time in our nation's history, a non-state organization carried out its terrorist attacks on such a scale as to be recognized as acts of war, and as a result, the United States is now engaged in a legally cognizable armed conflict to which the laws of war apply.[2] President Bush's objective to eradicate the evils of the war on terrorism meant that the conflict did not end with al-Qaida or the Afghan campaign against the Taliban for neither had been defeated. It also included other terrorist militant organizations in Iraq, Lebanon, Palestine, Chechnya, Indonesia, Pakistan, Iran, the Philippines and elsewhere where suspected terrorists presumably came within its potential scope of attack.[3]

Given the nature of al-Qaida and other transnational organizations equipped with covert cells of operatives capable of infiltrating into nation states to target and kill innocent civilian populations, it is safe to assume that there exists a very real possibility that we will be living with the war on terror for the foreseeable future, if not indefinitely. It is also safe to say that the scope and duration of the war on terror is expandable, based upon the determination of the President and the Congress. The principal question then is not whether the war on terror is justifiably considered a war, but rather is it of such a nature as to warrant expansion of the exercise of war power by the political branches of government and if so at what cost to individual liberty?

This last section of the study examines the critical long-term issues that must be addressed by the Congress and the Executive as we seek to balance civil liberties with national security policy in the continuing war on terrorism post-September 11.

****

The Separation of Powers and National Security

The courts have been most deferential to the President as Commander-in-Chief when he is exercising his war power in a military emergency situation, and such judicial deference is at its zenith when the Congress has specifically authorized the President's actions.[4] Yet it is also important to note that the United States Supreme Court has repeatedly indicated that judicial power does not disappear in times of war. There is no reason to believe, as Justice O'Connor has argued in *Hamdi*,[5] that the federal courts would unduly interfere with military operations or compromise national security by performing their expert role, that of resolving factual disputes.

In our system of government the three branches are separate, but co-equal. The principle of separation of powers does not immunize or isolate executive actions from judicial scrutiny even though governmental powers pertaining to the declaring and making of war are coordinated between the legislative and executive branches. As the Court noted in *Hirabayashi*:

> The war power of the national government is the power to wage war successfully. . . . Since the Constitution commits to the Executive and to the Congress the exercise of the war power in all the vicissitudes and conditions of warfare, it has necessarily given

them wide scope for the exercise of judgment and discretion in determining the nature and extent of the threatened injury or damages and the means for resisting it.[6]

Since actual hostilities began post-9/11 the Executive branch has identified, captured, and detained members of al-Qaida, the Taliban, and their supporters and held them as enemy combatants. The President prioritized appropriate security measures to be employed to protect national security interests of the United States and in doing so he justified his actions as part of an effort to successfully prosecute the war on terrorism. The nature of such policy decisions are political and essentially are for the President and Congress to determine, not the courts.

Congress agreed with the President that the attacks constituted acts of war, and enacted legislation which authorized him to use military force to respond accordingly. A whole host of actions were undertaken to ensure that enemy captives held in detention would no longer be able to take up arms against the United States, and that valuable intelligence information could be obtained from them in a timely fashion. Because of the unusual national security situation the United States faced, the President specifically wanted the option of a process that was distinct from the processes in the Federal Court and the Military Court system under the Uniform Code of Military Justice. Despite the fact that each distinct provision of the military detention and trial process created for enemy combatant detainees did not compare to all of the provisions of the federal court system or the court martial system, the Executive insisted that as a whole, the rules and procedures were designed to be fair, impartial and balanced and serve the needs of justice in their application.[7]

Although Justice O'Connor in *Hamdi* conceded that the courts are not ideally positioned to judge the Executive's particular military strategies or the conduct of war and recognized that "the scope of that discretion necessarily is wide,"[8] nonetheless, it is during our most challenging and uncertain moments that our courts are critical in enforcing due process principles.[9] When the President's policy of indefinite detention, justified on national security grounds, ran afoul of a legitimate individual liberty interest, a judicious constitutional review was required. The proper role of the courts then is to guard against a clear violation of authority and not to second-guess national security decisions of our elected leaders.

In his concurring opinion in *Hamdi,* Associate Justice David Souter expressed his concern that in a government of separated powers, "deciding finally on what is a reasonable degree of guaranteed liberty, whether in peace or war, is not well entrusted to the Executive Branch of Government, whose particular responsibility is to maintain security."[10] The Administration sees civil liberties as too costly for detainees including such elements as a presumption of innocence, the right to counsel and the right to compulsory process for calling witnesses. Except in the most pressing of emergency circumstances, there must be room to balance individual liberties with national security concerns, and to achieve that proper balance a separate branch of government is necessary to assess whether individuals are subjected to excesses in prosecuting the war on terror. It is for Congress to provide the express authorization that weighs the interests of due process with national security.

The Current Role of Congress

To date, Congress has failed to demonstrate a leadership role in the war on terrorism post-9/11. It has facilitated Presidential actions in this area by approving most directives introduced by the Administration, and generally it has stood on the sidelines when the President claimed his powers to act were pursuant to the Commander-in-Chief clause or were already available under existing law. As a body that tends to be far more sensitive to parochial interests than institutional concerns, individual members of Congress have been overwhelmed by the public support for most of the President's war-time limitations on civil liberties for enemy combatants, particularly those of non-citizens at Guantanamo Bay.

Congress's limited and largely deferential role to the President is most clearly demonstrated by the issuance of the President's Military Order (PMO) establishing Military Commissions in November 2001, and the Military Commission Order No. 1 issued in March 2002 by the Department of Defense (DoD Order).[11] The initial Order among other things, provided an enemy combatant could be convicted and sentenced to death based upon secret evidence, and on a vote of two-thirds of the members of the commission, and that trial proceedings might not be public. The March 2002 regulations and instructions that were issued by the Department of Defense responded to several of the due process complaints identified in the PMO including a presumption of innocence, a right to counsel, a right to cross-examine witnesses, and a right not to testify during trial with no adverse inferences to be drawn. The DoD Order allowed for public hearings and required that the death penalty be by unanimous vote, with guilt proven beyond a reasonable doubt.[12] Although several Fundamental Fairness Issues related to due process and civil liberties were not addressed,[13] the DoD Order was a marked improvement over the PMO.

Congress was not the principal catalyst for modification of the initial proposals. While oversight hearings were held by a few legislative committees, and isolated television and newspaper interviews were given by congressional leaders, the hue and cry of former judges and military officials, civil liberties groups, editorial writers, law professors and members of the European Union provided the principal impetus for change.

In general, Congress has been generously responsive and supportive of the President's terrorism initiatives. In addition to approving the military interventions and detentions of enemy combatants, Congress passed the USA PATRIOT Act that gave the Executive most of its wish list priorities concerning expanded wiretap authority, detention of immigrants, nationwide search warrants, and access to e-mail.[14] Despite criticism from civil liberties groups the final version of the PATRIOT Act essentially demonstrated that national security concerns far outweighed civil liberties interests with one notable exception, indefinite detention. The original Administration proposal would have authorized the Attorney General to detain indefinitely any non-citizen whom he had reason to believe might commit or facilitate acts of terrorism. Senior leadership of Congress from both parties opposed this provision and in Senate and House Judiciary Committee hearings strong concerns were expressed about the constitutional validity of indefinite detention. In negotiations between Senator Leahy, Chair of the Judiciary Committee, and the Department of Justice the following language was agreed to: "The Attorney General shall place an alien detained in removal proceedings, or shall charge the alien with a criminal offense, not later than 7 days after the commencement of such detention."[15] The full Congress imposed this limitation on detainment authority granted to the Attorney General in Section 412 of the USA PATRIOT Act, which President Bush signed into law on October 26, 2001.[16] Ironically, although Attorney General Ashcroft was denied authority to detain indefinitely any non-citizen suspected of terrorism, this explicit power was subsequently granted to the Secretary of Defense by the President when he issued the November 13, 2001 Military Order.[17]

For the most part Congress clearly deferred to the Executive on the USA PATRIOT Act because it was presented by the Department of Justice just one week after the September 11 attacks, and was overwhelmingly adopted by both houses of the Congress on October 24, 2001. The President's political support for such measures was at its peak during this time period.[18] Notwithstanding Congress's rejection of the Executive's proposal for indefinite detention to the extent that members of Congress valued civil liberties, it was simply too difficult to launch a frontal challenge to a popular president before the practical results of his polices were known.[19]

Long-Term Issues to be Addressed by Congress

What the recent Supreme Court decisions have determined is that the Executive, with proper congressional authorization, can detain terrorism suspects as enemy combatants, and whether they are held at home or at an offshore United

States base, they must be provided access to public review of that detention by an independent judicial authority. Additional concerns, not addressed by the Court, must be considered if detention is to be utilized as a principal weapon in the war on terror. A long-term legal framework is essential for our democratic society as we confront a new type of enemy and new kind of war in which we seek to properly balance civil liberties and national security interests.

Justice O'Connor in *Hamdi* creates a hearing system in which the citizen detainee bears the burden of proof, testimony is by hearsay rather than direct witness testimony, and the presiding officer may well be a neutral military officer rather than a judge or jury.[20] While some type of judicial review of detention is required, it should be authorized specifically by the law-making branch of government, the Congress, rather than be mandated by the Court. It is not appropriate for the Court to impose standards by itself because it places the judiciary in a potential position of managing conditions of confinement, interrogation methods as well as the use of intelligence information. Congressional authorization, oversight and review of a system of detention is a must, with judicial review interceding when the system exceeds Constitutional tolerance.

Legislation is warranted to establish standards and procedures for detaining United States citizens and non-citizens as enemy combatants.[21] Among the relevant issues that Congress needs to address are the following:

• **What is the threshold level of terrorist activity that warrants detention by the government?** Should it apply only to those who are directly engaged in terrorist hostilities against the United States or should it be extended to those who provide support for a terrorist organization as the Executive has consistently argued? It would appear that the Court in *Hamdi* considered the threshold level of activity as a narrow limited one of "fighting against the United States in Afghanistan as part of the Taliban."[22]

• **What standard of proof must the government meet before an impartial adjudicator to justify detention?** The Court in *Hamdi* rejected the

Government's position that a citizen is determined to be an enemy combatant under a very deferential "some evidence" standard.[23] Justice O'Connor for the plurality proposes a schema whereby the Government puts forth credible evidence that the habeas petitioner meets the enemy-combatant criteria for detention, than the onus shifts to the detainee to rebut that evidence with more persuasive evidence that he falls outside the criteria. This burden-sharing scheme, in her view, would effectively balance the Executive's needs during a period of on-going combat against terrorists with that of avoiding the risk of erroneous deprivation of a civil liberty interest for the detainees.[24] The Department of Defense in establishing its Combatant Status Review Tribunal post-*Hamdi* and *Rasul* operates with the presumption in favor of the government's evidence and a preponderance of evidence standard to determine whether a detained suspect is properly classified as an enemy combatant.[25] Should the Congress adopt a more demanding standard of proof for the government to justify, e.g. probable cause or the clear and convincing standard, which is higher than the usual civil evidentiary standard of preponderance of the evidence, but somewhat lower than the standard beyond a reasonable doubt?

• **What type of hearing must the impartial adjudicator conduct to determine the government's position for classifying a detainee an enemy combatant?** Although a majority of the Court in *Hamdi* supported a "fair opportunity to rebut the Government's factual assertion of detention as an enemy combatant before a neutral decision maker,[26] only the plurality advocated a proceeding tailored to alleviate any potential burden to the Executive in time of combat, and one which could be met by an appropriately authorized and properly constituted military tribunal.[27] The Department of Defense's Combatant Status Review Tribunal, established by Military Order, is comprised of three neutral military officers who had no role in capturing, interrogating or determining the status of the detainee before them. Although detainees who choose to appear before the tribunal are permitted to call witnesses, it must be deemed a reasonable request by the reviewing authority. Detainees are permitted a personal representative to assist them in the proceeding; however, that individual is appointed by the convening authority and may not be a lawyer. In addition to being denied access to legal counsel, the detainee may be excluded from all proceedings where his presence may compromise national security interests as determined by the Review Tribunal, and rules of evidence do not apply. The convening authority provides the final review of Tribunal decisions as to whether detainees were properly classified as enemy combatants. This process calls into serious question elements of fairness and balance.

• **For how long and for what purposes can the detention be continued, and what standard of proof applies to such a showing by the government?** An eight-member majority of the Court in *Hamdi* concluded that indefinite detention for the purpose of interrogation is not authorized; however, the plurality ruled that the United States may detain for the duration of hostilities those who are engaged in an armed conflict against the United States, provided that the right to notice and an opportunity to be heard is granted at a meaningful time and in a meaningful manner.[28] What does meaningful time and meaningful manner mean?

The Department of Defense by military rule has established an annual administrative review process to reassess the need to continue to detain an enemy combatant at Guantanamo Bay Naval Base. The process involves an Administrative Review Board which may sit in panels of three military officers, who are to make a written assessment as to whether the enemy combatants continue to be a threat to the national security of the United States, and if not whether it is in the interest of the United States and its allies to release them.[29]

Prior to the enemy combatant's hearing, the Review Board is required to provide notice to him. The enemy combatant is entitled to appear personally before the Review Board to explain why he is no longer a threat to American national security interests. The process permits him to be aided by an Assisting Military Officer in preparing his presentation to the Board, and the designated military officer may, if the enemy combatant chooses, present information to the

Review Board on his behalf. The Assisting Military Officer is entitled to see all information and documentation provided to the Review Board as part of the assessment procedure. The enemy combatant is not entitled to representation by counsel during this process.

Upon completion of its review the Board makes a written assessment concerning the enemy combatant's continued threat potential to the United States and based upon that assessment, the Review Board provides to the Presidentially-appointed designated civilian official (DCO) a written recommendation as to whether detention should be continued. The determination to continue to detain, release, or to seek the transfer of the enemy combatant to another government rests exclusively with the DCO, who is required to give full consideration to the written assessment and recommendation of the Review Board.[30]

The Administration has proclaimed that this nonadversarial fact-based administrative proceeding is designed to be deliberate and thoughtful in balancing the security needs of our nation with the human rights of detained individuals at Guantanamo. Although the Department of Defense met with and requested input from the Department of State, the Department of Justice, the CIA, and the Department of Homeland Security for developing this "comprehensive process," Congress was never formally consulted. Congressional leaders were briefed once the system was in place.

The denial of legal representation for detainees creates a gap in the process that potentially taints the entire review system. It is of interest to note that accused terrorists are guaranteed by statute the right to appointed counsel in proceedings under the Alien Terrorist Removal Act,[31] and in other Western democracies, Britain and Israel, detainees must have access to counsel to contest their status and appeal their designation to the judiciary. The review system put in place by the Executive for continued detention of enemy combatants at Guantanamo falls far short of an effective balancing of national security interests with that of assuring civil liberties for the detainees. There is clearly established a preferred position for the Executive in these proceedings. Congress must act to not permit national security to prevent it from subjecting military authority to legitimate oversight and review. Congress must also ensure that the rule of law and not the law of war as unilaterally determined by the Executive provides the standards and procedures for detention review.

• **Do enemy combatants have the right to an appeal, and if so where and to whom?** The Department of Defense in creating the Combatant Status Review Tribunal and the Administrative Review Board for continued detention of enemy combatants placed both systems under the jurisdiction of the Secretary of the Navy, Gordon England, who serves as DCO for the Administrative Review Board and Appointing Authority for the Combatant Status Review Tribunal. Rear Admiral James M. McGarrah, convening authority for the combatant status Review Tribunals, is appointed by Secretary England. The appeal buck stops there. Under the current system established by the Executive there is no built-in appeal to a higher civilian authority, including the judicial system. Additionally, the non-citizen detainee subject to these administrative proceedings at Guantanamo must face an Executive that serves as investigator, prosecutor, judge and jury in determining whether he is properly designated an enemy combatant and whether continued detention is warranted.

This same lack of independent review outside of the military system exists with respect to the rulings of military commissions that try enemy combatants for violations of the laws of war. Under the Defense Secretary's Rules and Instructions, an Appellate Review Panel comprised of three members of the military is exclusively responsible for appellate jurisdiction subject to any final action taken by the President or Secretary of Defense. The President's Military Order specifically bars any appellate review by any state or federal court. The availability of an appeal to an independent civilian body, which is part of American court martial proceedings, is crucial to ensure the integrity and impartiality of the commission process as well as providing venues of relief by defense counsels seeking to maximally protect the interests of their accused clients.[32] In the regular military justice system, a case proceeds through three levels of appellate review, The Court(s) of Military Review in each service and The United State Court of Military Appeals, which is located within, but is independent of, the Department of Defense, and in some instances, review by the United States Supreme Court.

This concern is well illustrated in an exchange between Attorney General John Ashcroft and Senator John Edwards, at a Senate Judiciary Committee hearing on the President's Military Order where attention was given to developing a potential and framework for appeals of military commission decisions. Attorney General Ashcroft believed, according to the Order, that the President and Secretary of Defense constituted the appellate authorities and that "those appellate authorities are consistent with systems that provide the kind of justice that is less likely to have error."[33] Senator Edwards, in response, suggested that the President and Secretary of Defense "are the people who decided the prosecution should be brought in the first case."[34] He believed that in the interest of justice and fairness, an objective third party should look at the trial, the conviction, and the imposition of the death penalty if it was imposed. Although Attorney General Ashcroft did not refute or reject Senator Edward's independent appeal procedure, he observed that the Secretary of Defense had "the authority to develop appellate procedures under the order, and if he chooses to confer with me, I'll provide advice to him about that."[35]

Why Congress Must Act

Undoubtedly at some point in the not too distant future the entire enemy combatant review and trial process will become the grist for judicial review with respect to weighing the interests of due process and national security policy. While the Administration suggested that the Joint Congressional Resolution, the Authorization for Use of Military Force, and Title 10 of the U.S. Code, provide the legal and practical ratification for the President's November 13, 2001 Military Order establishing military commissions,[36] legal scholars and members of Congress have expressed their collective wisdom that the Military Commissions contemplated by the President's Order are legally deficient, Article I of the Constitution provides that Congress, not the President has the power to "define and punish . . . offenses against the Law of Nations" and absent specific congressional authorization, the Order undermines the tradition of Separation of Powers.

It would therefore be far more advantageous for our system of government if the Congress stepped up now, to review, debate, and decide whether the standards and procedures put in place by the Executive for military trials of enemy combatants are acceptable rather than having the courts do their work for them. When the President issued his Military Order, both the Senate Judiciary and Armed Forces Committees held hearings with administrative officials and experts to assess the Executive's approach. What we learn from the testimony provided in those hearings is that: (a) the administration had not yet promulgated the procedures and standards to be employed by military commissions; (b) the Secretary of Defense was charged with drafting the procedures and standards; (c) the procedural safeguards and trial proceedings for the detainees would be full and fair; (d) it was premature to try to anticipate exactly what the framework and safeguards would be; (e) there was interest from members on both sides of the aisle to work with the Executive to establish a congressional authority for military tribunals in a certain framework; and (f) by having a congressional mandate and framework for military tribunals the position of the Executive would be strengthened in its ability to act effectively.[37]

The Executive as Law Maker, Law Enforcer, and Law Adjudicator

Under the President's Military Order the Executive is lawmaker, law enforcer, and law adjudicator. As lawmaker, the President delegates to the Secretary of Defense the power to promulgate orders and regulations. As law enforcer the Executive has the power to detain and prosecute enemy combatants, and as law adjudicator the President or the Secretary of Defense, if so designated by the President for that purpose, provides for review and final decision of the military commission.[38]

Under both systems of punishment created to deal with enemy combatant terrorists, detention and military commissions, the Executive assumes unilateral lawmaking, enforcing, and adjudicating power by Order, Rule, and Instruction. That is the very concern that James Madison warned about in Federalist No. 47 when he wrote: "The accumulation of all powers legislative, executive, and judiciary in the same hands, whether of one, a few, or many, and whether hereditary, self-appointed or elective, may justly be pronounced the very definition of tyranny."[39]

No one branch in a constitutional system of government has a total monopoly of authority, nor should it. In successfully pursuing our nation's antiterrorism efforts Congress should be recognized as a full partner in taking tough action on the terrorists while being true to the principles of the Constitution. That does not mean that Congress should exercise its deliberative and oversight role to the point that it becomes counter productive. It must perform its legitimate constitutional role in assuring that the Executive is effectively protecting our national security interests while sufficiently assuring our civil liberties.

Congressional authorization is necessary for the establishment of procedures, standards and military commissions to detain, adjudicate, and punish offenses arising from the September 11, 2001 attacks or future al-Qaida terrorist attacks against the United States and to provide a clear and unambiguous legal foundation for such proceedings. While Congress has authorized the President to use all necessary and appropriate force it has yet to expressly authorize the use of detention or military commissions. Congressional action would make it abundantly clear that detention and military commissions are the appropriate venues for treating enemy combatants. Spelling out in detail the requirements for detention and military commissions and the procedural protections afforded to enemy combatant detainees[40] would ensure that decisions when handed down survive judicial scrutiny.

Indispensable Safeguards in a Detention and Military Commission System

Some may think that it is not only inevitable but entirely proper for liberty to give way to security in times of national crisis, but that view has no place in the application of a Constitution which is designed precisely to confront war and, in a manner that accords with principles of due process, accommodate it.[41] There are certain indispensable safeguards to civil liberty that must be preserved even during periods of military emergency.

The writ of habeas corpus cannot be infringed since it is a critical tenet of our justice system. As Justice Scalia recognized in the *Hamdi* case, the very core of liberty served by our Anglo-Saxon system of separated powers has been freedom from indefinite imprisonment at the will of the Executive. This basic tenet dates back to 1215 when it stood in the Magna Carta as a critical individual right against arbitrary arrest and imprisonment.[42] Military Tribunals, Boards, and Commissions cannot deny detained individuals from the privilege of seeking a remedy in an appropriate court jurisdiction of the United States. The right to file a writ of habeas corpus provides access to the federal courts to test the legality of a detention. This principle is certainly reaffirmed in the *Hamdi and Rasul* decisions of the Supreme Court.

For the right of access and the right to a hearing to have substance, legal representation is a virtual necessity. The right to be heard is of far less significance in many instances if it is not accompanied by the right to be heard by counsel.[43] In *Hamdi*, Justice Sandra Day O'Connor wrote that the accused was entitled to receive notice and be provided a fair opportunity to rebut the government's position, adding that he unquestionably had the right to access to counsel.[44]

It has been consistently argued throughout this work that a fatal flaw that exists in the Executive's detention review process is denial of legal representation for the accused.[45] Any detainee faced with extended periods of physical custody has a due process right to counsel to legitimately challenge the legality of that detention, because as a practical matter, if he loses in the hearing process, he essentially loses his physical liberty.

Finally, there must be built into the punishment systems an independent appeals process beyond the Secretary of Defense. In legislation introduced by Representative Schiff and Senator Leahy, the United States Court of Appeals for the Armed Forces would be available as an appellate body to review all detention proceedings, convictions, and sentences of military commissions. The Supreme Court would be available as a court of last resort through writ of certiorari.[46] By Congress providing for an appeal to an independent entity, it will ensure that due process is protected, and the accused detainee is afforded basic protection.

Conclusion

Although there is no explicitly articulated language in the Constitution and minimal language in statutory code that refers to military commissions there is rich historical precedent for their application which has been authorized by Congress and upheld by the United States Supreme Court. Such commissions have been employed by the President to meet urgent governmental responsibilities relating to war without Congress specifically declaring war.[47]

The detention power, which includes the authority to incarcerate or restrain enemy combatants and suspected terrorists beyond their initial capture on the battlefield or within the United States, deprives the detainees of their freedom and normal procedural protection for judicial review. Such a power, invoked in emergency situations, has always belonged to Congress, to delegate to the Executive, or to restrain, as it sees fit.[48]

Prior to September 11, the power to detain was clearly the province of the Congress, which was critically reinforced by the enactment of Title 18, § 4001(a) of the U.S Code which provides that "[n]o citizen shall be imprisoned or otherwise detained by the United States except pursuant to an Act of Congress."[49] After September 11, in *Hamdi*, the Court ruled that by enacting the Joint Congressional Resolution Authorizing the Use of Force (AUMF) the Congress had authorized Hamdi's detention, and satisfied § 4001(a)'s requirement that a detention be pursuant to an Act of Congress.[50] As the text of the AUMF clearly demonstrates there is nothing said about the detention of anyone in connection with the use of military force, and particularly the detention of United States citizens.

As we face continuing threats from global terrorism, as well as demands for our government to respond in the interest of national security, more responsibility and authority will be placed in the President's arsenal as preeminent decision maker. It is essential that Congress, as the President's decision making partner in the war on terrorism, perform its critical deliberative role in properly balancing national security interests with civil liberties rights of citizens and non-citizens alike. As Alexander Bickel argues, "singly either the president or Congress can fall into bad errors. . . . So they can together too, but that is somewhat less likely and in any event, together they are all we've got."[51]

Summary

After the unprecedented and devastating attack of September 11, 2001, President Bush indicated that the enemy we face, terrorism, is one that we may be living with for the foreseeable future. A principal question to be considered is whether the war on terror is of such a nature to warrant expansion of war power by the political branches of government, and if so, at what cost to individual liberty?

The courts have historically been most deferential to the President as Commander-in-Chief when he exercises his war power in a military emergency situation, and it is at its peak when Congress specifically authorizes his actions. Such was the case post 9/11 when the President prioritized a series of security measures to be undertaken to ensure that enemy combatants held in detention at Guantanamo would no longer be able to take up arms against the United States, and that valuable intelligence information could be obtained from them in a timely fashion. The Congress, agreeing with the President that the terrorist attacks constituted acts of war, enacted legislation which authorized him to use military force to respond accordingly.

The Supreme Court in *Hamdi* concluded that the President, with proper congressional authorization, can detain terrorism suspects as enemy combatants; however, they cannot be detained indefinitely, and they must be afforded access to public review of that detention by an independent judicial authority.

Additional questions not fully addressed by the Court must be considered as we utilize detention as a principal weapon in the war on terror. A long-term legal framework is essential for our democratic society as we confront a new type of enemy and new kind of war in which we seek to properly balance civil liberties and national security interests. The nature of such policy considerations are political and essentially are for the President and Congress to determine, not the courts.

To date Congress has failed to demonstrate a leadership role in the war on terrorism as it relates to the treatment of enemy combatants. In light of the *Hamdi* and *Rasul* decisions, Congress must step forward as the Executive's partner in establishing appropriate standards and procedures for detention and trial of United States citizen and non-citizen detainees. Among the relevant issues to be addressed are:

(1) determination of the threshold level of terrorist authority that warrants detention by the government;

(2) the standard of proof required of the government to justify detention;

(3) the type of hearing conducted to determine the government's position for classifying a detainee an enemy combatant;

(4) the length, purpose, and standard of proof required for continued detention;

(5) the type of trial for the enemy combatant; and

(6) the right of appeal for an enemy combatant.

The Supreme Court decision in *Hamdi* provides the following guidelines:

- It would appear that the threshold level is a narrow limited one of "fighting against the United States in Afghanistan as part of the Taliban;"[52]

- the government puts forth credible evidence that the habeas petitioner meets the enemy combatant criteria for detention, than the onus shifts to the detainee to rebut the evidence with more persuasive evidence that he falls outside the criteria;[53]

- a hearing is provided before a neutral decision maker which supports a fair opportunity to rebut the Government's factual assertion of detention;[54]

- indefinite detention for the purpose of interrogation is not authorized; however, the government may detain for the duration of hostilities those engaged in armed conflict against the United States, provided the right to notice and an opportunity to be heard is granted with access to counsel, at a meaningful time in a meaningful manner.[55]

The Executive in response to the *Hamdi* and *Rasul* decisions established Combatant Status Review Tribunals to permit detainees at Guantanamo to contest their status as enemy combatants.[56] The following rules are provided:

- It would appear the threshold level is expansive as it applies to those directly engaged in terrorist activities against the United States and those who provide support for terrorist organizations;

- the presumption is in favor of the government's evidence and a preponderance of evidence standard is employed to determine whether a detained suspect is properly classified an enemy combatant;

- a neutral tribunal of three military officers preside affording the detainee the opportunity to appear if his presence does not compromise national security interests; the detainee is permitted witnesses to be called, if it is deemed a reasonable request; and he is permitted a personal representative to assist him in the proceeding although that individual is not permitted to be a lawyer;

- the tribunal determines that the detainee should be classified an enemy combatant and reports to the appointing authority who decides whether that classification is accepted, or requires additional deliberation.

Additionally, the Executive has created Administrative Review Boards to determine annually whether each Guantanamo detainee enemy combatant remains a threat to the United States and its allies.[57] The following guidelines apply:

- Each detainee enemy combatant will have a formal opportunity each year to appear before a board of three military officers and explain why he believes that he should be released. The burden of proof is on the detainee;

- he is provided a military officer who is not a lawyer to assist him in his appearance;

- the review board accepts written information from the family and national government of the enemy combatant detainee;

- the review board assesses the current threat posed by the enemy combatant detainee and recommends to a designated civilian defense official (DCO) whether he should remain in detention;

- the DCO then decides whether the detainee remains in detention.

Finally, the Executive has established military commissions to prosecute non-U.S. citizens who have allegedly participated in international terrorism against the United States, for war crimes and other offenses.[58] The following guidelines apply:

- Each military commission is composed of three to seven members, all of whom are current or retired members of the U.S. armed forces;

- the enemy combatant must be represented by an assigned defense counsel, but is permitted to hire a civilian defense lawyer at his own expense;

- a presumption of innocence exists for the accused;

- hearsay evidence can be admissible;

- the government must establish proof beyond any reasonable doubt;

- decisions are based on a two-thirds majority of commission members, except in death penalty cases where a unanimous verdict is required;

- cases are reviewed by a military review panel, but there is no appeal to a civilian court; and

- final review rests with either the Secretary of Defense or the President.

Detention and trial procedures of detainee enemy combatants under the Combatant Status Review Tribunals, Administrative Review Boards, and Military Commissions permit the Executive to act as a unilateral lawmaker, law enforcer and law adjudicator. No one branch in a constitutional system of government has a total monopoly of authority, nor should it. Congress should exercise its legitimate constitutional role in assuring that the Executive is effectively protecting our national security interest while sufficiently assuring our civil liberties.

While Congress has authorized the President to use all necessary and appropriate force it has yet to expressly authorize the use of detention or military commissions. Spelling out in detail the requirements for detention and military commissions and the procedural protections afforded to detainee enemy combatants would ensure that decisions when handed down survive judicial scrutiny.

Under our Constitution, there are certain indispensable safeguards to civil liberty that must be preserved even during periods of national crisis and military emergency. Military Tribunals, Boards, and Commissions cannot deny detained individuals from the privilege of seeking a remedy in an appropriate court jurisdiction of the United States. The right to be heard, which is certainly reaffirmed in *Hamdi* and *Rasul*, must be accompanied by the right to be heard by counsel. Any detainee enemy combatant facing extended periods of physical custody has a basic right to counsel to legitimately challenge that detention, because as a practical matter, if he loses in the hearing process, he essentially loses his physical liberty. Finally, there must be built into the punishment system an independent appeal process beyond the Secretary of Defense. By Congress providing for an appeal to an independent entity, it will ensure basic fairness and protection for the accused detainee enemy combatant.

As we face continuing threats from global terrorism, as well as demands for our government to respond in the interests of national security, more responsibility and authority will be placed in the President's arsenal of decision-making. It is essential for Congress, as the President's decision-making partner in the war on terrorism, to perform its critical deliberative role in properly balancing national security interests, with civil liberties rights of citizens and non-citizens alike.

Notes

[1] Remarks by the President at the signing of HR 5005, the Homeland Security Act of 2002, http://www.whitehouse.gov/news/releases/2002/11/20021125-6.html, November 25, 2002.

[2] *See* discussion in Chapter I, n.2 at 1, and Chapter II at 32-35. *See also,* John C. Yoo, "Perspectives on the Rules of War," http://www.sfgate.com/cgi-bin/article.cgi?file=/chronicle /archive/2004/06/15/EDGKJ66AM1.DTL June 15, 2004 and David B. Rivkin, Lee A. Casey, "The Law and War," http://www.washingtontimes.com/op-ed/20040125-103747-9111r.htm.

[3] *See* discussion in Chapter I at 2 and U.S. Department of State Press Statement, Oct. 3, 2003 (2003/1007).

[4] *See Youngstown Sheet and Tube v. Sawyer,* 343 U.S. 579 (1952) and discussion, Chapter V, n.19-22 at 148-49, and the decision of Justice Sandra Day O'Connor in *Hamdi* in which she concludes that individuals who fought against the United States in Afghanistan as part of the Taliban are individuals the President can detain because Congress targeted them in passing the Joint Resolution Authorizing the Use of Military Force (AUMF). *See Hamdi v. Rumsfeld* 542 U.S. __(2004), 124 S. Ct. 2633 (2004), No. 03-6696 at 10.

[5] "We have long since made clear that a state of war is not a blank check for the President when it comes to the rights of the nation's citizens" . . . and "while we accord the greatest respect and consideration to the judgments of military authorities . . . relating to the prosecution of war . . . it does not infringe on the core role of the military for the courts, to exercise their own constitutionally mandated roles of reviewing and resolving claims." *Id.* at 27, 28.

[6] 320 U.S. 81, at 93 (1943).

[7] *See* discussion in Chapter III at 58-59.

[8] *Hamdi v. Rumsfeld,* 542 U.S. __ (2004), 124 S. Ct. 2633 (2004), No. 03-6696 at 28.

[9] *Id.* at 25.

[10] *Id.* Souter opinion at 7.

[11] *See* Appendix A and Appendix C for full discussion of each document. Additional Military Commission Orders and Instructions were issued in 2004.

[12] *See* Chapter III at 58-60.

[13] *Id.* at 63-68.

[14] Pub. L. No. 107-56, 115 Stat. 272 (2001).

[15] S. 1510, 107th Cong. 412 (2001), reprinted at 147 Cong. Rec. S10621.

[16] Uniting and Strengthening America by Providing Appropriate Tools Required to Intercept and Obstruct Terrorism (USA PATRIOT) Act of 2001, Pub. L. No. 107-56, 412(a) 115 Stat. 272, 351 (2001).

200

[17] Military Order of November 13, 2001, Detention, Treatment, and Trial of Certain Non-Citizens in the War Against Terrorism, 66 Fed. Reg. 57, 833 (Nov. 16, 2001).

[18] The House voted 357 to 66 and the Senate voted 98 to 1 in support of the USA PATRIOT Act. In a survey by the *Washington Post* and ABC News, six in ten Americans agreed with President Bush that suspected terrorists should be tried in special military tribunals and not U.S. criminal courts. In addition, seven in ten Americans believed that the government was sufficiently protecting the civil rights of suspected terrorists; nine in ten believed the United States was justified in detaining foreign nationals for violating immigration laws and 89 percent supported President Bush's war in Afghanistan. *See* Richard Morin and Claudia Deane, "Most Americans Back U.S. Tactics: Poll Finds Little Worry Over Rights," *Washington Post,* November 29, 2001.

[19] Neal Devins, "Congress, Civil Liberties, and the War on Terrorism," 11 *Wm. and Mary Bill of Rights J.* 1139 (2003) at 1145. *See also*, Elizabeth A. Palmer and Adriel Bettelheim, "War and Civil Liberties: Congress Gropes for a Role," 59 *Cong. Weekly* 2820 (Dec. 1, 2001).

[20] *See* discussion in Chapter V at 151-152.

[21] Rep. Adam Schiff (D-CA) introduced H.R. 5684, "The Detention of Enemy Combatants Act" on October 16, 2002. Section 4 of the bill entitled Procedural Requirements provides for the promulgation of rules with "clear standards, and procedures" governing detention of a United States person or resident, and provides that such rules shall guarantee timely access to judicial review to challenge the basis for a detention, and permit the detainee access to counsel. Other bills introduced include S. 1941, 107th Cong. (2002); HR 3468, 107th Cong. (2002); HR 4035, 107th Cong. (2002). They all have specific limitations placed on military commissions to try alleged war crimes.

[22] The Court plurality in *Hamdi* held that Congress authorized the detention of combatants in a narrow sense, namely being part of, or supporting forces hostile to the United States or coalition partners in Afghanistan, and who engaged in an armed conflict against the United States there. *See* Chapter V at 150. The President's Military Order applies to non-citizens who engage in terrorist acts against the United States or who *aid* and *abet* in terrorist acts against the United States (emphasis added). What of rank and file members of terrorist organizations who do not bear arms, and what of American citizens who live in the United States and donate money to a terrorist organization or network? Are these classes of individuals to be detained? *See* Chapter II, n.25 at 50 and accompanying discussion.

[23] *See Hamdi v. Rumsfeld*, 542 U.S. __ (2004), 124 S. Ct. 2633 (2004), No. 03-6696, O'Connor at 9, 10.

[24] *Id.* at 27 citing *Mathews v. Eldridge*, 424 U.S. 319 at 335 (1976).

[25] *See* Chapter V, n.133 at 176. *See also*, Appendix E for the Order creating the Combatant Status Review Tribunal.

[26] *See Hamdi v. Rumsfeld*, 542 U.S. __ (2004), 124 S. Ct. 2633 (2004), No. 03-6696, Souter (concurring in part) at 16.

[27] *Id.* O'Connor opinion at 31.

[28] *Id.* O'Connor opinion at 26, citing *Fuentes v. Shevin*, 407 U.S. 67, 80 (1972) quoting *Baldwin v. Hale*, 1 Wall 223, 233 (1864); *Armstrong v. Manzo* 380 U.S. 545, 552 (1965).

[29] The Military Order, Administrative Review Procedures for Enemy Combatants in Control of the Department of Defense at Guantanamo Bay Naval Base, Cuba stated that similar administrative review procedures would be issued for enemy combatants in the control of DoD in the United States. *See* Appendix D.

[30] *Id. see* Section 3, E at 7-8.

[31] *See* 8 U.S.C. § 1534 (c)(1) and The Association of the Bar of the City of New York Committee on Federal Courts. *The Indefinite Detention of Enemy Combatants: Balancing Due Process and National Security in the Context of the War on Terror,* March 18, 2004 at 24. *See also,* discussion Chapter V, n.4 at 169.

[32] *See* discussion of this issue in Chapter III at 66-67, and Appendix A The Military Order on the Detention, Treatment, and Trial of Certain Non-Citizens in the War Against Terrorism (November 13, 2001), 66 Fed. Reg. 57, 833 (November 16, 2001).

[33] *See* the Department of Justice and Terrorism: Hearing Before the Senate Committee on the Judiciary, 107th Cong. (2001) at 52.

[34] *Id.*

[35] *Id.*

[36] *See* discussion in Chapter II at 28-29 and n.18.

[37] *See* the Department of Justice and Terrorism: Hearing Before the Senate Committee on the Judiciary, 107th Cong. (2002); To Receive Testimony on the Department of Defense's Implementation of the President's Military Order on Detention, Treatment, and Trial of Certain Non-Citizens in the War on Terrorism: Hearing Before the Senate Committee on Armed Services, 107th Cong. (2001). As a direct result of the Judiciary Committee hearings testimony, Senator Patrick Leahy introduced S 1941, Military Tribunal Authorization Act of 2002, 107th Cong. (2002), which would provide the Executive with specific authorization to use extraordinary tribunals to try members of the al-Qaida terrorist network and those who cooperated with them. Senator Leahy's proposed legislation would circumscribe military detainment and military trials very narrowly. It would have exempted from military trial or detainment individuals arrested while in the United States, since the civilian court system was well equipped to handle such cases, and it would also have exempted aliens lawfully admitted for permanent residence from detainment and military trial. It would have authorized for military detainment and trial only those persons "apprehended in Afghanistan fleeing from Afghanistan, or in fleeing from any other place outside the United States where there is armed conflict involving the Armed Forces of the United States." [S 1941, 3(a) (3)]

In addition to imposing these limitations on the scope of the Executive to detain persons and try them in military commissions, Senator Leahy's proposal would have provided individuals who were subject to these extraordinary powers significant procedural protections which neither the Bush Order nor the subsequent DoD Order implementing the directive afforded. Most relevant was the provision which subjected detentions under its authority to the supervision of the United States Court of Appeals for the District of Columbia Circuit. [S 1941 5(d)] The suggested measure would have provided for appellate review of military tribunals' judgments in the United States Court of Appeals for the Armed Forces – an all-civilian court comprised of judges whom the President appoints, with Senate advice and consent, to fifteen-year terms – as well as further review in the United States Supreme Court through writ of certiorari. [S 1941 4(e)(2) & (3)] The bill introduced by Senator Leahy was referred to the Senate Armed Services Committee, which took no further action on the measure.

[38] For a full discussion of this approach see Chapter III at 59-60 and Appendix C.

[39] *See* Neal K. Katyal and Laurence H. Tribe, "Waging War, Deciding Guilt: Trying the Military Tribunals," 111 *Yale L.J.* 1259 (2002) at 1277. *See also, Reid v. Covert*, 354 U.S.1, 11 (1957) (declaring that the "blending of executive, legislative, and judicial powers in one person or even one branch of government is ordinarily regarded as the very acme of absolutism); *Duncan v. Kahanamoku*, 327 U.S. 304, 322 (1946) (Burton, J. Dissenting) (proclaiming that the Founders "were opposed to governments that placed in the hands of one man the power to make interpret and enforce the laws"); and *Hamdi v. Rumsfeld*, 542 U.S. __ (2004), 124 S. Ct. 2633 (2004), No. 03-6696 at 291 (O'Connor, J.) (rejecting the governments position that separation of powers mandate a heavily circumscribed role for the courts in such circumstances. . . . "because such an approach serves only to condense power into a single branch of government.")

[40] The rights of the accused included in Military Commission Order No. 1 provide an initial basis upon which fair, impartial and balanced proceedings can occur. There are several rights that are omitted that are counter to fundamental fairness guarantees that should be considered. *See* discussion in Chapter III at 63-72.

[41] *See Hamdi v. Rumsfeld*, 542 U.S.__(2004), 124 S. Ct. 2633 (2004), No. 03-6696, Scalia (dissent) at 27.

[42] *Id.* at 3.

[43] *See Powell v. Alabama*, 287 U.S. 45, 68-69 (1932).

[44] It was left to the lower courts and the government to resolve areas of procedural controversy including the timing and type of hearing to be afforded to detainees. *See Hamdi*, O'Connor opinion at 29-32. In a memorandum opinion and order of October 20, 2004, Judge Colleen Kollar-Kotelly of the United States District Court for the District of Columbia, ruled that three Kuwaiti nationals detained at Guantanamo Bay since shortly after the September 11, 2001 terrorist attacks were entitled to be represented by counsel while pursing their claims in federal court. The Court further ruled that the Government could not encroach on the detainees' relationship with counsel by subjecting them to real time monitoring of meetings with their attorneys, and post hoc classification review of meeting notes and legal mail sent between the attorneys and detainees. While the Court was "acutely aware of the delicate balance that must be struck when weighing the importance of national security against the rights of the individual, . . . the Government has supplied only the most slender legal support for its argument, which cannot withstand the weight of the authority surrounding the importance of the attorney-client privilege." *See Fawzi Khalid Abdullah Fahad Al Odah, et al., v. United States of America*, No. 02-828 (CKK) (D.D.C. October 20, 2004).

[45] *See* Chapter V, n.4 and n.133 and accompanying text, and Chapter VI at 184-187.

[46] *See* discussion in n.21 and n.37 op. cit. and accompanying text.

[47] *See* Chapter I for full discussion of the historic background of Military Commissions.

[48] In *Ex Parte Quirin*, the Court read the President's power to detain combatants, be they unlawful or otherwise, on his power to enforce the Article of War, a statutory authorization, 317 U.S. 1

(1942) at 26-27; in *Ex Parte Endo*, the Court, in a discussion released on the same day as *Korematsu,* ordered Endo's discharge from confinement because Congress had not explicitly authorized her detention, 323 U.S. 214 (1944) at 300-02.

[49] *See,* Chapter IV at 112-114 for a full discussion of § 4001(a) and its impact upon Padilla and Hamdi's ongoing detention.

[50] *See* Chapter V, n.31 at 171 and accompanying text.

[51] *See* Ely, John Hart *War and Responsibility: Constitutional Lessons of Vietnam and Its Aftermath* (Princeton, N.J., Princeton University Press 1993) at 5.

[52] *See Hamdi v. Rumsfeld*, 542 U.S. __ (2004), 124 S. Ct. 2633 (2004), No. 03-6696, O'Connor at 3 cited in n.22.

[53] *Id.* O'Conner at 27, cited in n.24.

[54] *Id.* cited in n.26.

[55] *Id.* O'Connor at 26, cited in n.28.

[56] *See* Appendix E for full discussion of the document.

[57] *See* Appendix D for a full discussion of the document.

[58] *See* Appendixes A & C1-13 for a full discussion of the Order and Instructions.

APPENDIX A

the
White House
President George W. Bush

For Immediate Release
Office of the Press Secretary
November 13, 2001

President Issues Military Order
Detention, Treatment, and Trial of Certain Non-Citizens in the War Against
Terrorism

By the authority vested in me as President and as Commander in Chief of the
Armed Forces of the United States by the Constitution and the laws of the United
States of America, including the Authorization for Use of Military Force Joint
Resolution (Public Law 107-40, 115 Stat. 224) and sections 821 and 836 of title
10, United States Code, it is hereby ordered as follows:

Section 1. Findings.

(a) International terrorists, including members of al Qaida, have carried out
attacks on United States diplomatic and military personnel and facilities abroad
and on citizens and property within the United States on a scale that has created a
state of armed conflict that requires the use of the United States Armed Forces.

(b) In light of grave acts of terrorism and threats of terrorism, including the
terrorist attacks on September 11, 2001, on the headquarters of the United States
Department of Defense in the national capital region, on the World Trade Center
in New York, and on civilian aircraft such as in Pennsylvania, I proclaimed a
national emergency on September 14, 2001 (Proc. 7463, Declaration of National
Emergency by Reason of Certain Terrorist Attacks).

(c) Individuals acting alone and in concert involved in international terrorism
possess both the capability and the intention to undertake further terrorist attacks
against the United States that, if not detected and prevented, will cause mass
deaths, mass injuries, and massive destruction of property, and may place at risk
the continuity of the operations of the United States Government.

(d) The ability of the United States to protect the United States and its citizens,
and to help its allies and other cooperating nations protect their nations and their
citizens, from such further terrorist attacks depends in significant part upon using
the United States Armed Forces to identify terrorists and those who support them,
to disrupt their activities, and to eliminate their ability to conduct or support such
attacks.

(e) To protect the United States and its citizens, and for the effective conduct of military operations and prevention of terrorist attacks, it is necessary for individuals subject to this order pursuant to section 2 hereof to be detained, and, when tried, to be tried for violations of the laws of war and other applicable laws by military tribunals.

(f) Given the danger to the safety of the United States and the nature of international terrorism, and to the extent provided by and under this order, I find consistent with section 836 of title 10, United States Code, that it is not practicable to apply in military commissions under this order the principles of law and the rules of evidence generally recognized in the trial of criminal cases in the United States district courts.

(g) Having fully considered the magnitude of the potential deaths, injuries, and property destruction that would result from potential acts of terrorism against the United States, and the probability that such acts will occur, I have determined that an extraordinary emergency exists for national defense purposes, that this emergency constitutes an urgent and compelling government interest, and that issuance of this order is necessary to meet the emergency.

Sec. 2. Definition and Policy.

(a) The term "individual subject to this order" shall mean any individual who is not a United States citizen with respect to whom I determine from time to time in writing that:

(1) there is reason to believe that such individual, at the relevant times, (i) is or was a member of the organization known as al Qaida; (ii) has engaged in, aided or abetted, or conspired to commit, acts of international terrorism, or acts in preparation therefore, that have caused, threaten to cause, or have as their aim to cause, injury to or adverse effects on the United States, its citizens, national security, foreign policy, or economy; or (iii) has knowingly harbored one or more individuals described in subparagraphs (i) or (ii) of subsection 2(a)(1) of this order; and

(2) it is in the interest of the United States that such individual be subject to this order.

(b) It is the policy of the United States that the Secretary of Defense shall take all necessary measures to ensure that any individual subject to this order is detained in accordance with section 3, and, if the individual is to be tried, that such individual is tried only in accordance with section 4.

(c) It is further the policy of the United States that any individual subject to this order who is not already under the control of the Secretary of Defense but who is under the control of any other officer or agent of the United States or any State shall, upon delivery of a copy of such written determination to such officer or agent, forthwith be placed under the control of the Secretary of Defense.

Sec. 3. Detention Authority of the Secretary of Defense. Any individual subject to this order shall be –

(a) detained at an appropriate location designated by the Secretary of Defense outside or within the United States;

(b) treated humanely, without any adverse distinction based on race, color, religion, gender, birth, wealth, or any similar criteria;

(c) afforded adequate food, drinking water, shelter, clothing, and medical treatment;

(d) allowed the free exercise of religion consistent with the requirements of such detention; and

(e) detained in accordance with such other conditions as the Secretary of Defense may prescribe.

Sec. 4. Authority of the Secretary of Defense Regarding Trials of Individuals Subject to this Order.

(a) Any individual subject to this order shall, when tried, be tried by military commission for any and all offenses triable by military commission that such individual is alleged to have committed, and may be punished in accordance with the penalties provided under applicable law, including life imprisonment or death.

(b) As a military function and in light of the findings in section 1, including subsection (f) thereof, the Secretary of Defense shall issue such orders and regulations, including orders for the appointment of one or more military commissions, as may be necessary to carry out subsection (a) of this section.

(c) Orders and regulations issued under subsection (b) of this section shall include, but not be limited to, rules for the conduct of the proceedings of military commissions, including pretrial, trial, and post-trial procedures, modes of proof, issuance of process, and qualifications of attorneys, which shall at a minimum provide for –

(1) military commissions to sit at any time and place, consistent with such guidance regarding time and place as the Secretary of Defense may provide;

(2) a full and fair trial, with the military commission sitting as the triers of both fact and law;

(3) admission of such evidence as would, in the opinion of the presiding officer of the military commission (or instead, if any other member of the commission so requests at the time the presiding officer renders that opinion, the opinion of the commission rendered at that time by a majority of the commission), have probative value to a reasonable person;

(4) in a manner consistent with the protection of information classified or classifiable under Executive Order 12958 of April 17, 1995, as amended, or any successor Executive Order, protected by statute or rule from unauthorized disclosure, or otherwise protected by law, (A) the handling of, admission into evidence of, and access to materials and information, and (B) the conduct, closure of, and access to proceedings;

(5) conduct of the prosecution by one or more attorneys designated by the Secretary of Defense and conduct of the defense by attorneys for the individual subject to this order;

(6) conviction only upon the concurrence of two-thirds of the members of the commission present at the time of the vote, a majority being present;

(7) sentencing only upon the concurrence of two-thirds of the members of the commission present at the time of the vote, a majority being present; and

(8) submission of the record of the trial, including any conviction or sentence, for review and final decision by me or by the Secretary of Defense if so designated by me for that purpose.

Sec. 5. Obligation of Other Agencies to Assist the Secretary of Defense.

Departments, agencies, entities, and officers of the United States shall, to the maximum extent permitted by law, provide to the Secretary of Defense such assistance as he may request to implement this order.

Sec. 6. Additional Authorities of the Secretary of Defense.

(a) As a military function and in light of the findings in section 1, the Secretary of Defense shall issue such orders and regulations as may be necessary to carry out any of the provisions of this order.

(b) The Secretary of Defense may perform any of his functions or duties, and may exercise any of the powers provided to him under this order (other than under section 4(c)(8) hereof) in accordance with section 113(d) of title 10, United States Code.

Sec. 7. Relationship to Other Law and Forums.

(a) Nothing in this order shall be construed to – (1) authorize the disclosure of state secrets to any person not otherwise authorized to have access to them; (2) limit the authority of the President as Commander in Chief of the Armed Forces or the power of the President to grant reprieves and pardons; or (3) limit the lawful authority of the Secretary of Defense, any military commander, or any other officer or agent of the United States or of any State to detain or try any person who is not an individual subject to this order.

(b) With respect to any individual subject to this order – (1) military tribunals shall have exclusive jurisdiction with respect to offenses by the individual; and (2) the individual shall not be privileged to seek any remedy or maintain any proceeding, directly or indirectly, or to have any such remedy or proceeding sought on the individual's behalf, in (i) any court of the United States, or any State thereof, (ii) any court of any foreign nation, or (iii) any international tribunal.

(c) This order is not intended to and does not create any right, benefit, or privilege, substantive or procedural, enforceable at law or equity by any party, against the United States, its departments, agencies, or other entities, its officers or employees, or any other person.

(d) For purposes of this order, the term "State" includes any State, district, territory, or possession of the United States.

(e) I reserve the authority to direct the Secretary of Defense, at any time hereafter, to transfer to a governmental authority control of any individual subject to this order. Nothing in this order shall be construed to limit the authority of any such governmental authority to prosecute any individual for whom control is transferred.

Sec. 8. Publication.

This order shall be published in the Federal Register.

GEORGE W. BUSH
THE WHITE HOUSE

November 13, 2001.

# # #

APPENDIX B

S.J. Res. 23

One Hundred Seventh Congress
of the
United States of America

AT THE FIRST SESSION

*Begun and held at the City of Washington on Wednesday,
the third day of January, two thousand and one*

JOINT RESOLUTION

To authorize the use of United States Armed Forces against those responsible
for the recent attacks launched against the United States.

Whereas, on September 11, 2001, acts of treacherous violence were committed
against the United States and its citizens; and

Whereas, such acts render it both necessary and appropriate that the United States
exercise its rights to self-defense and to protect United States citizens both at
home and abroad; and

Whereas, in light of the threat to the national security and foreign policy of the
United States posed by these grave acts of violence; and

Whereas, such acts continue to pose an unusual and extraordinary threat to the
national security and foreign policy of the United States; and

Whereas, the President has authority under the Constitution to take action to deter
and prevent acts of international terrorism against the United States: Now,
therefore, be it

*Resolved by the Senate and House of Representatives of the United States
of America in Congress assembled,*

SECTION 1. SHORT TITLE.

This joint resolution may be cited as the "Authorization for Use of
Military Force".

SEC. 2. AUTHORIZATION FOR USE OF UNITED STATES ARMED FORCES.

(a) IN GENERAL.—That the President is authorized to use all necessary
and appropriate force against those nations, organizations, or persons he
determines planned, authorized, committed, or aided the terrorist attacks that
occurred on September 11, 2001, or harbored such organizations or persons, in

order to prevent any future acts of international terrorism against the United States by such nations, organizations or persons.

(b) WAR POWERS RESOLUTION REQUIREMENTS.—

(1) SPECIFIC STATUTORY AUTHORIZATION.—Consistent with section 8(a)(1) of the War Powers Resolution, the Congress declares that this section is intended to constitute specific statutory authorization within the meaning of section 5(b) of the War Powers Resolution.

(2) APPLICABILITY OF OTHER REQUIREMENTS.—Nothing in this resolution supercedes any requirement of the War Powers Resolution.

Speaker of the House of Representatives.

Vice President of the United States and President of the Senate.

APPENDIX C

Department of Defense Fact Sheet

Military Commission Procedures

- Military Commissions have historically been used to prosecute enemy combatants who violate the laws of war; the last time the United States used the Military Commission process was during World War II.

- Military Commissions provide:
  - o A full and fair trial;
  - o Protection for classified and sensitive information; and
  - o Protection and safety for all personnel participating in the process, including the accused.

- In accordance with his Military Order of November 13, 2001, the President must determine if an individual is subject to his Military Order. This decision is the jurisdictional basis for prosecution; until the President determines that an individual is subject to his Military Order, no prosecution is possible. However, this determination does not require that criminal charges be brought against the individual, that decision is made by the Appointing Authority (currently the Deputy Secretary of Defense) after the Chief Prosecutor recommends that charges be approved.

- An individual may be subject to the President's Military Order if the individual is not a U.S. citizen and the President determines that there is a reason to believe that the individual:
  - o Is or was a member of al Qaeda;
  - o Has engaged in, aided or abetted, or conspired to commit acts of international terrorism against the United States; or
  - o Knowingly harbored one or more of the individuals described above; and
  - o It is the interest of the United States that such individual be subject to this order.

- The Chief Prosecutor will draft charges, when appropriate, on individuals subject to the President's Military Order.

- The Appointing Authority approves and refers appropriate charges to a Military Commission and appoints Military Commission members.

- Each Military Commission panel has a minimum of three and a maximum of seven military officer members. One of the members must be a Judge Advocate who will serve as the Presiding Officer. All members of the Military Commission panel, including the Presiding Officer, vote on findings and, if necessary, on a sentence.

- Each accused tried by a Military Commission has the following procedural safeguards:
    o the presumption of innocence,
    o proof of guilt beyond a reasonable doubt,
    o the right to call and cross examine witnesses (subject to the rules regarding production of witnesses and protection of information),
    o nothing said by an accused to his attorney, or anything derived therefrom, may be used against him at trial,
    o no adverse inference for remaining silent,
    o and the overall requirement that any military commission proceeding be full and fair.
    o Finally, to assist him in preparing a defense, each accused has Military Defense Counsel provided at no cost to him.

- The accused may also hire a civilian defense counsel at no cost to the government as long as that counsel:
    o Is a United States citizen;
    o Is admitted to practice in a United States jurisdiction;
    o Has not been the subject of sanction or disciplinary action;
    o Is eligible for and obtains at least a SECRET level clearance; and
    o Agrees to follow the Military Commission rules.

- The Presiding Officer may admit any evidence that "would have probative value to a reasonable person." This standard of evidence takes into account the unique battlefield environment that is different than traditional peacetime law enforcement practices in the U.S. For example, soldiers are not required to obtain a search warrant when someone is shooting at them from a cave. This standard of evidence allows both the defense and the prosecution to admit evidence that was acquired during military operations.

- A finding of guilt and the imposition of a sentence must be with the concurrence of two-thirds of the Military Commission panel members.

- If there is a finding of guilt, the Military Commission panel members may impose any appropriate sentence, including death. A sentence of death requires a unanimous vote from a seven-member Military Commission panel.

- After the panel has delivered its verdict and imposed a sentence:
    o All records of trial must be reviewed by the Appointing Authority who may return the case to the Military Commission for further proceedings if he determines it is not administratively complete.

    o A three-member Review Panel of Military Officers, one of whom must have prior experience as a judge, will review all cases for material errors of law, and may consider matters submitted by the Prosecution and Defense. Review Panel members may be civilians who were specifically commissioned to serve on the panel. If a majority of the Review Panel members believe a material error of law has occurred, they may return the case to the Military Commission for further proceedings.

    o The Secretary of Defense will review the record of trial and, if appropriate, may return it to the Military Commission for further proceedings, or forward the case to the President with a recommendation as to disposition.

    o The President may either return the case to the Military Commission for further proceedings or make the final decision as to its disposition.

        ▪ The President may delegate final decision authority to the Secretary of Defense, in which case the Secretary may approve or disapprove the findings or change a finding of Guilty to a finding of Guilty to a lesser-included offense, or mitigate, commute, defer, or suspend the sentence imposed, or any portion thereof. A finding of Not Guilty as to a charge shall not be changed to a finding of Guilty.

- After a Final Decision is made, a sentence shall be carried out promptly.

Commission Process

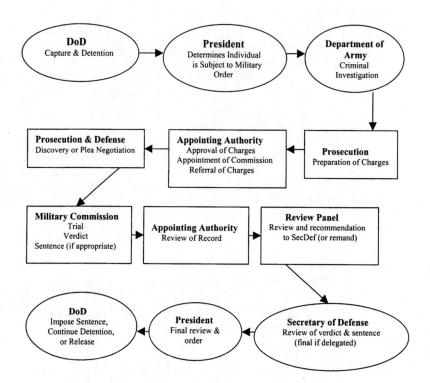

APPENDIX C 1

Department of Defense

Military Commission Order No. 1

March 21, 2002

SUBJECT: Procedures for Trials by Military Commissions of Certain Non-United States Citizens in the War Against Terrorism

References: (a) United States Constitution, Article II, section 2

(b) Military Order of November 13, 2001, "Detention, Treatment, and Trial of Certain Non-Citizens in the War Against Terrorism," 66 F.R. 57833 (Nov. 16, 2001) ("President's Military Order")

(c) DoD 5200.2-R, "Personnel Security Program," current edition

(d) Executive Order 12958, "Classified National Security Information" (April 17, 1995, as amended, or any successor Executive Order)

(e) Section 603 of title 10, United States Code

(f) DoD Directive 5025.1, "DoD Directives System," current edition

1. PURPOSE

This Order implements policy, assigns responsibilities, and prescribes procedures under references (a) and (b) for trials before military commissions of individuals subject to the President's Military Order. These procedures shall be implemented and construed so as to ensure that any such individual receives a full and fair trial before a military commission, as required by the President's Military Order. Unless otherwise directed by the Secretary of Defense, and except for supplemental procedures established pursuant to the President's Military Order or this Order, the procedures prescribed herein and no others shall govern such trials.

2. ESTABLISHMENT OF MILITARY COMMISSIONS

In accordance with the President's Military Order, the Secretary of Defense or a designee ("Appointing Authority") may issue orders from time to time appointing one or more military commissions to try individuals subject to the President's Military Order and appointing any other personnel necessary to facilitate such trials.

3. JURISDICTION

A. Over Persons

A military commission appointed under this Order ("Commission") shall have jurisdiction over only an individual or individuals ("the Accused") (1) subject to the President's Military Order and (2) alleged to have committed an offense in a charge that has been referred to the Commission by the Appointing Authority.

B. Over Offenses

Commissions established hereunder shall have jurisdiction over violations of the laws of war and all other offenses triable by military commission.

C. Maintaining Integrity of Commission Proceedings

The Commission may exercise jurisdiction over participants in its proceedings as necessary to preserve the integrity and order of the proceedings.

4. COMMISSION PERSONNEL

A. Members

(1) Appointment

The Appointing Authority shall appoint the members and the alternate member or members of each Commission. The alternate member or members shall attend all sessions of the Commission, but the absence of an alternate member shall not preclude the Commission from conducting proceedings. In case of incapacity, resignation, or removal of any member, an alternate member shall take the place of that member. Any vacancy among the members or alternate members occurring after a trial has begun may be filled by the Appointing Authority, but the substance of all prior proceedings and evidence taken in that case shall be made known to that new member or alternate member before the trial proceeds.

(2) Number of Members

Each Commission shall consist of at least three but no more than seven members, the number being determined by the Appointing Authority. For each such Commission, there shall also be one or two alternate members, the number being determined by the Appointing Authority.

(3) Qualifications

Each member and alternate member shall be a commissioned officer of the United States armed forces ("Military Officer"), including without limitation reserve personnel on active duty, National Guard personnel on active duty in Federal service, and retired personnel recalled to active duty. The Appointing Authority shall appoint members and alternate members determined to be competent to perform the duties involved. The Appointing Authority may remove members and alternate members for good cause.

(4) Presiding Officer

From among the members of each Commission, the Appointing Authority shall designate a Presiding Officer to preside over the proceedings of that Commission. The Presiding Officer shall be a Military Officer who is a judge advocate of any United States armed force.

(5) Duties of the Presiding Officer

(a) The Presiding Officer shall admit or exclude evidence at trial in accordance with Section 6(D). The Presiding Officer shall have authority to close proceedings or portions of proceedings in accordance with Section 6(B)(3) and for any other reason necessary for the conduct of a full and fair trial.

(b) The Presiding Officer shall ensure that the discipline, dignity, and decorum of the proceedings are maintained, shall exercise control over the proceedings to ensure proper implementation of the President's Military Order and this Order, and shall have authority to act upon any contempt or breach of Commission rules and procedures. Any attorney authorized to appear before a Commission who is thereafter found not to satisfy the requirements for eligibility or who fails to comply with laws, rules, regulations, or other orders applicable to the Commission proceedings or any other individual who violates such laws, rules, regulations, or orders may be disciplined as the Presiding Officer deems appropriate, including but not limited to revocation of eligibility to appear before that Commission. The Appointing Authority may further revoke that attorney's or any other person's eligibility to appear before any other Commission convened under this Order.

(c) The Presiding Officer shall ensure the expeditious conduct of the trial. In no circumstance shall accommodation of counsel be allowed to delay proceedings unreasonably.

(d) The Presiding Officer shall certify all interlocutory questions, the disposition of which would effect a termination of proceedings with respect to a charge, for decision by the Appointing Authority. The Presiding Officer may certify other interlocutory questions to the Appointing Authority as the Presiding Officer deems appropriate.

B. Prosecution

(1) Office of the Chief Prosecutor

The Chief Prosecutor shall be a judge advocate of any United States armed force, shall supervise the overall prosecution efforts under the President's Military Order, and shall ensure proper management of personnel and resources.

(2) Prosecutors and Assistant Prosecutors

Consistent with any supplementary regulations or instructions issued under Section 7(A), the Chief Prosecutor shall detail a Prosecutor and, as appropriate, one or more Assistant Prosecutors to prepare charges and conduct the prosecution for each case before a Commission ("Prosecution"). Prosecutors and Assistant Prosecutors shall be (a) Military Officers who are judge advocates of any United States armed force, or (b) special trial counsel of the Department of Justice who may be made available by the Attorney General of the United States. The duties of the Prosecution are:

(a) To prepare charges for approval and referral by the Appointing Authority;

(b) To conduct the prosecution before the Commission of all cases referred for trial; and

(c) To represent the interests of the Prosecution in any review process.

C. Defense

(1) Office of the Chief Defense Counsel

The Chief Defense Counsel shall be a judge advocate of any United States armed force, shall supervise the overall defense efforts under the President's Military Order, shall ensure proper management of personnel and resources, shall preclude conflicts of interest, and shall facilitate proper representation of all Accused.

(2) Detailed Defense Counsel.

Consistent with any supplementary regulations or instructions issued under Section 7(A), the Chief Defense Counsel shall detail one or more Military Officers who are judge advocates of any United States armed force to conduct the defense for each case before a Commission ("Detailed Defense Counsel"). The duties of the Detailed Defense Counsel are:

(a) To defend the Accused zealously within the bounds of the law without regard to personal opinion as to the guilt of the Accused; and

(b) To represent the interests of the Accused in any review process as provided by this Order.

(3) Choice of Counsel

(a) The Accused may select a Military Officer who is a judge advocate of any United States armed force to replace the Accused's Detailed Defense Counsel, provided that Military Officer has been determined to be available in accordance with any applicable supplementary regulations or instructions issued under Section 7(A). After such selection of a new Detailed Defense Counsel, the original Detailed Defense Counsel will be relieved of all duties with respect to that case. If requested by the Accused, however, the Appointing Authority may allow the original Detailed Defense Counsel to continue to assist in representation of the Accused as another Detailed Defense Counsel.

(b) the Accused may also retain the services of a civilian attorney of the Accused's own choosing and at no expense to the United States Government ("Civilian Defense Counsel"), provided that attorney: (i) is a United States citizen; (ii) is admitted to the practice of law in a State, district, territory, or possession of the United States, or before a Federal court; (iii) has not been the subject of any sanction or disciplinary action by any court, bar, or other competent governmental authority for relevant misconduct;

(iv) has been determined to be eligible for access to information classified at the level SECRET or higher under the authority of and in accordance with the procedures prescribed in reference (c); and (v) has signed a written agreement to comply with all applicable regulations or instructions for counsel, including any rules of court for conduct during the course of proceedings. Civilian attorneys may be pre-qualified as members of the pool of available attorneys if, at the time of application, they meet the relevant criteria, or they may be qualified on an *ad hoc* basis after being requested by an Accused. Representation by Civilian Defense Counsel will not relieve Detailed Defense Counsel of the duties specified in Section 4(C)(2). The qualification of a Civilian Defense Counsel does not guarantee that person's presence at closed Commission proceedings or that person's access to any information protected under Section 6(D)(5).

(4) Continuity of Representation

The Accused must be represented at all relevant times by Detailed Defense Counsel. Detailed Defense Counsel and Civilian Defense Counsel shall be herein referred to collectively as "Defense Counsel." The Accused and Defense Counsel shall be herein referred to collectively as "the Defense."

D. Other Personnel

Other personnel, such as court reporters, interpreters, security personnel, bailiffs, and clerks may be detailed or employed by the Appointing Authority, as necessary.

5. PROCEDURES ACCORDED THE ACCUSED

The following procedures shall apply with respect to the Accused:

A. The Prosecution shall furnish to the Accused, sufficiently in advance of trial to prepare a defense, a copy of the charges in English and, if appropriate, in another language that the Accused understands.

B. The Accused shall be presumed innocent until proven guilty.

C. A Commission member shall vote for a finding of Guilty as to an offense if and only if that member is convinced beyond a reasonable doubt, based on the evidence admitted at trial, that the Accused is guilty of the offense.

D. At least one Detailed Defense Counsel shall be made available to the Accused sufficiently in advance of trial to prepare a defense and until any findings and sentence become final in accordance with Section 6(H)(2).

E. The Prosecution shall provide the Defense with access to evidence the Prosecution intends to introduce at trial and with access to evidence known to the Prosecution that tends to exculpate the Accused. Such access shall be consistent with Section 6(D)(5) and subject to Section 9.

F. The Accused shall not be required to testify during trial. A Commission shall draw no adverse inference from an Accused's decision not to testify. This subsection shall not preclude admission of evidence of prior statements or conduct of the Accused.

G. If the Accused so elects, the Accused may testify at trial on the Accused's own behalf and shall then be subject to cross-examination.

H. The Accused may obtain witnesses and documents for the Accused's defense, to the extent necessary and reasonably available as determined by the Presiding Officer. Such access shall be consistent with the requirements of Section 6(D)(5) and subject to Section 9. The Appointing Authority shall order that such investigative or other resources be made available to the Defense as the Appointing Authority deems necessary for a full and fair trial.

I. The Accused may have Defense Counsel present evidence at trial in the Accused's defense and cross-examine each witness presented by the Prosecution who appears before the Commission.

J. The Prosecution shall ensure that the substance of the charges, the proceedings, and any documentary evidence are provided in English and, if appropriate, in another language that the Accused understands. The Appointing Authority may appoint one or more interpreters to assist the Defense, as necessary.

K. The Accused may be present at every stage of the trial before the Commission, consistent with Section 6(B)(3), unless the Accused engages in disruptive conduct that justifies exclusion by the Presiding Officer. Detailed Defense Counsel may not be excluded from any trial proceeding or portion thereof.

L. Except by order of the Commission for good cause shown, the Prosecution shall provide the Defense with access before sentencing proceedings to evidence the Prosecution intends to present in such proceedings. Such access shall be consistent with Section 6(D)(5) and subject to Section 9.

M. The Accused may make a statement during sentencing proceedings.

N. The Accused may have Defense Counsel submit evidence to the Commission during sentencing proceedings.

O. The Accused shall be afforded a trial open to the public (except proceedings closed by the Presiding Officer), consistent with Section 6(B).

P. The Accused shall not again be tried by any Commission for a charge once a Commission's finding on that charge becomes final in accordance with Section 6(H)(2).

6. CONDUCT OF THE TRIAL

A. Pretrial Procedures

(1) Preparation of the Charges

The Prosecution shall prepare charges for approval by the Appointing Authority, as provided in Section 4(B)(2)(a).

(2) Referral to the Commission

The Appointing Authority may approve and refer for trial any charge against an individual or individuals within the jurisdiction of a Commission in accordance with Section 3(A) and alleging an offense within the jurisdiction of a Commission in accordance with Section 3(B).

(3) Notification of the Accused

The Prosecution shall provide copies of the charges approved by the Appointing Authority to the Accused and Defense Counsel. The Prosecution also shall submit the charges approved by the Appointing Authority to the Presiding Officer of the Commission to which they were referred.

(4) Plea Agreements

The Accused, through Defense Counsel, and the Prosecution may submit for approval to the Appointing Authority a plea agreement mandating a sentence limitation or any other provision in exchange for an agreement to plead guilty, or any other consideration. Any agreement to plead guilty must include a written stipulation of fact, signed by the Accused, that confirms the guilt of the Accused and the voluntary and informed nature of the plea of guilty. If the Appointing Authority approves the plea agreement, the Commission will, after determining the voluntary and informed nature of the plea agreement, admit the plea agreement and stipulation into evidence and be bound to adjudge findings and a sentence pursuant to that plea agreement.

(5) Issuance and Service of Process; Obtaining Evidence

The Commission shall have power to:

> (a) Summon witnesses to attend trial and testify;
> (b) Administer oaths or affirmations to witnesses and other persons and to question witnesses;
> (c) Require the production of documents and other evidentiary material; and
> (d) Designate special commissioners to take evidence.

The Presiding Officer shall exercise these powers on behalf of the Commission at the Presiding Officer's own initiative, or at the request of the Prosecution or the Defense, as necessary to ensure a full and fair trial in accordance with the President's Military Order and this Order. The Commission shall issue its process in the name of the Department of Defense over the signature of the Presiding Officer. Such process shall be served as directed by the Presiding Officer in a manner calculated to give reasonable notice to persons required to take action in accordance with that process.

B. Duties of the Commission During Trial

The Commission shall:

> (1) Provide a full and fair trial.
>
> (2) Proceed impartially and expeditiously, strictly confining the proceedings to a full and fair trial of the charges, excluding irrelevant evidence, and preventing any unnecessary interference or delay.
>
> (3) Hold open proceedings except where otherwise decided by the Appointing Authority or the Presiding Officer in accordance with the President's Military Order and this Order. Grounds for closure include the protection of information classified or classifiable under reference (d); information protected by law or rule from unauthorized disclosure; the physical safety of participants in Commission proceedings, including prospective witnesses; intelligence and law enforcement sources, methods, or activities;

and other national security interests. The Presiding Officer may decide to close all or part of a proceeding on the Presiding Officer's own initiative or based upon a presentation, including an ex *parte, in camera* presentation by either the Prosecution or the Defense. A decision to close a proceeding or portion thereof may include a decision to exclude the Accused, Civilian Defense Counsel, or any other person, but Detailed Defense Counsel may not be excluded from any trial proceeding or portion thereof. Except with the prior authorization of the Presiding Officer and subject to Section 9, Defense Counsel may not disclose any information presented during a closed session to individuals excluded from such proceeding or part thereof. Open proceedings may include, at the discretion of the Appointing Authority, attendance by the public and accredited press, and public release of transcripts at the appropriate time. Proceedings should be open to the maximum extent practicable. Photography, video, or audio broadcasting, or recording of or at Commission proceedings shall be prohibited, except photography, video, and audio recording by the Commission pursuant to the direction of the Presiding Officer as necessary for preservation of the record of trial.

(4) Hold each session at such time and place as may be directed by the Appointing Authority. Members of the Commission may meet in closed conference at any time.

(5) As soon as practicable at the conclusion of a trial, transmit an authenticated copy of the record of trial to the Appointing Authority.

C. Oaths

(1) Members of a Commission, all Prosecutors, all Defense Counsel, all court reporters, all security personnel, and all interpreters shall take an oath to perform their duties faithfully.

(2) Each witness appearing before a Commission shall be examined under oath, as provided in Section 6(D)(2)(b).

(3) An oath includes an affirmation. Any formulation that appeals to the conscience of the person to whom the oath is administered and that binds that person to speak the truth, or, in the case of one other than a witness, properly to perform certain duties, is sufficient.

D. Evidence

(1) Admissibility

Evidence shall be admitted if, in the opinion of the Presiding Officer (or instead, if any other member of the Commission so requests at the time the Presiding Officer renders that opinion, the opinion of the Commission rendered at that time by a majority of the Commission), the evidence would have probative value to a reasonable person.

(2) Witnesses

(a) Production of Witnesses

The Prosecution or the Defense may request that the Commission hear the testimony of any person, and such testimony shall be received if found to be admissible and not cumulative. The Commission may also summon and hear witnesses on its own initiative. The Commission may permit the testimony of witnesses by telephone, audiovisual means, or other means; however, the Commission shall consider the ability to test the veracity of that testimony in evaluating the weight to be given to the testimony of the witness.

(b) Testimony

Testimony of witnesses shall be given under oath or affirmation. The Commission may still hear a witness who refuses to swear an oath or make a solemn undertaking; however, the Commission shall consider the refusal to swear an oath or give an affirmation in evaluating the weight to be given to the testimony of the witness.

(c) Examination of Witnesses

A witness who testifies before the Commission is subject to both direct examination and cross-examination. The Presiding Officer shall maintain order in the proceedings and shall not permit badgering of witnesses or questions that are not material to the issues before the Commission. Members of the Commission may question witnesses at any time.

(d) Protection of Witnesses

The Presiding Officer shall consider the safety of witnesses and others, as well as the safeguarding of Protected Information as defined in Section 6(D)(5)(a), in determining the appropriate methods of receiving testimony and evidence. The Presiding Officer may hear any presentation by the Prosecution or the Defense, including an *ex parte, in camera* presentation, regarding the safety of potential witnesses before determining the ways in which witnesses and evidence will be protected. The Presiding Officer may authorize any methods appropriate for the protection of witnesses and evidence. Such methods may include, but are not limited to: testimony by telephone, audiovisual means, or other electronic means; closure of the proceedings; introduction of prepared declassified summaries of evidence; and the use of pseudonyms.

(3) Other Evidence

Subject to the requirements of Section 6(D)(1) concerning admissibility, the Commission may consider any other evidence including, but not limited to, testimony from prior trials and proceedings, sworn or unsworn written statements, physical evidence, or scientific or other reports.

(4) Notice

The Commission may, after affording the Prosecution and the Defense an opportunity to be heard, take conclusive notice of facts that are not subject to reasonable dispute either because they are generally known or are capable of determination by resort to sources that cannot reasonably be contested.

(5) Protection of Information

(a) Protective Order

The Presiding Officer may issue protective orders as necessary to carry out the Military Order and this Order, including to safeguard "Protected Information," which includes: (i) information classified or classifiable pursuant to reference (d); (ii) information protected by law or rule from unauthorized disclosure; (iii) information the disclosure of which may endanger the physical safety of participants in Commission proceedings, including prospective witnesses; (iv) information concerning intelligence and law enforcement sources, methods, or activities; or (v) information concerning other national security interests. As soon as practicable, counsel for either side will notify the Presiding Officer of any intent to offer evidence involving Protected Information.

(b) Limited Disclosure

The Presiding Officer, upon motion of the Prosecution or *sua sponte*, shall, as necessary to protect the interests of the United States and consistent with Section 9, direct (i) the deletion of specified items of Protected Information from documents to be made available to the Accused, Detailed Defense Counsel, or Civilian Defense Counsel; (ii) the substitution of a portion or summary of the information for such Protected Information; or (iii) the substitution of a statement of the relevant facts that the Protected Information would tend to prove. The Prosecution's motion and any materials submitted in support thereof or in response thereto shall, upon request of the Prosecution, be considered by the Presiding Officer *ex parte, in camera*, but no Protected Information shall be admitted into evidence for consideration by the Commission if not presented to Detailed Defense Counsel.

(c) Closure of Proceedings

The Presiding Officer may direct the closure of proceedings in accordance with Section 6(B)(3).

(d) Protected Information as Part of the Record of Trial

All exhibits admitted as evidence but containing Protected Information shall be sealed and annexed to the record of trial. Additionally, any Protected Information not admitted as evidence but reviewed *in camera* and subsequently withheld from the Defense over Defense objection shall, with the associated motions and responses and any materials submitted in support thereof, be sealed and annexed to the record of trial as additional exhibits. Such sealed material shall be made available to reviewing authorities in closed proceedings.

E. Proceedings During Trial

The proceedings at each trial will be conducted substantially as follows, unless modified by the Presiding Officer to suit the particular circumstances:

(1) Each charge will be read, or its substance communicated, in the presence of the Accused and the Commission.

(2) The Presiding Officer shall ask each Accused whether the Accused pleads "Guilty" or "Not Guilty." Should the Accused refuse to enter a plea, the Presiding Officer shall enter a plea of "Not Guilty" on the Accused's behalf. If the plea to an offense is "Guilty," the Presiding Officer shall enter a finding of Guilty on that offense after conducting sufficient inquiry to form an opinion that the plea is voluntary and informed. Any plea of Guilty that is not determined to be voluntary and informed shall be changed to a plea of Not Guilty. Plea proceedings shall then continue as to the remaining charges. If a plea of "Guilty" is made on all charges, the Commission shall proceed to sentencing proceedings; if not, the Commission shall proceed to trial as to the charges for which a "Not Guilty" plea has been entered.

(3) The Prosecution shall make its opening statement.

(4) The witnesses and other evidence for the Prosecution shall be heard or received.

(5) The Defense may make an opening statement after the Prosecution's opening statement or prior to presenting its case.

(6) The witnesses and other evidence for the Defense shall be heard or received.

(7) Thereafter, the Prosecution and the Defense may introduce evidence in rebuttal and surrebuttal.

(8) The Prosecution shall present argument to the Commission. Defense Counsel shall be permitted to present argument in response, and then the Prosecution may reply in rebuttal.

(9) After the members of the Commission deliberate and vote on findings in closed conference, the Presiding Officer shall announce the Commission's findings in the presence of the Commission, the Prosecution, the Accused, and Defense Counsel. The individual votes of the members of the Commission shall not be disclosed.

(10) In the event a finding of Guilty is entered for an offense, the Prosecution and the Defense may present information to aid the Commission in determining an appropriate sentence. The Accused may testify and shall be subject to cross-examination regarding any such testimony.

(11) The Prosecution and, thereafter, the Defense shall present argument to the Commission regarding sentencing.

(12) After the members of the Commission deliberate and vote on a sentence in closed conference, the Presiding Officer shall announce the Commission's sentence in the presence of the Commission, the Prosecution, the Accused, and Defense Counsel. The individual votes of the members of the Commission shall not be disclosed.

F. Voting

Members of the Commission shall deliberate and vote in closed conference. A Commission member shall vote for a finding of Guilty as to an offense if and only if that member is convinced beyond a reasonable doubt, based on the evidence admitted at trial, that the Accused is guilty of the offense. An affirmative vote of two-thirds of the members is required for a finding of Guilty. When appropriate, the Commission may adjust a charged offense by exceptions and substitutions of language that do not substantially change the nature of the offense or increase its seriousness, or it may vote to convict of a lesser-included offense. An affirmative vote of two-thirds of the members is required to determine a sentence, except that a sentence of death requires a unanimous, affirmative vote of all of the members. Votes on findings and sentences shall be taken by secret, written ballot.

G. Sentence

Upon conviction of an Accused, the Commission shall impose a sentence that is appropriate to the offense or offenses for which there was a finding of Guilty, which sentence may include death, imprisonment for life or for any lesser term, payment of a fine or restitution, or such other lawful punishment or condition of punishment as the Commission shall determine to be proper. Only a Commission of seven members may sentence an Accused to death. A Commission may (subject to rights of third parties) order confiscation of any property of a convicted Accused, deprive that Accused of any stolen property, or order the delivery of such property to the United States for disposition.

H. Post-Trial Procedures

(1) Record of Trial

Each Commission shall make a verbatim transcript of its proceedings, apart from all Commission deliberations, and preserve all evidence admitted in the trial (including any sentencing proceedings) of each case brought before it, which shall constitute the record of trial. The court reporter shall prepare the official record of trial and submit it to the Presiding Officer for authentication upon completion. The Presiding Officer shall transmit the authenticated record of trial to the Appointing Authority. If the Secretary of Defense is serving as the Appointing Authority, the record shall be transmitted to the Review Panel constituted under Section 6(H)(4).

(2) Finality of Findings and Sentence

A Commission finding as to a charge and any sentence of a Commission becomes final when the President or, if designated by the President, the Secretary of Defense makes a final decision thereon pursuant to Section 4(c)(8) of the President's Military Order and in accordance with Section 6(H)(6) of this Order. An authenticated finding of Not Guilty as to a charge shall not be changed to a finding of Guilty. Any sentence made final by action of the President or the Secretary of Defense shall be carried out promptly. Adjudged confinement shall begin immediately following the trial.

(3) Review by the Appointing Authority

If the Secretary of Defense is not the Appointing Authority, the Appointing Authority shall promptly perform an administrative review of the record of trial. If satisfied that the proceedings of the Commission were administratively complete, the Appointing Authority shall transmit the record of trial to the Review Panel constituted under Section 6(H)(4). If not so satisfied, the Appointing Authority shall return the case for any necessary supplementary proceedings.

(4) Review Panel

The Secretary of Defense shall designate a Review Panel consisting of three Military Officers, which may include civilians commissioned pursuant to reference (e). At least one member of each Review Panel shall have experience as a judge. The Review Panel shall review the record of trial and, in its discretion, any written submissions from the Prosecution and the Defense and shall deliberate in closed conference. The Review Panel shall disregard any variance from procedures specified in this Order or elsewhere that would not materially have affected the outcome of the trial before the Commission. Within thirty days after receipt of the record of trial, the Review Panel shall either (a) forward the case to the Secretary of Defense with a recommendation as to disposition, or (b) return the case to the Appointing Authority for further proceedings, provided that a majority of the Review Panel has formed a definite and firm conviction that a material error of law occurred.

(5) Review by the Secretary of Defense

The Secretary of Defense shall review the record of trial and the recommendation of the Review Panel and either return the case for further proceedings or, unless making the final decision pursuant to a Presidential designation under Section 4(c)(8) of the President's Military Order, forward it to the President with a recommendation as to disposition.

(6) Final Decision

After review by the Secretary of Defense, the record of trial and all recommendations will be forwarded to the President for review and final decision (unless the President has designated the Secretary of Defense to perform this function). If the President has so designated the Secretary of Defense, the Secretary may approve or disapprove findings or change a finding of Guilty to a finding of Guilty to a lesser-included offense, or mitigate, commute, defer, or suspend the sentence imposed or any portion thereof. If the Secretary of Defense is authorized to render the final decision, the review of the Secretary of Defense under Section 6(H)(5) shall constitute the final decision.

7. REGULATIONS

A. Supplementary Regulations and Instructions

The Appointing Authority shall, subject to approval of the General Counsel of the Department of Defense if the Appointing Authority is not the Secretary of Defense, publish such further regulations consistent with the President's Military Order and this Order as are necessary or appropriate for the conduct of proceedings by Commissions under the President's Military Order. The General Counsel shall issue such instructions consistent with the President's military Order and this Order as the General Counsel deems necessary to facilitate the conduct of proceedings by such Commissions, including those governing the establishment of Commission-related offices and performance evaluation and reporting relationships.

B. Construction

In the event of any inconsistency between the President's Military Order and this Order, including any supplementary regulations or instructions issued under Section 7(A), the provisions of the President's Military Order shall govern. In the event of any inconsistency between this Order and any regulations or instructions issued under Section 7(A), the provisions of this Order shall govern.

8. AUTHORITY

Nothing in this Order shall be construed to limit in any way the authority of the President as Commander in Chief of the Armed Forces or the power of the President to grant reprieves and pardons. Nothing in this Order shall affect the authority to constitute military commissions for a purpose not governed by the President's Military Order.

9. PROTECTION OF STATE SECRETS

Nothing in this Order shall be construed to authorize disclosure of state secrets to any person not authorized to receive them.

10. OTHER

This Order is not intended to and does not create any right, benefit, or privilege, substantive or procedural, enforceable by any party, against the United States, its departments, agencies, or other entities, its officers or employees, or any other person. No provision in this Order shall be construed to be a requirement of the United States Constitution. Section and subsection captions in this document are for convenience only and shall not be used in construing the requirements of this Order. Failure to meet a time period specified in this Order, or supplementary regulations or instructions issued under Section 7(A), shall not create a right to relief for the Accused or any other person. Reference (f) shall not apply to this Order or any supplementary regulations or instructions issued under Section 7(A).

11. AMENDMENT

The Secretary of Defense may amend this Order from time to time.

12. DELEGATION

The authority of the Secretary of Defense to make requests for assistance under Section 5 of the President's Military Order is delegated to the General Counsel of the Department of Defense. The Executive Secretary of the Department of Defense shall provide such assistance to the General Counsel as the General Counsel determines necessary for this purpose.

13. EFFECTIVE DATE

This Order is effective immediately.

Donald H. Rumsfeld
Secretary of Defense

APPENDIX C 2

Department of Defense

Military Commission Order No. 2

June 21, 2003

SUBJECT: Designation of Deputy Secretary of Defense as Appointing Authority

References: (a) Military Order of November 13, 2001, "Detention, Treatment, and Trial of Certain Non-Citizens in the War Against Terrorism," 66 F.R. 57833 (Nov. 16, 2001) ("President's Military Order")

(b) Military Commission Order No. 1 (Mar. 21, 2002)

(c) 32 C.F.R. sec. 341.1

1. PURPOSE

This Order implements policy and assigns responsibilities under references (a) and (b) for trials before military commissions of individuals subject to the President's Military Order.

2. DESIGNATION OF APPOINTING AUTHORITY

In accordance with the President's Military Order and Military Commission Order No.1, the Deputy Secretary of Defense, Dr. Paul D. Wolfowitz, is designated as the Appointing Authority.

3. RE-DESIGNATION OF APPOINTING AUTHORITY

The Deputy Secretary of Defense shall not re-designate another as the Appointing Authority without the approval of the Secretary of Defense.

4. EFFECTIVE DATE

This Order is effective immediately.

Donald H. Rumsfeld
Secretary of Defense

APPENDIX C 3

Department of Defense

Military Commission Order No. 3

February 5, 2004

SUBJECT: Special Administrative Measures for Certain Communications Subject to Monitoring

References: (a) Military Commission Order No. 1 (Mar. 21, 2002)

(b) Military Order of November 13, 2001, "Detention, Treatment, and Trial of Certain Non-Citizens in the War Against Terrorism," 66 F.R. 57833 (Nov. 16, 2001)

(c) Section 113(d) of Title 10 of the United States Code

(d) Section 140(b) of Title 10 of the United States Code

1. PURPOSE

This Order promulgates policy, assigns responsibilities, and prescribes procedures for matters related to monitoring certain communications of persons who are subject to trial by military commission pursuant to references (a) and (b).

2. AUTHORITY

This Order is issued pursuant to section 7(A) of reference (a) and in accordance with references (b), (c), and (d).

3. COMMUNICATIONS SUBJECT TO MONITORING

This Order applies solely to the monitoring of communications (including oral, electronic, written, or any other means) between individuals whom the President has determined to be subject to reference (b) and their defense counsel (including Civilian Defense Counsel, Detailed Defense Counsel, and any interpreter or other person detailed or employed to assist in the defense of such person), for security or intelligence purposes. For purposes of this Order, "monitoring" includes both real-time interception and analysis and recording of the subject communications by any means.

4. POLICIES AND PROCEDURES

A.   *Approval of Monitoring.* The Commander of the Combatant Command with control of the detainee, or that commander's designee, shall approve any communications monitoring that may be conducted pursuant to this Order. Communications monitoring conducted pursuant to this Order shall be approved only upon a determination that such monitoring is (1) likely to produce information for security or intelligence purposes (including information related to the conduct, furtherance, facilitation, or prevention of future terrorist or other illegal acts) or (2) may prevent communications aimed at facilitating terrorist operations.

B.   *Notification to Defense Counsel.* In cases in which the Combatant Commander, or designee, determines that communications subject to this Order will be monitored, the Detailed Defense Counsel and Civilian Defense Counsel shall be notified in advance of any monitoring of their communications. The Detailed Defense Counsel and Civilian Defense Counsel may, in turn, notify the individual with whom they are communicating that their communications will be monitored.

C.   *Action Agent.* A Department of Defense intelligence collecting entity ("monitoring entity") will conduct any monitoring approved pursuant to this Order.

D.   *Review of Monitored Communications.* Monitoring entity personnel shall review any monitored communications for security and intelligence purposes as well as for purposes of assessing distribution restrictions consistent with this Order.

E.   *Prohibited Monitoring.* Communications solely between two or more defense counsel shall not be monitored.

F.   *Use and Disclosure of Monitored Communications.* Information derived from communications monitored pursuant to this Order shall not be used in proceedings against the individual who made or received the relevant communication; and such information shall not be disclosed to personnel involved in the prosecution or underlying prosecution investigation of said individual. Information related to (1) the conduct, furtherance, facilitation, or prevention of future terrorist or other illegal acts or (2) which may prevent communications aimed at facilitating terrorist operations and derived from monitored communications may be disclosed to appropriate persons other than those involved in such prosecutions.

G. *Reporting Requirements.* The monitoring entity will report promptly to the Combatant Commander, or that commander's designee, any monitored communication deemed relevant to security or intelligence (including information related to the conduct, furtherance, facilitation, or prevention of future terrorist or other illegal acts or acts harmful to the national security). If the Combatant Commander, or designee, is satisfied that a reasonable suspicion exists to believe that such communications are (1) relevant to security or intelligence (including information related to the conduct, furtherance, facilitation, or prevention of future terrorist or other illegal acts) or (2) which may prevent communications aimed at facilitating terrorist operations, he shall report promptly such information through established intelligence or law enforcement reporting channels.

5. EFFECTIVE DATE

This Order is effective immediately.

Paul D. Wolfowitz
Deputy Secretary of Defense

APPENDIX C 4

Department of Defense

Military Commission Order No. 4

January 30, 2004

SUBJECT: Designation of Deputy Appointing Authority

References: (a) Military Order of November 13, 2001, "Detention, Treatment, and Trial of Certain Non-Citizens in the War Against Terrorism," 66 F.R. 57833 (Nov. 16, 2001)

(b) Military Commission Order No. 1 (Mar. 21, 2002)

1. PURPOSE

This order assigns responsibilities under references (a) and (b) for trials before military commissions of individuals subject to the President's Military Order.

2. DESIGNATION OF DEPUTY APPOINTING AUTHORITY

Brigadier General Thomas L. Hemingway, U.S. Air Force, is designated as the Deputy Appointing Authority. This designation is in addition to the designation of Brigadier General Hemingway as the Legal Advisor to the Appointing Authority.

3. POWERS OF DEPUTY APPOINTING AUTHORITY

The Deputy Appointing Authority has full authority to exercise the authority and perform the duties of the Appointing Authority. While exercising the authority or performing the duties of the Deputy Appointing Authority or the Acting Appointing Authority, Brigadier General Hemingway will obtain legal advice from another attorney in the Office of the Legal Advisor to the Appointing Authority.

4.   EFFECTIVE DATE

This Order is effective immediately.

Paul Wolfowitz
Deputy Secretary of Defense

APPENDIX C 5

Department of Defense

Military Commission Instruction No. 1

April 30, 2003

SUBJECT: Military Commission Instructions

References: (a)   Military Commission Order No. 1 (Mar. 21, 2002)

(b)   Military Order of November 13, 2001, "Detention, Treatment, and Trial of Certain Non-Citizens in the War Against Terrorism," 66 F.R. 57833 (Nov. 16, 2001)

(c)   Section 113(d) of Title 10 of the United States Code

(d)   Section 140(b) of Title 10 of the United States Code

(e)   Section 898 of Title 10 of the United States Code

1. PURPOSE

This Instruction establishes policies for the issuance and interpretation of Military Commission Instructions promulgated pursuant to references (a) and (b).

2. AUTHORITY

This Instruction is issued pursuant to Section 7(A) of reference (a) and in accordance with references (c) and (d).

3. APPLICABILITY

This Instruction, and, unless stated otherwise, all other Military Commission Instructions apply throughout the Department of Defense, including to the Office of the Secretary of Defense, the Military Departments, the Chairman and Vice Chairman of the Joint Chiefs of Staff and the Joint Staff, the Combatant Commands, the Office of the Inspector General of the Department of Defense, the Defense Agencies, the Department of Defense Field Activities, and all other organizational entities within the Department of Defense, to any special trial counsel of the Department of Justice who may be made available by the Attorney General of the United States to serve as a prosecutor in trials before military commissions pursuant to Section 4(B)(2) of reference (a), to any civilian attorney who seeks qualification as a member of the pool of qualified Civilian Defense Counsel authorized in Section 4(C)(3)(b) of reference (a), and to any attorney who has been qualified as a member of that pool.

4. POLICIES AND PROCEDURES

A. *Promulgation.* Military Commission Instructions will be issued by the General Counsel of the Department of Defense (hereinafter General Counsel). Each Instruction will issue over the signature of the General Counsel and, unless otherwise specified therein, shall take effect upon the signature of the General Counsel. Instructions will be numbered in sequence.

B. *Professional Responsibility.* Compliance with these Instructions shall be deemed a professional responsibility obligation for the practice of law within the Department of Defense.

C. *Compliance Breaches.* Failure to adhere to these Instructions or any other failure to comply with any rule, regulation, or Instruction applicable to trials by military commission convened pursuant to references (a) and (b) may be subject to appropriate action by the Appointing Authority, the General Counsel of the Department of Defense, or the Presiding Officer of a military commission. Such action may include permanently barring an individual from participating in any military commission proceeding convened pursuant to references (a) and (b), punitive measures imposed under reference (e), and nay other lawful sanction.

5. CONSTRUCTION

Military Commission Instructions shall be construed in a manner consistent with references (a) and (b). Nothing in these Military Commission Instructions applies with respect to the trial of crimes by military commissions convened under other authority. In the event of an inconsistency, the provisions of references (a) and (b) shall govern as provided in Section 7(B) of reference (b). Pronouns referring to the male gender shall be construed as applying to both male and female.

6. NON-CREATION OF RIGHT

Neither this Instruction nor any Military Commission Instruction issued hereafter, is intended to and does not create any right, benefit, privilege, substantive or procedural, enforceable by any party, against the United States, its departments, agencies, or other entities, its officers or employees, or any other person. Alleged noncompliance with an Instruction does not, of itself, constitute error, give rise to judicial review, or establish a right to relief for the Accused or any other person

7. RESERVATION OF AUTHORITY

Neither this Instruction nor any Military Commission Instruction issued hereafter shall be construed to limit, impair, or otherwise affect any authority granted by the Constitution or laws of the United States or Department of Defense regulation or directive.

8. AMENDMENT

The General Counsel may issue, supplement, amend, or revoke any Military Commission Instruction at any time.

9. EFFECTIVE DATE

This Instruction is effective immediately.

                    William J. Haynes II
                    General Counsel of the Department of Defense

APPENDIX C 6

Department of Defense

Military Commission Instruction No. 2

April 30, 2003

SUBJECT: Crimes and Elements for Trials by Military Commission

References: (a) Military Commission Order No. 1 (Mar. 21, 2002)

(b) Military Order of November 13, 2001, "Detention, Treatment, and Trial of Certain Non-Citizens in the War Against Terrorism," 66 F.R. 57833 (Nov. 16, 2001)

(c) Section 113(d) of Title 10 of the United States Code

(d) Section 140(b) of Title 10 of the United States Code

(e) Section 821 of Title 10 of the United States Code

(f) Military Commission Instruction No. 1, current edition

1. PURPOSE

This Instruction provides guidance with respect to crimes that may be tried by military commissions established pursuant to references (a) and (b) and enumerates the elements of those crimes.

2. AUTHORITY

This Instruction is issued pursuant to Section 7(A) of reference (a) and in accordance with references (b) through (e). The provisions of reference (f) are applicable to this Instruction.

3. GENERAL

A. *Background.* The following crimes and elements thereof are intended for use by military commissions established pursuant to references (a) and (b), the jurisdiction of which extends to offenses or offenders that by statute or the law of armed conflict may be tried by military commission as limited by reference (b). No offense is cognizable in a trial by military commission if that offense did not exist prior to the conduct in question. These crimes and elements derive from the law of armed conflict, a body of law that is sometimes referred to as the law of war. They constitute violations of the law of armed conflict or offenses that, consistent with that body of law, are triable by military commission. Because this document is declarative of existing law, it does not preclude trial for crimes that occurred prior to its effective date.

B. *Effect of Other Laws.* No conclusion regarding the applicability or persuasive authority of other bodies of law should be drawn solely from the presence, absence, or similarity of particular language in this Instruction as compared to other articulations of law.

C. *Non-Exclusivity.* This Instruction does not contain a comprehensive list of crimes triable by military commission. It is intended to be illustrative of applicable principles of the common law of war but not to provide an exclusive enumeration of the punishable acts recognized as such by that law. The absence of a particular offense from the corpus of those enumerated herein does not preclude trial for that offense.

4. APPLICABLE PRINCIPLES OF LAW

A. *General Intent.* All actions taken by the Accused that are necessary for completion of a crime must be performed with general intent. This intent is not listed as a separate element. When the mens rea required for culpability to attach involves an intent that a particular consequence occur, or some other specific intent, an intent element is included. The necessary relationship between such intent element and the conduct constituting the actus reus is not articulated for each set of elements, but is presumed; a nexus between the two is necessary.

B. *The Element of Wrongfulness and Defense.* Conduct must be wrongful to constitute one of the offenses enumerated herein or any other offense triable by military commission. Conduct is wrongful if it is done without justification or excuse cognizable under applicable law. The element of wrongfulness (or the absence of lawful justification or excuse), which may be required under the customary law of armed conflict, is not repeated in the elements of crimes below. Conduct satisfying the elements found herein shall be inferred to be wrongful in the absence of evidence to the contrary. Similarly, this Instruction does not enunciate defenses that may apply for specific offenses, though an Accused is entitled to raise any defense available under the law of armed conflict. Defenses potentially available to an Accused under the law of armed conflict, such as self-defense, mistake of fact, and duress, may be applicable to certain offenses subject to trial by military commission. In the absence of evidence to the contrary, defenses in individual cases shall be presumed not to apply. The burden of going forward with evidence of lawful justification or excuse or any applicable defense shall be upon the Accused. With respect to the issue of combatant immunity raised by the specific enumeration of an element requiring the absence thereof, the prosecution must affirmatively prove that element regardless of whether the issue is raised by the defense. Once an applicable defense or an issue of lawful justification or lawful excuse is fairly raised by the evidence presented, except for the defense of lack of mental responsibility, the burden is on the prosecution to establish beyond a reasonable doubt that the conduct was wrongful or that the defense does not apply. With respect to the defense of lack of mental responsibility, the Accused has the burden of proving by clear and convincing evidence that, as a result of a severe mental disease or defect, the Accused was unable to appreciate the nature and quality of the wrongfulness of the Accused's acts. As provided in Section 5(C) of reference (a), the prosecution bears the burden of establishing the Accused's guilt beyond a reasonable doubt in all cases tried by a military commission. Each element of an offense enumerated herein must be proven beyond a reasonable doubt.

C. *Statue of Limitations.* Violations of the laws of war listed herein are not subject to any statue of limitations.

5. DEFINITIONS

A. *Combatant immunity.* Under the law of armed conflict, only a lawful combatant enjoys "combatant immunity" or "belligerent privilege" for the lawful conduct of hostilities during armed conflict.

B. *Enemy.* "Enemy" includes any entity with which the United States or allied forces may be engaged in armed conflict, or which is preparing to attack the United States. It is not limited to foreign nations, or foreign military organizations or members thereof. "Enemy" specifically includes any organization of terrorists with international reach.

C. *In the context of and was associated with armed conflict.* Elements containing this language require a nexus between the conduct and armed hostilities. Such nexus could involve, but is not limited to, time, location, or purpose of the conduct in relation to the armed hostilities. The existence of such factors, however, may not satisfy the necessary nexus (e.g., murder committed between members of the same armed force for reasons of personal gain unrelated to the conflict, even if temporally and geographically associated with armed conflict, is not "in the context of" the armed conflict). The focus of this element is not the nature or characterization of the conflict, but the nexus to it. This element does not require a declaration of war, ongoing mutual hostilities, or confrontation involving a regular national armed force. A single hostile act or attempted act may provide sufficient basis for the nexus so long as its magnitude or severity rises to the level of an "armed attack" or an "act of war," or the number, power, stated intent or organization of the force with which the actor is associated is such that the act or attempted act is tantamount to an attack by an armed force. Similarly, conduct undertaken or organized with knowledge or intent that it initiate or contribute to such hostile act or hostilities would satisfy the nexus requirement.

D. *Military objective.* "Military objectives" are those potential targets during an armed conflict which, by their nature, location, purpose, or use, effectively contribute to the opposing force's war-fighting or war-sustaining capability and whose total or partial destruction, capture, or neutralization would constitute a military advantage to the attacker under the circumstances at the time of the attack.

E. *Object of the attack.* "Object of the attack" refers to the person, place, or thing intentionally targeted. In this regard, the term includes neither collateral damage nor incidental injury or death.

F. *Protected property.* "Protected property" refers to property specifically protected by the law of armed conflict such as buildings dedicated to religion, education, art, science or charitable purposes, historic monuments, hospitals, or places where the sick and wounded are collected, provided they are not being used for military purposes or are not otherwise military objectives. Such property would include objects properly identified by one of the distinctive emblems of the Geneva Conventions but does not include all civilian property.

G. *Protected under the law of war.* The person or object in question is expressly "protected" under one or more of the Geneva Conventions of 1949 or, to the extent applicable, customary international law. The term does not refer to all who enjoy some form of protection as a consequence of compliance with international law, but those who are expressly designated as such by the applicable law of armed conflict. For example, persons who either are *hors de combat* or medical or religious personnel taking no active part in hostilities are expressly protected, but other civilians may not be.

H. *Should have known.* The facts and circumstances were such that a reasonable person in the Accused's position would have had the relevant knowledge or awareness.

6. CRIMES AND ELEMENTS

A. *Substantive Offenses—War Crimes.* The following enumerated offenses, if applicable, should be charged in separate counts. Elements are drafted to reflect conduct of the perpetrator. Each element need not be specifically charged.

1) Willful Killing of Protected Persons

a. *Elements.*

(1) The accused killed one or more persons;

(2) The accused intended to kill such person or persons;

(3) Such person or persons were protected under the law of war;

(4) The accused knew or should have known of the factual circumstances that established that protected status; and

(5) The killing took place in the context of and was associated with armed conflict.

b. *Comments.*

(1) The intent required for this offense precludes its applicability with regard to collateral damage or injury incident to a lawful attack.

2) Attacking Civilians

a. *Elements.*

(1) The accused engaged in an attack;

(2) The object of the attack was a civilian population as such or individual civilians not taking direct or active part in hostilities;

(3) The accused intended the civilian population as such or individual civilians not taking direct or active part in hostilities to be an object of the attack; and

(4) The attack took place in the context of and was associated with armed conflict.

b. *Comments*

(1) The intent required for this offense precludes its applicability with regard to collateral damage or injury incident to a lawful attack.

3) Attacking Civilian Objects

a. *Elements.*

(1) The accused engaged in an attack;

(2) The object of the attack was civilian property, that is, property that was not a military objective;

(3) The accused intended such property to be an object of the attack;

(4) The accused knew or should have known that such property was not a military objective; and

(5) The attack took place in the context of and was associated with armed conflict.

b. *Comments.*

(1) The intent required for this offense precludes its applicability with regard to collateral damage or injury incident to a lawful attack.

4) Attacking Protected Property

a. *Elements.*

(1) The accused engaged in an attack;

(2) The object of the attack was protected property;

(3) The accused intended such property to be an object of the attack;

(4) The accused knew or should have known of the factual circumstances that established that protected status; and

(5) The attack took place in the context of and was associated with armed conflict.

b. *Comments.*

(1) The intent required for this offense precludes its applicability with regard to collateral damage or injury incident to a lawful attack.

5) Pillaging

a. *Elements.*

(1) The accused appropriated or seized certain property;

(2) The accused intended to appropriate or seize such property for private or personal use;

(3) The appropriation or seizure was without the consent of the owner of the property or other person with authority to permit such appropriation or seizure; and

(4) The appropriation or seizure took place in the context of and was associated with armed conflict.

b. *Comments.*

(1) As indicated by the use of the term "private or personal use," legitimate captures or appropriations, or seizures justified by military necessity, cannot constitute the crime of pillaging.

6) Denying Quarter

a. *Elements.*

(1) The accused declared, ordered, or otherwise indicated that there shall be no survivors or surrender accepted;

(2) The accused thereby intended to threaten an adversary or to conduct hostilities such that there would be no survivors or surrender accepted;

(3) It was foreseeable that circumstances would be such that a practicable and reasonable ability to accept surrender would exist;

(4) The accused was in a position of effective command or control over the subordinate forces to which the declaration or order was directed; and

(5) The conduct took place in the context of and was associated with armed conflict.

b. *Comments.*

(1) Element (3) precludes this offense from being interpreted as limiting the application of lawful means or methods of warfare against enemy combatants. For example, a remotely delivered attack cannot give rise to this offense.

7) Taking Hostages

a. *Elements.*

(1) The accused seized, detained, or otherwise held hostage one or more persons;

(2) The accused threatened to kill, injure, or continue to detain such person or persons;

(3) The accused intended to compel a State, an international organization, a natural or legal person, or a group of persons to act or refrain from acting as an explicit or implicit condition for the safety or release of such person or persons; and

(4) The conduct took place in the context of and was associated with armed conflict.

b. *Comments.*

(1) Consistent with Section 4(B) of this Instruction, this offense cannot be committed by lawfully detaining enemy

combatants or other individuals as authorized by the law of armed conflict.

8) Employing Poison or Analogous Weapons

a. *Elements.*

(1) The accused employed a substance or a weapon that releases a substance as a result of its employment;

(2) The substance was such that exposure thereto causes death or serious damage to health in the ordinary course of events, through its asphyxiating, poisonous, or bacteriological properties;

(3) The accused employed the substance or weapon with the intent of utilizing such asphyxiating, poisonous, or bacteriological properties as a method of warfare;

(4) The accused knew or should have known of the nature of the substance or weapon; and

(5) The conduct took place in the context of and was associated with armed conflict.

b. *Comments.*

(1) The "death or serious damage to health" required by Element (2) of this offense must be a direct result of the substance's effect or effects on the human body (e.g., asphyxiation caused by the depletion of atmospheric oxygen secondary to a chemical or other reaction would not give rise to this offense).

(2) The clause "serious damage to health" does not include temporary incapacitation or sensory irritation.

(3) The use of the "substance or weapon" at issue must be proscribed under the law of armed conflict. It may include chemical or biological agents.

(4) The specific intent element for this offense precludes liability for mere knowledge of potential collateral consequences (e.g., mere knowledge of a secondary

asphyxiating or toxic effect would be insufficient to complete the offense).

9) Using Protected Persons as Shields

a. *Elements.*

(1) The accused positioned, or took advantage of the location of, one or more civilians or persons protected under the law of war;

(2) The accused intended to use the civilian or protected nature of the person or persons to shield a military objective from attack or to shield, favor, or impede military operations; and

(3) The conduct took place in the context of and was associated with armed conflict.

10) Using Protected Property as Shields

a. *Elements.*

(1) The accused positioned, or took advantage of the location of, civilian property or property protected under the law of war;

(2) The accused intended to shield a military objective from attack or to shield, favor, or impede military operations; and

(3) The conduct took place in the context of and was associated with armed conflict.

11) Torture

a. *Elements.*

(1) The accused inflicted severe physical or mental pain or suffering upon one or more persons;

(2) The accused intended to inflict such severe physical or mental pain or suffering;

(3) Such person or persons were in the custody or under the control of the accused; and

(4) The conduct took place in the context of and was associated with armed conflict.

b. *Comments.*

(1) Consistent with Section 4(B) of this Instruction, this offense does not include pain or suffering arising only from, inherent in, or incidental to, lawfully imposed punishments. This offense does not include the incidental infliction or pain or suffering associated with the legitimate conduct of hostilities.

(2) Severe "mental pain or suffering" is the prolonged mental harm caused by or resulting from:

(a) the intentional infliction or threatened infliction of severe physical pain or suffering;

(b) the administration or application, or threatened administration or application, or mind-altering substances or other procedures calculated to disrupt profoundly the senses or the personality;

(c) the threat of imminent death; or

(d) the threat that another person will imminently be subjected to death, severe physical pain or suffering, or the administration or application of mind-altering substances or other procedures calculated to disrupt profoundly the senses or personality.

(3) "Prolonged mental harm" is a harm of some sustained duration, though not necessarily permanent in nature, such as a clinically identifiable mental disorder.

(4) Element (3) of this offense does not require a particular formal relationship between the accused and the victim. Rather, it precludes prosecution for pain or suffering consequent to a lawful military attack.

12) Causing Serious Injury

a) *Elements.*

(1) The accused caused serious injury to the body or health of one or more persons;

(2) The accused intended to inflict such serious injury;

(3) Such person or persons were in the custody or under the control of the accused; and

(4) The conduct took place in the context of and was associated with armed conflict.

b) *Comments.*

(1) "Serious injury" includes fractured or dislocated bones, deep cuts, torn members of the body, and serious damage to internal organs.

13) Mutilation or Maiming

a) *Elements.*

(1) The accused subjected one or more persons to mutilation, in particular by permanently disfiguring the person or persons, or by permanently disabling or removing an organ or appendage;

(2) The accused intended to subject such person or persons to such mutilation;

(3) The conduct caused death or seriously damaged or endangered the physical or mental health or appearance of such person or persons.

(4) The conduct was neither justified by the medical treatment of the person or persons concerned nor carried out in the interest of such person or persons;

(5) Such person or persons were in the custody or control of the accused; and

(6) The conduct took place in the context of and was associated with armed conflict.

14) Use of Treachery or Perfidy

a. *Elements.*

(1) The accused invited the confidence or belief of one or more persons that they were entitled to, or were obliged to accord, protection under the law of war;

(2) The accused intended to betray that confidence or belief;

(3) The accused killed, injured, or captured one or more persons;

(4) The accused made use of that confidence or belief in killing, injuring, or capturing such person or persons; and

(5) The conduct took place in the context of and was associated with armed conflict.

15) Improper Use of Flag of Truce

a. *Elements.*

(1) The accused used a flag of truce;

(2) The accused made such use in order to feign an intention to negotiate, surrender, or otherwise to suspend hostilities when there was no such intention on the part of the accused; and

(3) The conduct took place in the context of and was associated with armed conflict.

16) Improper Use of Protective Emblems

a. *Elements.*

(1) The accused used a protective emblem recognized by the law of armed conflict;

(2) The accused undertook such use for combatant purposes in a manner prohibited by the law of armed conflict;

(3) The accused knew or should have known of the prohibited nature of such use; and

(4) The conduct took place in the context of and was associated with armed conflict.

b. *Comments.*

(1) "Combatant purposes," as used in Element (2) of this offense, means purposes directly related to hostilities and does not include medical, religious, or similar activities.

17) Degrading Treatment of a Dead Body

a. *Elements.*

(1) The accused degraded or otherwise violated the dignity of the body of a dead person;

(2) The accused intended to degrade or otherwise violate the dignity of such body;

(3) The severity of the degradation or other violation was of such degree as to be generally recognized as an outrage upon personal dignity; and

(4) The conduct took place in the context of and was associated with armed conflict.

b. *Comments.*

(1) Element (2) of this offense precludes prosecution for actions justified by military necessity.

18) Rape

a. *Elements.*

(1) The accused invaded the body of a person by conduct resulting in penetration, however slight, or any part of the body of the victim or of the accused with a sexual organ, or of the anal or genital opening of the victim with any object or any other part of the body;

(2) The invasion was committed by force, threat of force or coercion, or was committed against a person incapable of giving consent; and

(3) The conduct took place in the context of and was associated with armed conflict.

b. *Comments.*

(1) Element (2) of this offense recognizes that consensual conduct does not give rise to this offense.

(2) It is understood that a person may be incapable of giving consent if affected by natural, induced, or age-related incapacity.

(3) The concept of "invasion" is linked to the inherent wrongfulness requirement for all offenses. In this case, for example, a legitimate body cavity search could not give rise to this offense.

(4) The concept of "invasion" is gender neutral.

B. *Substantive Offenses—Other Offenses Triable by Military Commission.* The following enumerated offenses, if applicable, should be charged in separate counts. Elements are drafted to reflect conduct of the perpetrator. Each element need not be specifically charged.

1) **Hijacking or Hazarding a Vessel or Aircraft**

a. *Elements.*

(1) The accused seized, exercised control over, or endangered the safe navigation of a vessel or aircraft;

(2) The accused intended to so seize, exercise control over, or endanger such vessel or aircraft; and

(3) The conduct took place in the context of and was associated with armed conflict.

b. *Comments.*

(1) A seizure, exercise of control, or endangerment required by military necessity, or against a lawful military objective

undertaken by military forces of a State in the exercise of their official duties, would not satisfy the wrongfulness requirement for this crime.

2) Terrorism

a. *Elements.*

(1) The accused killed or inflicted bodily harm on one or more persons or destroyed property;

(2) The accused:

    (a) intended to kill or inflict bodily harm on one or more persons;

or

    (b) intentionally engaged in an act that is inherently dangerous to another and evinces a wanton disregard of human life;

(3) The killing, harm or destruction was intended to intimidate or coerce a civilian population, or to influence the policy of a government by intimidation or coercion; and

(4) The killing, harm or destruction took place in the context of and was associated with armed conflict.

b. *Comments.*

(1) Element (1) of this offense includes the concept of causing death or bodily harm, even if indirectly.

(2) The requirement that the conduct be wrongful for this crime necessitates that the conduct establishing this offense not constitute an attack against a lawful military objective undertaken by military forces of a State in the exercise of their official duties.

3) Murder by an Unprivileged Belligerent

a. Elements.

(1) The accused killed one or more persons;

(2) The accused:

    (a) intended to kill or inflict great bodily harm on such person or persons

        or

    (b) intentionally engaged in an act that is inherently dangerous to another and evinces a wanton disregard of human life;

(3) The accused did not enjoy combatant immunity; and

(4) The killing took place in the context of and was associated with armed conflict.

  b. *Comments*

(1) The term "kill" includes intentionally causing death, whether directly or indirectly.

(2) Unlike the crimes of willful killing or attacking civilians, in which the victim's status is a prerequisite to criminality, for this offense the victim's status is immaterial. Even an attack on a soldier would be a crime if the attacker did not enjoy "belligerent privilege" or "combatant immunity."

4) Destruction of Property by an Unprivileged Belligerent

  a. *Elements.*

(1) The accused destroyed property;

(2) The property belonged to another person, and the destruction was without that person's consent;

(3) The accused intended to destroy such property;

(4) The accused did not enjoy combatant immunity; and

(5) The destruction took place in the context of and was associated with armed conflict.

5) Aiding the Enemy

a. Elements.

(1) The accused aided the enemy;

(2) The accused intended to aid the enemy; and

(3) The conduct took place in the context of and was associated with armed conflict.

b. *Comments.*

(1) Means of accomplishing Element (1) of this offense include, but are not limited to: providing arms, ammunition, supplies, money, other items or services to the enemy; harboring or protecting the enemy; or giving intelligence or other information to the enemy.

(2) The requirement that conduct be wrongful for this crime necessitates that the accused act without proper authority. For example, furnishing enemy combatants detained during hostilities with subsistence or quarters in accordance with applicable orders or policy is not aiding the enemy.

(3) The requirement that conduct be wrongful for this crime may necessitate that, in the case of a lawful belligerent, the accused owe allegiance or some duty to the United States of America or to an ally or coalition partner. For example, citizenship, resident alien status, or a contractual relationship in or with the United States or an ally or coalition partner is sufficient to satisfy this requirement so long as the relationship existed at the time relevant to the offense alleged.

6) Spying

a. *Elements.*

(1) The accused collected or attempted to collect certain information;

(2) The accused intended to convey such information to the enemy;

(3) The accused, in collecting or attempting to collect the information, was lurking or acting clandestinely, while acting under false pretenses; and

(4) The conduct took place in the context of and was associated with armed conflict.

b. *Comments.*

(1) Members of a military organization not wearing a disguise and others who carry out their missions openly are not spies, if, though they may have resorted to concealment, they have not acted under false pretenses.

(2) Related to the requirement that conduct be wrongful or without justification or excuse in this case is the fact that, consistent with the law of war, a lawful combatant who, after rejoining the armed force to which that combatant belongs, is subsequently captured, can not be punished for previous acts of espionage. His successful rejoining of his armed force constitutes a defense.

7)   Perjury or False Testimony

a. *Elements.*

(1) The accused testified at a military commission, in proceedings ancillary to a military commission, or provided information in a writing executed under an oath to tell the truth or a declaration acknowledging the applicability of penalties of perjury in connection with such proceedings;

(2) Such testimony or information was material;

(3) Such testimony or information was false; and

(4) The accused knew such testimony or information to be false.

8)   Obstruction of Justice Related to Military Commissions

a. *Elements.*

(1) The accused did an act;

(2) The accused intended to influence, impede, or otherwise obstruct the due administration of justice; and

(3) The accused did such act in the case of a certain person against whom the accused had reason to believe:

(a) there were or would be proceedings before a military commission.

or

(b) there was an ongoing investigation of offenses triable by military commission.

C. *Other Forms of Liability and Related Offenses.* A person is criminally liable as a principal for a completed substantive offense if that person commits the offense (perpetrator), aids or abets the commission of the offense, solicits commission of the offense, or is otherwise responsible due to command responsibility. Such a person would be charged as a principal even if another individual more directly perpetrated the offense. In proving culpability, however, the below listed definitions and elements are applicable. Additionally, if a substantive offense was completed, a person may be criminally liable for the separate offense of accessory after the fact. If the substantive offense was not completed, a person may be criminally liable of the lesser-included offense of attempt or the separate offense of solicitation. Finally, regardless of whether the substantive offense was completed, a person may be criminally liable of the separate offense of conspiracy in addition to the substantive offense. Each element need not be specifically charged.

1)   Aiding or Abetting

a. *Elements.*

(1) The accused committed an act that aided or abetted another person or entity in the commission of a substantive offense triable by military commission;

(2) Such other person or entity committed or attempted to commit the substantive offense; and

(3) The accused intended to or knew that the act would aid or abet such other person or entity in the commission of the substantive offense or an associated criminal purpose or enterprise.

b. *Comments.*

(1) The term "aided or abetted" in Element (1) includes: assisting, encouraging, advising, instigating, counseling, ordering, or procuring another to commit a substantive offense; assisting, encouraging, advising, counseling, or ordering another in the commission of a substantive offense; and in any other way facilitating the commission of a substantive offense.

(2) In some circumstances, inaction may render one liable as an aider or abettor. If a person has legal duty to prevent or thwart the commission of a substantive offense, but does not do so, that person may be considered to have aided or abetted the commission of the offense if such noninterference is intended to and does operate as an aid or encouragement to the actual perpetrator.

(3) An accused charged with aiding or abetting should be charged with the related substantive offense as a principal.

2) Solicitation

a. *Elements.*

(1) The accused solicited, ordered, induced, or advised a certain person or persons to commit one or more substantive offenses triable by military commission; and

(2) The accused intended that the offense actually be committed.

b. *Comments.*

(1) The offense is complete when a solicitation is made or advice is given with the specific wrongful intent to induce a person or persons to commit any offense triable by military commission. It is not necessary that the person or persons solicited, ordered, induced, advised, or assisted agree to or act upon the solicitation or advice. If the offense solicited is actually committed, however, the accused is liable under the law of armed conflict for the substantive offense. An accused should not be convicted of both solicitation and the

268

substantive offense solicited if criminal liability for the substantive offense is based upon the solicitation.

(2) Solicitation may be by means other than speech or writing. Any act or conduct that reasonably may be construed as a serious request, order, inducement, advice, or offer of assistance to commit any offense triable by military commission may constitute solicitation. It is not necessary that the accused act alone in the solicitation, order, inducement, advising, or assistance. The accused may act through other persons in committing this offense.

(3) An accused charged with solicitation of a completed substantive offense should be charged for the substantive offense as a principal. An accused charged with solicitation of an uncompleted offense should be charged for the separate offense of solicitation. Solicitation is not a lesser-included offense of the related substantive offense.

3)   Command/Superior Responsibility – Perpetrating

a. *Elements.*

(1) The accused had command and control, or effective authority and control, over one or more subordinates;

(2) One or more of the accused's subordinates committed, attempted to commit, conspired to commit, solicited to commit, or aided or abetted the commission of one or more substantive offenses triable by military commission;

(3) The accused either knew or should have known that the subordinate or subordinates were committing, attempting to commit, conspiring to commit, soliciting, or aiding or abetting such offense or offenses; and

(4) The accused failed to take all necessary and reasonable measures within his power to prevent or repress the commission of the offense or offenses.

b. *Comments.*

(1) The phrase "effective authority and control" in Element (1) of this offense includes the concept of relative authority over the subject matter or activities associated with the

perpetrator's conduct. This may be relevant to a civilian superior who should not be held responsible for the behavior of subordinates involved in activities that have no relationship to such superior's sphere of authority. Subject matter authority need not be demonstrated for command responsibility as it applies to a military commander.

(2) A commander or other military or civilian superior, not in command, charged with failing adequately to prevent or repress a substantive offense triable by military commission should be charged for the related substantive offense as a principal.

4) **Command/Superior Responsibility – Misprision**

a. *Elements.*

(1) The accused had command and control, or effective authority and control, over one or more subordinates;

(2) One or more of the accused's subordinates had committed, attempted to commit, conspired to commit, solicited to commit, or aided or abetted the commission of one or more substantive offenses triable by military commissions;

(3) The accused knew or should have known that the subordinate or subordinates had committed, attempted to commit, conspired to commit, solicited, or aided or abetted such offense or offenses; and

(4) The accused failed to submit the matter to competent authorities for investigation or prosecution as appropriate.

b. *Comments.*

(1) The phrase, "effective authority and control" in Element (1) of this offense includes the concept of relative authority over the subject matter or activities associated with the perpetrator's conduct. This may be relevant to a civilian superior who cannot be held responsible under this offense for the behavior of subordinates involved in activities that have nothing to do with such superior's sphere of authority.

(2) A commander or superior charged with failing to take appropriate punitive or investigative action subsequent to

the perpetration of a substantive offense triable by military commission should not be charged for the substantive offense as a principal. Such commander or superior should be charged for the separate offense of failing to submit the matter for investigation and/or prosecution as detailed in these elements. This offense is not a lesser-included offense of the related substantive offense.

5)   Accessory After the Fact

a. *Elements.*

(1) The accused received, comforted, or assisted a certain person;

(2) Such person had committed an offense triable by military commission;

(3) The accused knew that such person had committed such offense or believed such person had committed a similar or closely related offense; and

(4) The accused intended to hinder or prevent the apprehension, trial, or punishment of such person.

b. *Comments.*

(1) Accessory after the fact should be charged separately from the related substantive offense. It is not a lesser-included offense of the related substantive offense.

6)   Conspiracy

a. *Elements.*

(1) The accused entered into an agreement with one or more persons to commit one or more substantive offenses triable by military commission or otherwise joined an enterprise of persons who shared a common criminal purpose that involved, at least in part, the commission or intended commission of one or more substantive offenses triable by military commission;

(2) The accused knew the unlawful purpose of the agreement or the common criminal purpose of the enterprise and joined in it willfully, that is, with the intent to further the unlawful purpose; and

(3) One of the conspirators or enterprise members, during the existence of the agreement or enterprise, knowingly committed an overt act in order to accomplish some objective or purpose of the agreement or enterprise.

b. *Comments.*

(1) Two or more persons are required in order to have a conspiracy. Knowledge of the identity of co-conspirators and their particular connection with the agreement or enterprise need not be established. A person may be guilty of conspiracy although incapable of committing the intended offense. The joining of another conspirator after the conspiracy has been established does not create a new conspiracy or affect the status of the other conspirators. The agreement or common criminal purpose in a conspiracy need not be in a particular form or manifested in any formal words.

(2) The agreement or enterprise must, at least in part, involve the commission or intended commission of one or more substantive offenses triable by military commission. A single conspiracy may embrace multiple criminal objectives. The agreement need not include knowledge that any relevant offense is in fact "triable by military commission."

(3) The overt act must be done by one or more of the conspirators, but not necessarily the accused, and it must be done to effectuate the object of the conspiracy or in furtherance of the common criminal purpose. The accused need not have entered the agreement or criminal enterprise at the time of the overt act.

(4) The overt act need not be in itself criminal, but it must advance the purpose of the conspiracy. It is not essential that any substantive offense be committed.

(5) Each conspirator is liable for all offenses committed pursuant to or in furtherance of the conspiracy by any of

the co-conspirators, after such conspirator has joined the conspiracy and while the conspiracy continues and such conspirator remains a party to it.

(6) A party to the conspiracy who withdraws from or abandons the agreement or enterprise before the commission of an overt act by any conspirator is not guilty of conspiracy. An effective withdrawal or abandonment must consist of affirmative conduct that is wholly inconsistent with adherence to the unlawful agreement or common criminal purpose and that shows that the party has severed all connection with the conspiracy. A conspirator who effectively withdraws from or abandons the conspiracy after the performance of an overt act by one of the conspirators remains guilty of conspiracy and of any offenses committed pursuant to the conspiracy up to the time of the withdrawal or abandonment. The withdrawal of a conspirator from the conspiracy does not affect the status of the remaining members.

(7) That the object of the conspiracy was impossible to effect is not a defense to this offense.

(8) Conspiracy to commit an offense is a separate and distinct offense from any offense committed pursuant to or in furtherance of the conspiracy, and both the conspiracy and any related offense may be charged, tried, and punished separately. Conspiracy should be charged separately from the related substantive offense. It is not a lesser-included offense of the substantive offense.

. 7) **Attempts**

a. *Elements.*

(1) The accused committed an act;

(2) The accused intended to commit one or more substantive offenses triable by military commission;

(3) The act amounted to more than mere preparation; and

(4) The act apparently tended to effect the commission of the intended offense.

b. *Comments.*

(1) To constitute an attempt there must be a specific intent to commit the offense accompanied by an act that tends to accomplish the unlawful purpose. This intent need not involve knowledge that the offense is in fact "triable by military commission."

(2) Preparation consists of devising or arranging means or measures apparently necessary for the commission of the offense. The act need not be the last act essential to the consummation of the offense. The combination of specific intent to commit an offense, plus the commission of an act apparently tending to further its accomplishment, constitutes the offense of attempt. Failure to complete the offense, whatever the cause, is not a defense.

(3) A person who purposely engages in conduct that would constitute the offense if the attendant circumstances were as that person believed them to be is guilty of an attempt.

(4) It is a defense to an attempt offense that the person voluntarily and completely abandoned the intended offense, solely because of the person's own sense that it was wrong, prior to the completion of the substantive offense. The voluntary abandonment defense is not allowed if the abandonment results, in whole or in part, from other reasons, for example, the person feared detection or apprehension, decided to await a better opportunity for success, was unable to complete the crime, or encountered unanticipated difficulties or unexpected resistance.

(5) Attempt is a lesser-included offense of any substantive offense triable by military commission and need not be charged separately. An accused may be charge with attempt without being charge with the substantive offense.

7. EFFECTIVE DATE

This Instruction is effective immediately.

William J. Haynes II
General Counsel of the Department of Defense

APPENDIX C 7

Department of Defense

Military Commission Instruction No. 3

April 30, 2003

SUBJECT: Responsibilities of the Chief Prosecutor, Prosecutors, and Assistant Prosecutors

References: (a) Military Commission Order No. 1 (Mar. 21, 2002)

(b) Military Order of November 13, 2001, "Detention, Treatment, and Trial of Certain Non-Citizens in the War Against Terrorism," 66 F.R. 57833 (Nov. 16, 2001)

(c) Section 113(d) of Title 10 of the United States Code

(d) Section 140(b) of Title 10 of the United States Code

(e) Military Commission Instruction No. 1, current edition

(f) DoD Directive 5122.5, "Assistant Secretary of Defense for Public Affairs," current edition

1. PURPOSE

This Instruction establishes the responsibilities of the Office of the Chief Prosecutor and components thereof.

2. AUTHORITY

This Instruction is issued pursuant to Section 7(A) of reference (a) and in accordance with references (b), (c), and (d). The provisions of reference (e) are applicable to this Instruction.

3. OFFICE OF THE CHIEF PROSECUTOR

A. *General.* The Office of the Chief Prosecutor shall be a component of the Office of Military Commissions and shall be comprised of the

Chief Prosecutor, Prosecutors, and other persons properly under the supervision of the Chief Prosecutor.

B. *Chief Prosecutor.*

1) The Chief Prosecutor shall be a judge advocate of any United States armed force and shall be designated by the General Counsel of the Department of Defense.

2) The Chief Prosecutor shall report directly to the Deputy General Counsel (Legal Counsel) of the Department of Defense.

3) The Chief Prosecutor shall have authority to subpoena any individual to appear as a witness, to testify, or to produce any evidence in a case referred to military commissions or in a criminal investigation associated with a case that may be referred to a military commission.

4) The Chief Prosecutor shall direct the overall prosecution effort pursuant to references (a) and (b), ensuring proper supervision and management of all personnel and resources assigned to the Office of the Chief Prosecutor.

5) The Chief Prosecutor shall ensure that all personnel assigned to the Office of the Chief Prosecutor review, and attest that they understand and will comply with, references (a) and (b) and all Supplementary Regulations and Instructions issued in accordance therewith.

6) The Chief Prosecutor shall inform the Deputy General Counsel (Legal Counsel) of all requirements for personnel, office space, equipment, and supplies to ensure the successful functioning and mission accomplishment of the Office of the Chief Prosecutor.

7) The Chief Prosecutor shall supervise all Prosecutors and other personnel assigned to the Office of the Chief Prosecutor including any special trial counsel of the Department of Justice who may be made available by the Attorney General of the United States.

8) The Chief Prosecutor, or his designee, shall fulfill applicable performance evaluation requirements associated with

Prosecutors and other personnel properly under the supervision of the Office of the Chief Prosecutor.

9) The Chief Prosecutor shall detail a Prosecutor and, as appropriate, one or more Assistant Prosecutors to perform the duties of the prosecution as set forth in Section 4(B)(2) of reference (a). The Chief Prosecutor may detail himself to perform such duties.

10) The Chief Prosecutor shall ensure that all Prosecutors and Assistant Prosecutors faithfully represent the United States in discharging their prosecutorial duties before military commissions conducted pursuant to references (a) and (b).

11) The Chief Prosecutor shall ensure that all Prosecutors and Assistant Prosecutors have taken an oath to perform their duties faithfully.

12) The Chief Prosecutor shall ensure that all personnel properly under the supervision of the Office of the Chief Prosecutor possess the appropriate security clearances.

C. *Prosecutors.*

1) Prosecutors shall be detailed by the Chief Prosecutor and may be either judge advocates of any United States armed force or special trial counsel of the Department of Justice who may be made available by the Attorney General of the United States.

2) Prosecutors shall represent the United States as Prosecutors or Assistant Prosecutors as directed by the Chief Prosecutor and in accordance with references (a) and (b).

3) Prosecutors shall fulfill all responsibilities detailed in references (a) and (b), those set forth in this Instruction, and those assigned by the Chief Prosecutor.

4) Prosecutors shall ensure that all court reporters, security personnel, and interpreters who are to perform duties in relation to a military commission proceeding have taken an oath to perform their duties faithfully. As directed by the Presiding Officer, Prosecutors also shall administer appropriate oaths to witnesses during military commission proceedings.

4. DUTIES AND RESPONSIBILITIES OF THE PROSECUTION

A. *Regular Duties.* The Prosecution shall perform all duties specified or implied in reference (a) as responsibilities of the Prosecution.

B. *Administrative Duties.* The Prosecution shall, as directed by the Presiding Officer or the Appointing Authority, prepare any documentation necessary to facilitate the conduct of military commissions proceedings. The Prosecution shall, as directed by the Deputy General Counsel (Legal Counsel), prepare a trial guide to provide a standardized administrative plan for the conduct of military commission proceedings. Unless directed otherwise by the Appointing Authority, the Presiding Officer may, in his discretion, depart from this guide as appropriate.

C. *Special Duties.* The Prosecution shall perform all other functions, consistent with references (a) and (b), as may be directed by the Appointing Authority or the General Counsel of the Department of Defense.

5. POLICIES

A. *Prohibition on Prosecutors Serving as Defense Counsel.* Judge advocates assigned to the Office of the Chief Prosecutor shall be deemed unavailable for service as Defense Counsel under section 4(C)(3)(a) of reference (a).

B. *Prohibition on Certain Disclosures.* All Prosecutors must strictly comply with section 6(D)(5) and section 9 of reference (a) to ensure they do not improperly disclose classified information, national security information, or state secrets to any person not specifically authorized to receive such information.

C. *Statements To The Media.* Consistent with reference (f), the Assistant Secretary of Defense for Public Affairs shall serve as the sole release authority for DoD information and audiovisual materials regarding military commissions. Personnel assigned to the Office of the Chief Prosecutor may communicate with news media representatives regarding cases and other matters related to military commissions only when approved by the Appointing Authority or the General Counsel of the Department of Defense.

6. EFFECTIVE DATE

This Instruction is effective immediately.

William J. Haynes II
General Counsel of the Department of Defense

APPENDIX C 8

Department of Defense

Military Commission Instruction No. 4

April 30, 2003

SUBJECT: Responsibilities of the Chief Defense Counsel, Detailed Defense
Counsel, and Civilian Defense Counsel.

References: (a) Military Commission Order No. 1 (Mar. 21, 2002)

(b) Military Order of November 13, 2001, "Detention, Treatment,
and Trial of Certain Non-Citizens in the War Against
Terrorism," 66 F.R. 57833 (Nov. 16, 2001)

(c) Section 113(d) of Title 10 of the United States Code

(d) Section 140(b) of Title 10 of the United States Code

(e) Military Commission Instruction No. 1, current edition

(f) DoD Directive 5122.5 "Assistant Secretary of Defense for
Public Affairs," current edition.

1. PURPOSE

This Instruction establishes the responsibilities of the Office of Chief Defense
Counsel and components thereof.

2. AUTHORITY

This Instruction is issued pursuant to Section 7(A) of reference (a) and in
accordance with references (b), (c) and (d). The provisions of reference (e) are
applicable to this Instruction.

3. OFFICE OF THE CHIEF DEFENSE COUNSEL

A. *General.* The Office of the Chief Defense Counsel shall be a component of the Office of Military Commissions and shall be comprised of the Chief Defense Counsel, Defense Counsel, and other such persons properly under the supervision of the Chief Defense Counsel.

B. *Chief Defense Counsel*

1) The Chief Defense Counsel shall be a judge advocate of any United States armed force and shall be designated by the General Counsel of the Department of Defense.

2) The Chief Defense Counsel shall report directly to the Deputy General Counsel (Personnel and Health Policy) of the Department of Defense.

3) The Chief Defense Counsel shall supervise all defense activities and the efforts of Detailed Defense Counsel and other office personnel and resources pursuant to references (a) and (b), ensuring proper supervision and management of all personnel and resources assigned to the Office of the Chief Defense Counsel and facilitating the proper representation of all Accused referred to trial before a military commission appointed pursuant to references (a) and (b).

4) The Chief Defense Counsel shall ensure that all personnel assigned to the Office of the Chief Defense Counsel review, and attest that they understand and will comply with, references (a) and (b) and all Supplementary Regulations and Instructions issued in accordance therewith. Furthermore, the Chief Defense Counsel shall regulate the conduct of Detailed Defense Counsel as deemed necessary, consistent with references (a) and (b) and subordinate instructions and regulations, and specifically shall ensure that Detailed Defense Counsel have been directed to conduct their activities consistent with applicable prescriptions and proscriptions specified in Section II of the Affidavit And Agreement By Civilian Defense Counsel at Annex B. to Military Commission Instruction No. 5.

5) The Chief Defense Counsel shall inform the Deputy General Counsel (Personnel and Health Policy) of the Department of Defense of all requirements for personnel, office space, equipment, and supplies to ensure the successful functioning and mission accomplishment of the Office of the Chief Defense Counsel.

6) The Chief Defense Counsel shall supervise all Defense Counsel and other personnel assigned to the Office of the Chief Defense Counsel.

7) The Chief Defense Counsel, or his designee, shall fulfill applicable performance evaluation requirements associated with Defense Counsel and other personnel properly under the supervision of the Chief Defense Counsel.

8) The Chief Defense Counsel shall detail a judge advocate of any United States armed force to perform the duties of the Detailed Defense Counsel as set forth in Section 4(C)(2) of reference (a) and shall detail or employ any other personnel as directed by the Appointing Authority or the Presiding Officer in a particular case. The Chief Defense Counsel may not detail himself to perform the duties of Detailed Defense Counsel, nor does he form an attorney-client relationship with accused persons or incur any concomitant confidentiality obligations.

    a. The Chief Defense Counsel may, when appropriate, detail an additional judge advocate as Assistant Detailed Defense Counsel to assist in performing the duties of the Detailed Defense Counsel.

    b. The Chief Defense Counsel may structure the Office of the Chief Defense Counsel so as to include subordinate supervising attorneys who may incur confidentiality obligations in the context of fulfilling their supervisory responsibilities with regard to Detailed Defense Counsel.

9) The Chief Defense Counsel shall take appropriate measures to preclude Defense Counsel conflicts of interest arising from the representation of Accused before military commissions. The Chief Defense Counsel shall be provided sufficient information (potentially including protected information) to fulfill this responsibility.

10) The Chief Defense Counsel shall take appropriate measures to ensure that each Detailed Defense Counsel is capable of zealous representation, unencumbered by any conflict of interest. In this regard, the Chief Defense Counsel shall monitor the activities of all Defense Counsel (Detailed and Civilian) and take appropriate measures to ensure that Defense Counsel do not enter into agreements with other Accused or Defense Counsel that might cause them or the Accused they represent to incur an obligation of

confidentiality with such other Accused or Defense Counsel or to effect some other impediment to representation.

11) The Chief Defense Counsel shall ensure that an Accused tried before a military commission pursuant to references (a) and (b) is represented at all relevant times by Detailed Defense Counsel.

12) The Chief Defense Counsel shall administer all requests for replacement Detailed Defense Counsel requested in accordance with Section 4(C)(3) of reference (a). He shall determine the availability of such counsel in accordance with this Instruction.

13) The Chief Defense Counsel shall administer the Civilian Defense Counsel pool, screening all requests for pre-qualification and ad hoc qualification, making qualification determinations and recommendations in accordance with reference (a), this Instruction, and Military Commission Instruction No. 5, and ensuring appropriate notification to an Accused of civilian attorneys available to represent Accused before a military commission.

14) The Chief Defense Counsel shall ensure that all Detailed Defense Counsel and Civilian Defense Counsel who are to perform duties in relation to a military commission have taken an oath to perform their duties faithfully.

15) The Chief Defense Counsel shall ensure that all personnel properly under the supervision of the Office of the Chief Defense Counsel possess the appropriate security clearances.

C. *Detailed Defense Counsel*

1) Detailed Defense Counsel shall be judge advocates of any United States armed force.

2) Detailed Defense Counsel shall represent the Accused before military commissions when detailed in accordance with references (a) and (b). In this regard Detailed Defense Counsel shall: defend the Accused to whom detailed zealously within the bounds of the law and without regard to personal opinion as to guilt; represent the interests of the Accused in any review process as provided by reference (a); and comply with the procedures accorded the Accused pursuant to Sections 5 and 6 of reference (a). Detailed Defense Counsel shall so serve notwithstanding any intention expressed by the Accused to represent himself.

3) Detailed Defense Counsel shall have primary responsibility to prevent conflicts of interest related to the handling of the cases to which detailed.

4) Detailed Defense Counsel shall fulfill all responsibilities detailed in references (a) and (b), those set forth in this Instruction, and those assigned by the Chief Defense Counsel.

D. *Selected Detailed Defense Counsel*

1) The Accused may select a judge advocate of any United States armed force to replace the Accused's Detailed Defense Counsel, provided that judge advocate has been determined to be available by the Chief Defense Counsel in consultation with the Judge Advocate General of that judge advocate's military department.

2) A judge advocate shall be determined not to be available if assigned duties: as a general or flag officer; as a military judge; as a prosecutor in the Office of Military Commissions; as a judge advocate assigned to the Department of Defense Criminal Investigation Task Force or Joint Task Force Guantanamo; as a principal legal advisor to a command, organization, or agency; as an instructor or student at a service school, academy, college or university; or in any other capacity that the Judge Advocate General of the Military Department concerned may determine not to be available because of the nature or responsibilities of their assignments, exigent circumstances, military necessity, or other appropriate reasons.

3) Consistent with Section 6(B) or reference (a), the selection and replacement of new Detailed Defense Counsel shall not unreasonably delay military commission proceedings.

4) Unless otherwise directed by the Appointing Authority or the General Counsel of the Department of Defense, the Chief Defense Counsel will, after selection of a new Detailed Defense Counsel, relieve the original Detailed Defense Counsel of all duties with respect to that case.

E. *Qualified Civilian Defense Counsel*

1) The Accused may, at no expense to the United States, retain the services of a civilian attorney of the Accused's own choosing to assist in the conduct of his defense before a military commission,

provided that the civilian attorney retained has been determined to be qualified pursuant to Section 4(C)(3)(b) of reference (a).

2) Consistent with Section 6(B) of reference (a), the retention of Civilian Defense Counsel shall not unreasonably delay military commission proceedings.

3) Representation by Civilian Defense Counsel will not relieve Detailed Defense Counsel of duties specified in Section 4(C)(2) of reference (a).

4) Neither qualification of a Civilian Defense Counsel for membership in the pool of available Civilian Defense Counsel nor the entry of appearance in a specific cause guarantees that counsel's presence at closed military commission proceedings or access to information protected under Section 6(D)(5) of reference (a).

5) The Chief Defense Counsel shall monitor the conduct of all qualified Civilian Defense Counsel for compliance with all rules, regulations, and instructions governing military commissions. The Chief Defense Counsel will report all instances of noncompliance with the rules, regulations, and instructions governing military commissions to the Appointing Authority and to the General Counsel of the Department of Defense with a recommendation as to any appropriate action consistent with reference (a) and this Instruction.

4. DUTIES AND RESPONSIBILITIES OF THE DEFENSE

A. *Regular Duties.* The Defense shall perform all duties specified or implied in reference (a) as responsibilities of the Defense.

B. *Special Duties.* The Office of the Chief Defense Counsel shall perform such other functions, consistent with references (a) and (b) and the mission of the Office of the Chief Defense Counsel, as may be directed by the Appointing Authority or the General Counsel of the Department of Defense.

5. POLICES

A. *Prohibition on Certain Agreements.* No Defense Counsel may enter into agreements with any detainee other than his client, or such detainee's Defense Counsel, that might cause him or the client he represents to incur an obligation of confidentiality with such other detainee or Defense Counsel or to effect some other impediment to representation.

B. *Prohibition on Certain Disclosures.* All Defense Counsel must strictly comply with section 6(D)(5) and section 9 of reference (a) to ensure they do not improperly disclose classified information, national security information, or state secrets to an Accused or potential Accused or to any other person not specifically authorized to receive such information.

C. *Statements to the Media.* Consistent with reference (f), the Assistant Secretary of Defense for Public Affairs shall serve as the sole release authority for DoD information and audiovisual materials regarding military commissions. Personnel assigned to the Office of the Chief Defense Counsel, as well as all members of the Civilian Defense Counsel pool and associated personnel may communicate with news media representatives regarding cases and other matters related to military commissions only when approved by the Appointing Authority or the General Counsel of the Department of Defense.

6. EFFECTIVE DATE

This Instruction is effective immediately.

William J. Haynes II
General Counsel of the Department of Defense

APPENDIX C 9

Department of Defense

Military Commission Instruction No. 5

April 30, 2003

SUBJECT: Qualification of Civilian Defense Counsel

References: (a) Military Commission Order No. 1 (Mar. 21, 2002)

(b) Military Order of November 13, 2001, "Detention, Treatment, and Trial of Certain Non-Citizens in the War Against Terrorism," 66 F.R. 57833 (Nov. 16, 2001)

(c) Section 113(d) of Title 10 of the United States Code

(d) Section 140(b) of Title 10 of the United States Code

(e) Military Commission Instruction No. 1, current edition

(f) Section 1001 of Title 18 of the United States Code

(g) DoD 5200.2-R, "Personnel Security Program," current edition

1. PURPOSE

This Instruction establishes policies and procedures for the creation and management of the pool of qualified Civilian Defense Counsel authorized in Section 4(C)(3)(b) of reference (a) in accordance with reference (b).

2. AUTHORITY

This Instruction is issued pursuant to Section 7(A) of reference (a) and in accordance with references (c) and (d). The provisions of reference (e) are applicable to this Instruction.

3. POLICIES AND PROCEDURES

A. *Application Procedures*

1) Civilian attorneys may be prequalified as members of the pool of attorneys eligible to represent Accused before military commissions at no expense to the United States if, at the time of application, they meet the eligibility criteria set forth in Section 4(C)(3)(b) of reference (a) as further detailed in this Instruction, or they may be qualified on an ad hoc basis after being requested by an Accused. In both cases, qualification results in membership in the pool of available Civilian Defense Counsel.

2) An attorney seeking qualification as a member of the pool of available Civilian Defense Counsel shall submit an application, by letter, to:

Office of the General Counsel, Department of Defense
(Attn: Chief Defense Counsel, Office of Military Commissions)
1600 Defense Pentagon
Washington, DC 20301-1600

Applications will be comprised of the letter requesting qualification for membership, together with the following documents that demonstrate satisfaction of the criteria set forth in Section 4(C)(3)(b) of reference (a):

a. Section 4(C)(3)(b)(i), *Civilian Defense Counsel shall be United States citizens.* Applicants will provide proof of citizenship (e.g., certified true copy of passport, birth certificate, or certificate of naturalization).

b. Section 4(C)(3)(b)(ii), *Civilian Defense Counsel shall be admitted to the practice of law in a State, district, territory or possession of the United States, or before a Federal court.* Applicants will submit an official certificate showing that the applicant is an active member in good standing with the bar of a qualifying jurisdiction. The certificate must be dated within three months of the date of the Chief Defense Counsel's receipt of the application.

c. Section 4(C)(b)(iii), *Civilian Defense Counsel shall not have been the subject of any sanction or disciplinary action by any court, bar, or other competent governmental authority for relevant misconduct.*

    i. An applicant shall submit a statement detailing all sanctions or disciplinary actions, pending or final, to which he has been subject, whether by a court, bar or other competent governmental authority, for misconduct of any kind. The statement shall identify the jurisdiction or authority that imposed the sanction or disciplinary action, together with any explanation deemed appropriate by the applicant. Additionally, the statement shall identify and explain any formal challenge to the attorney's fitness to practice law, regardless of the outcome of any subsequent proceedings. In the event that no sanction, disciplinary action or challenge has been imposed on or made against an applicant, the statement shall so state. Further, the applicant's statement shall identify each jurisdiction in which he has been admitted or to which he has applied to practice law, regardless of whether the applicant maintains a current active license in that jurisdiction, together with any dates of admission to or rejection by each such jurisdiction and, if no longer active, the date of and basis for inactivation. The above information shall be submitted either in the form of a sworn notarized statement or as a declaration under penalty of perjury of the laws of the United States. The sworn statement or declaration must be executed and dated within three months of the date of the Chief Defense Counsel's receipt of the application.

    ii. Further, applicants shall submit a properly executed Authorization for Release of Information (Annex A), authorizing the Chief Defense Counsel or his designee to obtain information relevant to qualification of the applicant as a member of the Civilian Defense Counsel pool from each jurisdiction in which the applicant has been admitted or to which he has applied to practice law.

290

d. Section 4(C)(b)(iv), *Civilian Defense Counsel shall be determined to be eligible for access to information classified at the level SECRET or higher under the authority of and in accordance with the procedures described in Department of Defense Regulation, DoD 5200.2-R, "Personnel Security Program."*

i. Civilian Defense Counsel applicants who possess a valid current security clearance of SECRET or higher shall provide, in writing, the date of their background investigation, the date such clearance was granted, the level of the clearance, and the adjudicating authority.

ii. Civilian Defense Counsel applicants who do not possess a valid current security clearance of SECRET or higher shall state in writing their willingness to submit to a background investigation in accordance with reference (g) and to pay any actual costs associated with the processing of the same. The security clearance application, investigation, and adjudication process will not be initiated until the applicant has submitted an application that otherwise fully complies with this Instruction and the Chief Defense Counsel has determined that the applicant would otherwise be qualified for membership in the Civilian Defense Counsel pool. Favorable adjudication of the applicant's personnel security investigation must be completed before an applicant will be qualified for membership in the pool of Civilian Defense Counsel. The Chief Defense Counsel may, at his discretion, withhold qualification and wait to initiate the security clearance process until such time as the Civilian Defense Counsel's services are likely to be sought.

e. Section 4(C)(b)(v), *Civilian Defense Counsel shall have signed a written agreement to comply with all applicable regulations or instructions for counsel, including any rules of court for conduct .during the course of proceedings.* This requirement shall be satisfied by the execution of the Affidavit And

Agreement By Civilian Defense Counsel at Annex B to this Instruction. The Affidavit And Agreement By Civilian Defense Counsel shall be executed and agreed to without change, (*i.e.*, no omissions, additions or substitutions). Proper execution shall require the notarized signature of the applicant. The Affidavit And Agreement By Civilian Defense Counsel shall be dated within three months of the date of the Chief Defense Counsel's receipt of the application.

3) Applications mailed in a franked U.S. Government envelope or received through U.S. Government distribution will not be considered. Telefaxed or electronic mail application materials will not be accepted. Failure to provide all of the requisite information and documentation may result in rejection of the application. A false statement in any part of the application may preclude qualification and/or render the applicant liable for disciplinary or criminal sanction, including under reference (f).

B. *Application Review*

1) The Chief Defense Counsel or his designee shall review all Civilian Defense Counsel pool applications for compliance with references (a) and (b) and with this Instruction.

2) The Chief Defense Counsel shall consider all applicants for qualification as members of the Civilian Defense Counsel pool without regard to race, religion, color, sex, age, national origin, or other non-disqualifying physical or mental disability.

3) The Chief Defense Counsel may reject any Civilian Defense Counsel application that is incomplete or otherwise fails to comply with references (a) and (b) or with this Instruction.

4) Subject to review by the General Counsel of the Department of Defense, the Chief Defense Counsel shall determine the number of qualified attorneys that shall constitute the pool of available Civilian Defense Counsel. Similarly, subject to review by the General Counsel of the Department of Defense, the Chief Defense Counsel shall determine the qualification of applicants for membership in such pool. This shall include determinations as to whether any sanction, disciplinary action, or challenge is related to relevant misconduct that would disqualify the Civilian Defense Counsel applicant.

5) The Chief Defense Counsel's determination as to each applicant's qualification for membership in the pool of qualified Civilian Defense Counsel shall be deemed effective as of the date of the Chief Defense Counsel's written notification publishing such determination to the applicant. Subsequent to this notification, the retention of qualified Civilian Defense Counsel is effected upon written entry of appearance, communicated to the military commission through the Chief Defense Counsel.

6) The Chief Defense Counsel may reconsider his determination as to an individual's qualification as a member of the Civilian Defense Counsel pool on the basis of subsequently discovered information indicating material nondisclosure or misrepresentation in the application, or material violation of obligations of the Civilian Defense Counsel, or other good cause, or the matter may be referred to the Appointing Authority or the General Counsel of the Department of Defense, who may revoke or suspend the qualification of any member of the Civilian Defense Counsel pool.

4. EFFECTIVE DATE

This Instruction is effective immediately.

William J. Haynes II
General Counsel of the Department of Defense

ANNEX A to Department of Defense Military Commission Instruction No. 5, "Qualification of Civilian Defense Counsel"

UNITED STATES OF AMERICA
Authorization for Release of Information
(Carefully read this authorization to release information about you, then sign and date it in ink.)

I authorize the Chief Defense Counsel, Office of Military Commissions, Department of Defense, his designee or other duly authorized representative of the Department of Defense who may be charged with assessing or determining my qualification for membership in the pool of Civilian Defense Counsel available to represent Accused before military commissions, to obtain any information from any court, the bar of any State, locality, district, territory or possession of the United States, or from any other governmental authority.

This information may include, but is not limited to, information relating to: any application for a security clearance; my admission or application for admission to practice law in any jurisdiction, including action by the jurisdiction upon such application, together with my current status with regard to the practice of law in such jurisdiction; any sanction or disciplinary action to which I have been subject for misconduct of any kind; and any formal challenge to my fitness to practice law, regardless of the outcome of subsequent proceedings.

I authorize custodians of such records or information and other sources of information pertaining to me to release such at the request of the officials named above, regardless of any previous agreement to the contrary.

I understand that for certain custodians or sources of information a separate specific release may be required and that I may be contacted for the purposes of executing such at a later date.

I understand that the records or information released by custodians and other sources of information are for official use by the Department of Defense, only for the purposes provided herein, and that they may be redisclosed by the Department of Defense only as authorized by law.

Copies of this authorization that show my signature are as valid as the original signed by me. This authorization is valid for five (5) years from the date signed or upon termination of my affiliation with the Department of Defense, whichever is later.

_____   _____
Signature (sign in ink)   SSN   Date

ANNEX B to Department of Defense Military Commission Instruction No. 5, "Qualification of Civilian Defense Counsel"

AFFIDAVIT AND AGREEMENT BY CIVILIAN DEFENSE COUNSEL

Pursuant to Section 4(C)(3)(b) of Department of Defense Military Commission Order No. 1, "Procedures for Trials by Military Commissions of Certain Non-United States Citizens in the War Against Terrorism," dated March 21, 2002 ("MCO No. 1"), Military Commission Instructions No. 4, "Responsibilities of the Chief Defense Counsel, Detailed Defense Counsel, and Civilian Defense Counsel" ("MCI No. 4") and No. 5, "Qualification of Civilian Defense Counsel" ("MCI NO. 5"), and in accordance with the President's Military Order of November 13, 2001, "Detention, Treatment, and Trial of Certain Non-Citizens in the War Against Terrorism," 66 F.R. 57833 (Nov. 16, 2001) ("President's Military Order"), I [Name of Civilian Attorney], make this Affidavit and Agreement for the purposes of applying for qualification as a member of the pool of Civilian Defense Counsel available to represent Accused before military commissions and serving in that capacity.

I.   Oaths or Affirmations. I swear or affirm that the following information is true to the best of my knowledge and belief:

A.   I have read and understand the President's Military Order, MCO No. 1, MCI No. 4, MCI No. 5, and all other Military Commission Orders and Instructions concerning the rules, regulations and instructions applicable to trial by military commissions. I will read all future Orders and Instructions applicable to trials by military commissions.

B.   I am aware that my qualification as a Civilian Defense Counsel does not guarantee my presence at closed military commission proceedings or guarantee my access to any information protected under Section 6(D)(5) or Section 9 of MCO No. 1.

II.   Agreements. I hereby agree to comply with all applicable regulations and instructions for counsel, including any rules of court for conduct during the course of proceedings, and specifically agree, without limitation, to the following:

A.   I will notify the Chief Defense Counsel and, as applicable, the relevant Presiding Officer immediately if, after the execution of this Affidavit and Agreement but prior to the conclusion of proceedings (defined as the review and final decision of the President or, if designated, the Secretary of Defense), if there is any change in any of the information provided in my application, including this Affidavit and Agreement, for qualification as member of the Civilian Defense Counsel pool. I understand that such notification shall be in writing and shall set forth the substantive nature of the changed information.

B. I will be well-prepared and will conduct the defense zealously, representing the Accused throughout the military commission process, form the inception of my representation through the completion of any post trial proceedings as detailed in Section 6(H) of MCO No. 1. I will ensure that these proceedings are my primary duty. I will not seek to delay or to continue the proceedings for reasons relating to matters that arise in the course of my law practice or other professional or personal activities that are not related to military commission proceedings.

C. The Defense Team shall consist entirely of myself, Detailed Defense Counsel, and other personnel provided by the Chief Defense Counsel, the Presiding Officer, or the Appointing Authority. I will make no claim against the U.S. Government for any fees or costs associated with my conduct of the defense or related activities or efforts.

D. Recognizing that my representation does not relieve Detailed Defense Counsel of duties specified in Section 4(C)(2) of MCO No. 1, I will work cooperatively with such counsel to ensure coordination of efforts and to ensure such counsel is capable of conducting the defense independently if necessary.

E. During the pendency of the proceedings, unless I obtain approval in advance from the Presiding Officer to do otherwise, I will comply with the following restrictions on my travel and communications:

1. I will not travel or transmit documents from the site of the proceedings without the approval of the Appointing Authority or the Presiding Officer. The Defense Team and I will otherwise perform all of our work relating to the proceedings, including any electronic or other research, at the site of the proceedings (except that this shall not apply during post-trial proceedings detailed in Section 6(H) of MCO No. 1).

2. I will not discuss or otherwise communicate or share documents or information about the case with anyone except persons who have been designated as members of the Defense Team in accordance with this Affidavit and Agreement and other applicable rules, regulations and instructions.

F. At no time, to include any period subsequent to the conclusion of the proceedings, will I make any public or private statements regarding any closed sessions of the proceedings or any classified information or material, or document or material constituting protected information under MCO No. 1.

G. I understand and agree to comply with all rules, regulations and instructions governing the handling of classified information and material. Furthermore, no document or material constituting protected information under MCO No. 1, regardless of its classification level, may leave the site of the proceedings.

H. I understand that there may be reasonable restrictions on the time and duration of contact I may have with my client, as imposed by the Appointing Authority, the Presiding Officer, detention authorities, or regulation.

I. I understand that my communications with my client, even if traditionally covered by the attorney-client privilege, may be subject to monitoring or review by government officials, using any available means, for security and intelligence purposes. I understand that any such monitoring will only take place in limited circumstances when approved by proper authority, and that any evidence or information derived from such communications will not be used in proceedings against the Accused who made or received the relevant communication. I further understand that communications are not protected if they would facilitate criminal acts or a conspiracy to commit criminal acts, or if those communications are not related to the seeking or providing of legal advice.

J. I agree that I shall reveal to the Chief Defense Counsel and any other appropriate authorities, information relating to the representation of my client to the extent that I reasonably believe necessary to prevent the commission of a future criminal act that I believe is likely to result in death or substantial bodily harm, or significant impairment of national security.

K. I understand and agree that nothing in this Affidavit and Agreement creates any substantive, procedural, or other rights for me as counsel or for my client(s).

/s/ _____

Print Name: _____

Address: _____

_____

Date: _____

STATE OF   )

COUNTY OF   )

     Sworn to and subscribed before me, by _____, this _____ day
of _____, 20__.

                                                     Notary

My commission expires:

APPENDIX C 10

Department of Defense

Military Commission Instruction No. 6

_____
April 30, 2003
_____
_____

SUBJECT: Reporting Relationships for Military Commission Personnel

References: (a) Military Commission Order No. 1 (Mar. 21, 2002)

(b) Military Order of November 13, 2001, "Detention, Treatment, and Trial of Certain Non-Citizens in the War Against Terrorism," 66 F.R. 57833 (Nov. 16, 2001)

(c) Section 113(d) of Title 10 of the United States Code

(d) Section 140(b) of Title 10 of the United States Code

(e) Military Commission Instruction No. 1, current edition

1. PURPOSE

This Instruction establishes supervisory and performance evaluation relationships for military commission personnel.

2. AUTHORITY

This Instruction is issued pursuant to Section 7(A) of reference (a) and in accordance with references (b), (c), and (d). The provisions of reference (e) are applicable to this Instruction.

3. POLICIES AND PROCEDURES

A. *Supervisory and Performance Evaluation Relationships.* Individuals appointed, assigned, detailed, designated or employed in a capacity related to the conduct of military commission proceedings conducted in accordance with references (a) and (b) shall be subject to the relationship set forth below. Unless stated otherwise, the person to whom an individual "reports," as set forth below, shall be deemed to

300

be such individual's supervisor and shall, to the extent possible, fulfill all performance evaluation responsibilities normally associated with the function of direct supervisor in accordance with the subordinate's Military Service performance evaluation regulations.

1) Appointing Authority: any Appointing Authority designated by the Secretary of Defense pursuant to reference (a) shall report to the Secretary of Defense in accordance with reference (c).

2) Legal Advisor to Appointing Authority: The Legal Advisor to the Appointing Authority shall report to the Appointing Authority.

3) Chief Prosecutor: The Chief Prosecutor shall report to the Deputy General Counsel (Legal Counsel) of the Department of Defense and then to the General Counsel of the Department of Defense.

4) Prosecutors and Assistant Prosecutors: Prosecutors and Assistant Prosecutors shall report to the Chief Prosecutor and then to the Deputy General Counsel (Legal Counsel) of the Department of Defense.

5) Chief Defense Counsel: The Chief Defense Counsel shall report to the Deputy General Counsel (Personnel and Health Policy) of the Department of Defense and then to the General Counsel of the Department of Defense.

6) Detailed Defense Counsel: Detailed Defense Counsel shall report to the Chief Defense Counsel and then to the Deputy General Counsel (Personnel and Health Policy) of the Department of Defense.

7) Review Panel Members: Members of the Review Panel shall report to the Secretary of Defense.

8) Commission Members: Commission members shall continue to report to their parent commands. The consideration or evaluation of the performance of duty as a member of a military commission is prohibited in preparing effectiveness, fitness, or evaluation reports of a commission member.

9) Other Personnel: All other military commission personnel, such as court reporters, interpreters, security personnel, bailiffs, and clerks detailed or employed by the Appointing Authority pursuant to Section 4(D) of reference (a), if not assigned to the Office of the

Chief Prosecutor of the Office of the Chief Defense Counsel, shall report to the Appointing Authority or his designee.

B. *Responsibilities of Supervisory/Reporting Officials.* Officials designated in this Instruction as supervisory/reporting officials shall:

1) Supervise subordinates in the performance of their duties.

2) Prepare fitness or performance evaluation reports and, as appropriate, process awards and citations for subordinates. To the extent practicable, a reporting official shall comply with the rated subordinate's Military Service regulations regarding the preparation of fitness or performance evaluation reports and in executing related duties.

4. EFFECTIVE DATE

This Instruction is effective immediately.

William J. Haynes II
General Counsel of the Department of Defense

APPENDIX C 11

Department of Defense

Military Commission Instruction No. 7

April 30, 2003

SUBJECT: Sentencing

References: (a) Military Commission Order No. 1 (Mar. 21, 2002)

(b) Military Order of November 13, 2001, "Detention, Treatment, and Trial of Certain Non-Citizens in the War Against Terrorism," 66 F.R. 57833 (Nov. 16, 2001)

(c) Section 113(d) of Title 10 of the United States Code

(d) Section 140(b) of Title 10 of the United States Code

(e) Military Commission Instruction No. 1, current edition

1. PURPOSE

This Instruction promulgates policy, assigns responsibilities, and prescribes procedures for matters related to sentencing of persons with regard to whom a finding of guilty is entered for an offense referred for trial by a military commission appointed pursuant to references (a) and (b).

2. AUTHORITY

This Instruction is issued pursuant to section 7(A) of reference (a) and in accordance with references (b), (c), and (d). The provisions of reference (e) are applicable to this Instruction.

3. AVAILABLE SENTENCES

A. *General.* Reference (a) permits a military commission wide latitude in sentencing. Any lawful punishment or condition of punishment is authorized, including death, so long as the prerequisites detailed in reference (a) are met. Detention associated with an individual's status as an enemy combatant shall not be considered to fulfill any term of imprisonment imposed by a military commission. The sentence determination should be made while bearing in mind that there are several principal reasons for a sentence given to those who violate the law. Such reasons included: punishment of the wrongdoer; protection of society from the wrongdoer; deterrence of the wrongdoer and those who know of his crimes and sentence from committing the same or similar offenses; and rehabilitation of the wrongdoer. In determining an appropriate sentence, the weight to be accorded any or all of these reasons rests solely within the discretion of commission members. All sentences should, however, be grounded in a recognition that military commissions are a function of the President's war-fighting role as Commander-in-Chief of the Armed Forces of the United States and of the broad deterrent impact associated with a sentence's effect on adherence to the laws and customs of war in general.

B. *Conditions of Imprisonment.* Decisions regarding the location designated for any imprisonment, the conditions under which a sentence to imprisonment is served, or the privileges accorded one during any period of imprisonment should generally not be made by the commission. Those decisions and actions, however, may be appropriate subjects for recommendation to the person making a final decision on the sentence in accordance with Section 6(H) of reference (a).

C. *Prospective Recommendations for Sentence Modification.* A sentence imposed by military commission may be accompanied by a recommendation to suspend, remit, commute or otherwise modify the adjudged sentence in concert with one or more conditions upon which the suspension, remission, commutation, or other modification is contingent (usually relating to the performance, behavior or conduct of the Accused). Unless otherwise directed, a decision or action in accordance with such a recommendation will be effected by direction or delegation to the Appointing Authority by the official making a final decision on the sentence in accordance with Section 6(H) of reference (a).

4. SENTENCING PROCEDURES

A. *General.* Reference (a) permits the military commission substantial discretion regarding the conduct of sentencing proceedings. Sentencing proceedings should normally proceed expeditiously. In the discretion of the Presiding Officer, as limited by the Appointing Authority, reasonable delay between the announcement of findings and the commencement of sentencing proceedings may be authorized to facilitate the conduct of proceedings in accordance with Section 6(B) of reference (a).

B. *Information Relevant to Sentencing.* Section 6(E)(10) of reference (a) permits the Prosecution and Defense to present information to aid the military commission in determining an appropriate sentence. Such information may include a recommendation of an appropriate sentence, information regarding sentence ranges for analogous offenses (e.g., the sentencing range under the Federal Sentencing Guidelines that could be applicable to the Accused for the most analogous federal offenses), and other relevant information. Regardless of any presentation by the Prosecution or Defense, the military commission shall consider any evidence admitted for consideration prior to findings regarding guilt. The Presiding Officer may limit or require the presentation of certain information consistent with references (a) and (b).

C. *Cases Involving Plea Agreements.* In accordance with Section 6(A)(4) of reference (a), after determining the voluntary and informed nature of a plea agreement approved by the Appointing Authority, the military commission is bound to adjudge findings and a sentence pursuant to that plea agreement. Accordingly, the Presiding Officer may exercise the authority granted in Section 6(E) of reference (a) to curtail or preclude the presentation of information and argument relative to the military commission's determination of an appropriate sentence.

D. *Special Duties.* In cases involving plea agreements or recommendations for certain conditions of imprisonment or prospective sentence modification, the Prosecution and Defense shall provide whatever post-trial information or recommendation as is relevant to any subsequent decision regarding such condition or suspension, remission, commutation, or other modification recommendation associated with the sentence.

5. EFFECTIVE DATE

This Instruction is effective immediately.

William J. Haynes II
General Counsel of the Department of Defense

APPENDIX C 12

Department of Defense

Military Commission Instruction No. 8

<hr>

April 30, 2003

<hr>

SUBJECT: Administrative Procedures

References: (a) Military Commission Order No. 1 (Mar. 21, 2002)

(b) Military Order of November 13, 2001, "Detention, Treatment, and Trial of Certain Non-Citizens in the War Against Terrorism," 66 F.R. 57833 (Nov. 16, 2001)

(c) Section 113(d) of Title 10 of the United States Code

(d) Section 140(b) of Title 10 of the United States Code

(e) Military Commission Instruction No. 1, current edition

1. PURPOSE

This Instruction promulgates policy, assigns responsibilities, and prescribes procedures for the conduct of trials by a military commission appointed pursuant to references (a) and (b).

2. AUTHORITY

This Instruction is issued pursuant to Section 7(A) of reference (a) and in accordance with references (b), (c), and (d). The provisions of reference (e) are applicable to this Instruction.

3. COMMISSION PERSONNEL

A. *Appointment and Removal of Commission Members.*

1) In accordance with reference (a), the Appointing Authority shall appoint at least three but no more than seven members

and one or two alternate members. The Appointing Authority may remove members and alternate members for good cause. In the event a member (or alternate member) is removed for good cause, the Appointing Authority may replace the member, direct that an alternate member serve in the place of the original member, direct that proceedings simply continue without the member, or convene a new commission. In the absence of guidance from the Appointing Authority regarding replacement, the Presiding Officer shall select an alternate member to replace the member in question.

2) The Presiding Officer shall determine if it is necessary to conduct or permit questioning of members (including the Presiding Officer) on issues of whether there is good cause for their removal. The Presiding Officer may permit questioning in any manner he deems appropriate. Consistent with reference (a), any such questioning shall be narrowly focused on issues pertaining to whether good cause may exist for the removal of any member.

3) From time to time, it may be appropriate for a Presiding Officer to forward to the Appointing Authority information and, if appropriate, a recommendation relevant to the question of whether a member (including the Presiding Officer) should be removed for good cause. While awaiting the Appointing Authority's decision on such matter, the Presiding Officer may elect either to hold proceedings in abeyance or to continue. The Presiding Officer may issue any appropriate instructions to the member whose continued service is in question. A military commission shall not engage in deliberations on findings or sentence prior to the Appointing Authority's decision in any case in which the Presiding Officer has recommended a member's removal.

B. *Military Commission Security Officer.* The Appointing Authority may detail a Security Officer to advise a military commission on matters related to classified and protected information. In addition to any other duties assigned by the Appointing Authority, the Security Officer shall ensure that all classified or protected evidence and information is appropriately safeguarded at all times and that only personnel with the appropriate clearances and authorizations are present when classified or protected materials are presented before military commissions.

C. *Other Military Commission Personnel.* The Appointing Authority may detail court reporters, interpreters, security personnel, bailiffs, clerks, and any other personnel to a military commission as deemed necessary. In the absence of a detailing by the Appointing Authority, the Chief Prosecutor shall be responsible to ensure the availability of necessary or appropriate personnel to facilitate the impartial and expeditious conduct of full and fair trials by military commission.

4. INTERLOCUTORY QUESTIONS

A. *Certification of Interlocutory Questions.* The Presiding Officer shall generally adjudicate all motions and questions that arise during the course of a trial by military commission. In accordance with Section 4(A)(5)(d) of reference (a), however, the Presiding Officer shall certify all interlocutory questions, the disposition of which would effect a termination of proceedings with respect to a charge, for decision by the Appointing Authority. In addition, the Presiding Officer may certify other interlocutory questions to the Appointing Authority as the Presiding Officer deems appropriate.

B. *Submission of Interlocutory Questions.* The Presiding Officer shall determine what, if any, documentary or other materials should be forwarded to the Appointing Authority in conjunction with an interlocutory question.

C. *Effect of Interlocutory Question Certification on Proceedings.* While decision by the Appointing Authority is pending on any certified interlocutory question, the Presiding Officer may elect either to hold proceedings in abeyance or to continue.

5. IMPLIED DUTIES OF THE PRESIDING OFFICER

The Presiding Officer shall ensure the execution of all ancillary functions necessary for the impartial and expeditious conduct of a full and fair trial by military commission in accordance with reference (a). Such functions include, for example, scheduling the time and place of convening of a military commission, ensuring that an oath or affirmation is administered to witnesses and military commission personnel as appropriate, conducting appropriate *in camera* meetings to facilitate efficient trial proceedings, and providing necessary instructions to other commission members. The Presiding Officer shall rule on appropriate motions or, at his discretion consistent with reference (a), may submit them to the commission for decision or to the Appointing Authority as a certified interlocutory question.

6. DISCLOSURES

A. *General.* Unless directed otherwise by the Presiding Officer upon a showing of good cause or for some other reason, counsel for the Prosecution and the Defense shall provide to opposing counsel, at least one week prior to the scheduled convening of a military commission, copies of all information intended for presentation as evidence at trial, copies of all motions the party intends to raise before the military commission, and names and contact information of all witnesses a party intends to call. Motions shall also be provided to the Presiding Officer at the time they are provided to opposing counsel. Unless directed otherwise by the Presiding Officer, written responses to any motions will be provided to opposing counsel and the Presiding Officer no later than three days prior to the scheduled convening of a military commission.

B. *Notifications by the Prosecution.* The Prosecution shall provide the Defense with access to evidence known to the Prosecution that tends to exculpate the Accused as soon as practicable, and in no instance later than one week prior to the scheduled convening of a military commission.

C. *Notifications by the Defense.* The Defense shall give notice to the Prosecution of any intent to raise an affirmative defense to any charge at least one week prior to the scheduled convening of a military commission.

D. *Evidence Related to Mental Responsibility.* If the Defense indicates an intent to raise a defense of lack of mental responsibility or introduce expert testimony regarding an Accused's mental condition, the prosecution may require that the Accused submit to a mental examination by a military psychologist or psychiatrist, and both parties shall have access to the results of that examination.

7. EFFECTIVE DATE

This Instruction is effective immediately.

William J. Haynes II
General Counsel of the Department of Defense

APPENDIX C 13

Department of Defense

Military Commission Instruction No. 9

December 26, 2003

SUBJECT: Review of Military Commission Proceedings

References: (a) Military Commission Order No. 1 (Mar. 21, 2002)

(b) Military Order of November 13, 2001, "Detention, Treatment, and Trial of Certain Non-Citizens in the War Against Terrorism," 66 F.R. 57833 (Nov. 16, 2001)

(c) Section 113(d) of Title 10 of the United States Code

(d) Section 140(b) of Title 10 of the United States Code

(e) Section 603 of Title 10 of the United States Code

(f) Military Commission Instruction No. 1, current edition

(g) Military Commission Instruction No. 2, current edition

1. PURPOSE

This Instruction prescribes procedures and establishes responsibilities for the review of military commission proceedings.

2. AUTHORITY

This Instruction is issued pursuant to Section 7(A) of reference (a) and in accordance with references (b), (c), and (d). The provisions of reference (f) are applicable to this Instruction.

3. ADMINISTRATIVE REVIEW BY THE APPOINTING AUTHORITY

Pursuant to Section 6(H)(3) of reference (a), the Appointing Authority shall promptly perform an administrative review of the record of trial. Once satisfied that the proceedings of the military commission are administratively complete, the Appointing Authority shall transmit the record of trial to the Review Panel constituted under Section 6(H)(4) of reference (a) and in accordance with this Instruction. If not so satisfied, the Appointing Authority shall return the case to the military commission for any necessary supplementary proceedings.

4. REVIEW PANEL

A. *Generally.* A Review Panel shall consist of three Military Officers and shall commence its review of a military commission case upon the forwarding of a record of trial by the Appointing Authority.

B. *Members.* The Secretary of Defense will designate three or more Military Officers, including civilians commissioned pursuant to reference (e), as eligible to serve on a Review Panel. With regard to the internal operations of a Review Panel, civilians appointed as officers shall have the same authority, duties, and responsibilities as any other member of the armed forces serving on the Review Panel. Such officers whose total service under reference (e) and otherwise to the United States is not expected to exceed 130 days during any period of 365 consecutive days shall be special Government employees for the purposes of 10 U.S.C. §§ 202, 203, 205, 207, 208, and 209. Section 973(b) of Title 10, U.S. Code, does not apply to such officers. At least one member of each Review Panel shall have experience as a judge.

1) *Qualifications.*

a. In designating members as eligible to serve on a Review Panel, only individuals who are well qualified by virtue of their experience, impartiality, and judicial temperament shall be chosen.

b. No person shall be eligible to serve on a Review Panel if such person:

(1) Participated in the investigation of the case;
(2) Served as a member of the military commission that heard the case;
(3) Served as prosecutor or defense counsel before such commission; or
(4) Is otherwise incapable of providing an impartial review of military commissions as determined by the Secretary of Defense.

    c. No person who has served a term of appointment as a member eligible to serve on a Review Panel may be reappointed to a second term.

2) *Term of Appointment.* The Secretary of Defense will prescribe the term of each Review Panel member, which normally shall not exceed two years. The Secretary of Defense may permanently remove a Review Panel member only for good cause. "Good cause" includes, but is not limited to, physical disability, military exigency, or other circumstances that render the member unable to perform his duties.

3) *Review Panel Composition.* The Military Officers designated by the Secretary of Defense shall select from among themselves the three members of each Review Panel. The three members of each Review Panel may select, at their discretion, one member to act as the President of that Review Panel.

4) *Oath of Office.* An oath (or affirmation) of office shall be administered to each Review Panel member.

    a. *Procedure for administering oath.* The following oath (or affirmation) may be administered by the Secretary of Defense, the General Counsel of the Department of Defense, and any person duly authorized to administer oaths, "Do you (swear) (affirm) that you will faithfully and impartially perform, according to your conscience and the rules applicable to the review of trials by military commission, all the duties incumbent upon you as a member of this Review Panel (so help you God)?"

C. *Post-Trial Review by the Review Panel.*
1) *Action on the Record of Trial.* After it has completed its review, the Review Panel shall take action as specified in subparagraphs (a) or (b) below:

    a. Return the case to the Appointing Authority for further proceedings when a majority of the Review Panel has formed a definite and firm conviction that a material error of law occurred.

    (1) In cases where the only further proceedings necessitated by the Review Panel's conclusion that a material error of law occurred are proceedings where the charge(s) against the Accused shall be dismissed, the Appointing Authority shall dismiss the charge(s).

(2) In all other cases, the Appointing Authority shall refer the review Panel's conclusions to the military commission for proceedings consistent with those conclusions.

b. Forward the case directly to the Secretary of Defense with a written opinion, consistent with Section 4(C)(5) of this Instruction, when a majority of the Review Panel has not formed a definite and firm conviction that a material error of law occurred.

(1) As to each finding of Guilty, the review Panel shall recommend that it be approved, disapproved, or changed to a finding of Guilty to a lesser-included offense. The Review Panel may recommend disapproval of findings of guilty on a basis other than a material error of law.

(2) As to the sentence imposed or any portion thereof, the Review Panel shall recommend that it be approved, mitigated, commuted, deferred, or suspended.

2) *Standard of Review.*

a. *Material Error of Law.* Variance from the procedures specified in reference (a) and its implementing Instructions that would not have had a material effect on the outcome of the military commission shall not constitute a material error of law.

b. Material errors of law may include but are not limited to the following:

(1) A deficiency or error of such gravity and materiality that it deprives the accused of a full and fair trial;

(2) Conviction of a charge that fails to state an offense that by statute or the law of armed conflict may be tried by military commission pursuant to references (a), (b), and (g);

(3) Insufficiency of the evidence as a matter of law; and

(4) A sentence that is not consistent with Section 6(G) of reference (a).

3) *Timing of Post-Trial Review.* The Review Panel shall complete its review and forward the record of trial within 30 days of receipt of the record of trial. The Appointing Authority shall ensure that the Review Panel has

sufficient time to review the record of trial. Upon written application of the President of the Review Panel, the Secretary of Defense may grant extensions of time.

4) *Scope of Post-Trial Review.*

    a. The Review Panel shall review the entire record of trial as defined by Section 6(H)(1) of reference (a), including decisions by the Appointing Authority.

       (1) In making the determination specified in Section 4(C)(1)(a) of this Instruction and the recommendations required in Section 4(C)(1)(b) of this Instruction, the Review Panel may consider factual matters included in the record of trial.

       (2) In making the determination specified in Section 4(C)(1)(a) of this Instruction and the recommendations required in Section 4(C)(1)(b) of this Instruction, the Review Panel may review sentences as part of its review of the record of trial.

    b. The Review Panel shall ordinarily review submissions from the Prosecution and the Defense. In the event that the Review Panel reviews such written submissions, it may also in its discretion invite oral arguments on the written submissions.

    c. The Review Panel may in its discretion review any *amicus curiae* submissions, particularly from the government of the nation of which the accused is a citizen. The Review Panel shall ordinarily review any such governmental submissions.

5) *Written Opinions.* The Review Panel shall issue a written opinion in every case, addressing the determination specified in Section 4(C)(1)(a) of this Instruction and the recommendations required in Section 4(C)(1)(b) of this Instruction.

    a. The written opinion shall include a legal analysis in the form of a memorandum supporting the Review Panel's determination in Section 4(C)(1)(a) and recommendations in Section 4(C)(1)(b) of this Instruction and where it otherwise deems appropriate in the exercise of its discretion.

    b. Members of the Review Panel may write a separate opinion concurring with or dissenting from the majority opinion.

    c. The written opinions of each Review Panel shall constitute precedent for subsequent opinions of all Review Panels.

D. *Deliberation.* The members of the Review Panel shall deliberate in closed conference and shall not disclose the contents of their deliberations outside their closed conference.

E. *Publication.* Except as necessary to safeguard protected information (as defined by reference (a)), the written opinions of the Review Panel shall be published.

F. *Applicability of 10 U.S.C. § 837(a).* The provisions of 10 U.S.C. § 837(a), prohibiting any attempts to coerce or, by any unauthorized means, influence the action of any military tribunal or reviewing authority, apply to Review Panel members.

G. *Effectiveness, Fitness, or Evaluation Reports.* The consideration or evaluation of the substantive judicial decisions made by a member of a Review Panel is prohibited in preparing effectiveness, fitness, or evaluation reports of a Review Panel member.

H. *Administrative Support.* The Review Panel shall be provided any necessary administrative and logistical support required to perform its duties through the Office of the Appointing Authority.

5. REVIEW BY THE SECRETARY OF DEFENSE AFTER RECEIPT OF THE REVIEW PANEL'S RECOMMENDATION

Pursuant to Section 6(H)(5) of reference (a), the Secretary of Defense will review the record of trial and the recommendations of the Review Panel and either return the case for further proceedings or, unless making the final decision pursuant to a Presidential designation under Section 4(c)(8) of reference (b), forward it to the President with a recommendation as to disposition.

6. FINAL DECISION

Pursuant to Section 6(H)(6) of reference (a), after review by the Secretary of Defense, the record of trial and all recommendations will be forwarded to the President for review and final decision (unless the President has designated the Secretary of Defense to perform this function). If the President has so designated the Secretary of Defense: 1) The Secretary may approve or disapprove findings or change a finding of Guilty to a finding of Guilty to a lesser-included offense; or 2) The Secretary of Defense may mitigate, commute, defer, or suspend the sentence imposed or any portion thereof. If the Secretary of Defense is authorized to render the final decision, the review of the Secretary of Defense under Section 6(H)(5) of reference (a) shall constitute the final decision. Pursuant to Section 6(H)(2) of reference (a), an authenticated finding of Not Guilty as to a charge shall not be changed to a finding of Guilty.

7. EFFECTIVE DATE

This instruction is effective immediately.

William J. Haynes II
General Counsel of the Department of Defense.

APPENDIX D

May 11, 2004

ORDER

SUBJECT: Administrative Review Procedures for Enemy Combatants in the Control of the Department of Defense at Guantanamo Bay Naval Base, Cuba

1.   INTRODUCTION AND BACKGROUND

This Order establishes an administrative review process to assess annually the need to continue to detain each enemy combatant during the course of the current and ongoing hostilities. This process will permit each enemy combatant in the control of the Department of Defense ("DoD") at the Guantanamo Bay Naval Base, Cuba ("GTMO") to explain why he is no longer a threat to the United States and its allies in the ongoing armed conflict against al Qaida and its affiliates and supporters or to explain why his release would otherwise be appropriate.*

The law of war permits the detention of enemy combatants until the end of an armed conflict. It permits that detention for the practical purpose of preventing the enemy from rejoining the conflict. It does not require the use of a review process to support continued detention. Nevertheless, to address some unique and unprecedented characteristics of the current conflict, DoD has determined, as a matter of policy, to implement these procedures. These procedures may be amended from time to time, also as a matter of policy, as circumstances in the conflict warrant.

A.   *Existing Procedures.*

The procedures established by this Order offer a layer of review in addition to the other layers of review already in place for enemy combatants detained at GTMO. Under pre-existing guidance, captured individuals are assessed at the time of their capture by military officers in the field. Those officers determine whether those captured individuals were part of or supporting forces hostile to the United States or coalition partners, or otherwise engaged in an armed conflict against the United States. If the individuals detained meet those criteria, they are enemy combatants. If they do not, they are released.

Those persons determined to be enemy combatants are subsequently sent to a centralized holding facility where a military screening team reviews all available

---

* Similar administrative review procedures will be issued for enemy combatants in the control of DoD in the United States.

320

information regarding each detainee to again review whether the individual is an enemy combatant. With the assistance of other U.S. government officials (including military lawyers, intelligence officers, and federal law enforcement officials) and considering all relevant information (including the facts from capture and detention, the threat the individual poses, his intelligence value, and any law enforcement interest) the military screening team assesses whether the detainee is an enemy combatant and should continue to be detained and whether transfer to GTMO is warranted.

After the screening team makes this assessment, a general officer designated by the combatant commander reviews the central holding area screening team's recommendation. When determining whether a detainee should be transferred to GTMO, the combatant commander considers the threat posed by the detainee, his seniority within hostile forces, possible intelligence that may be gained from the detainee, possible law of war violations committed by the detainee, and any other relevant factors. DoD officials in Washington review those proposed for transfer to GTMO prior to their transfer. An internal DoD review panel, including legal advisors, reviews the recommendations of the combatant commander and advises the Secretary of Defense on proposed detainee transfers to GTMO. All available information is considered in those reviews, including information submitted by other governments or obtained from the detainees themselves. In the event that enemy combatants are transferred to GTMO, immediately upon their arrival at GTMO, they are interviewed and further assessments are made based on relevant information, including detainee interviews, U.S. intelligence and law enforcement sources, and information supplied by foreign governments.

Each enemy combatant detained at GTMO also undergoes an extensive assessment of the threat he poses. This threat assessment process is used to determine whether, notwithstanding his status as an enemy combatant, he can be transferred to the custody of another government, can be released, or should remain detained in the control of DoD. Threat assessments of each detainee are made by an integrated team of interrogators, analysts, behavioral scientists, and regional experts. Those threat assessments are provided to the Commander, U.S. Southern Command for review and recommendation. The Southern Command then forwards its recommendations to an interagency committee in Washington that includes law enforcement, intelligence, and defense representatives. That interagency committee makes an assessment and recommendation. The Secretary of Defense or his designee then decides whether transfer of the detainee to the custody of another government, release of that individual, or his continued detention in DoD control is appropriate.

B.   *Relationship of this Order to Existing Procedures.*

Once an enemy combatant has been reviewed by the interagency process described above and the Secretary of Defense or his designee has determined that his continued detention in the control of DoD is appropriate, he will be eligible for review of the need for his continued detention under the procedures this Order establishes. This Order provides the authority to empanel as many review board panels as are deemed necessary to accomplish the review of the enemy combatants in the control of DoD at GTMO.

2.   **ESTABLISHMENT OF ADMINISTRATIVE REVIEW PROCESS**

A.   *Administrative Review Process.* There is established the Administrative Review Board ("Review Board"). The Review Board will assess whether each enemy combatant remains a threat to the United States and its allies in the ongoing armed conflict against al Qaida and its affiliates and supporters or if there is any other reason that it is in the interest of the United States and its allies for the enemy combatant to remain in the control of DoD. Based on that assessment, the Review Board will recommend whether the enemy combatant should continue to be detained in the control of DoD.

B.   *Administrative Review Board.* The Review Board shall be composed of three or more military offices.
  i.   Establishment of Review Board.
      a.   The Review Board shall report to and be selected by a presidentially-appointed Senate-confirmed civilian in the Department of Defense whom the Secretary of Defense has designated to operate and oversee the administrative review process ("designated civilian official" or "DCO").
      b.   The Review Board may sit in panels of three members each.
      c.   The DCO may establish as many review board panels as he deems necessary.
  ii.   *Qualifications of Review Board Members.*
      a.   Military officers assigned to serve as Review Board members shall be those who are, in the DCO's view, qualified for the duty by reason of education, training, experience, length of service, temperament, and objectivity.
      b.   At least one member of a Review Board panel shall be experienced in the field of intelligence.

C.   *Presiding Officer.* For the purpose of its deliberations and any hearing held pursuant to this Order, the senior member of the Review Board, or any Review Board panel, shall be the presiding officer. The sole role of the presiding officer as presiding officer shall be to ensure the orderliness of board proceedings. The presiding officer's vote in board determinations will be accorded the same weight as the votes of the other members of the Review Board.

D. *Legal Counsel.* The General Counsel of DoD shall ensure that the Review Board has the assistance of legal counsel.

E. *Enemy Combatants Eligible for the Procedures in this Order.* Enemy combatants who are in the control of DoD at GTMO are eligible for the review procedures established in this Order.
   i.   Enemy combatants whom the President has determined to be subject to his Military Order of November 13, 2001 are excepted from the procedures established in this Order until the disposition of any charges against them or the service of any sentence imposed by a military commission.
   ii. An enemy combatant in the control of DoD at GTMO will become eligible for the review process once he has been reviewed through the previously established procedures described in Section 1 and the Secretary or his designee has determined that his continued detention is appropriate.
   iii. An enemy combatant may decline in writing to participate in the procedures established by this Order. If the enemy combatant is unable to provide a written declination, the assisting military officer provided under Section 3.B shall prepare and execute such a writing on the enemy combatant's behalf.

3. **ADMINISTRATIVE REVIEW BOARD PROCEEDINGS**

A. *Review Board Proceedings.* The proceedings before the Review Board shall be non-adversarial.
   i.   *Provision of Information by the Government of the State of Which the Enemy Combatant is a National.*
      a.   Unless the DCO determines that it is not consistent with national security, the DCO shall request that the Department of State notify the State of which the enemy combatant is a national ("the State") of the proceedings.
         1) The notice shall be provided in advance of the proceedings to permit the State to prepare and present information to the Review Board.
         2) The notice to the State shall provide that information submitted by the State shall be

> in writing, except as otherwise deemed appropriate by the Review Board, and that it shall be provided on or before a date specified by the Review Board.
>
> 3)   Unless the DCO concludes that it is not consistent with national security, the notice shall also include a request for the State to notify the enemy combatant's relatives of the proceedings and inform them that they may provide information relevant to the proceedings through the State's written submissions.

b.   Unless the DCO determines that it is not consistent with national security, the State may submit to the Review Board information of any nature, including information related to the threat posed by the enemy combatant to the United States and its allies in the ongoing armed conflict against al Qaida and its affiliates and supporters.

c.   In the event that the submission of a State is not received by the date established by the Review Board, the Review Board may disregard the State's submission.

ii.   *Provision of Information by a Designated Military Officer.*

a.   A designated military officer ("Designated Military Officer") shall provide to the Review Board all reasonably available threat information in the possession of DoD regarding the enemy combatant under review and any other information indicating whether it would be in the interest of the United States and its allies to release, transfer, or continue to detain the enemy combatant. That information shall include any information that tends to support continued detention as well as any information that tends to support release or transfer.

b.   The Designated Military Officer is not an advocate for or against the continued detention of the enemy combatant under review.

c.   The Designated Military Officer who shall be selected by the DCO must meet the same qualifications set forth for members of the Review Board under Section 2.B.ii.a.

d.   In addition to any other information or documentation presented to the Review Board, the Designated Military Officer shall prepare, in unclassified form, a written summary of the primary factors favoring continued detention of the enemy combatant and the primary factors favoring release or transfer. When the Review Board deems it appropriate, the Designated Military Officer may present information orally.

   iii.   *Presentation of Information by the Enemy Combatant.*

      a.   Notice. Prior to the enemy combatant's hearing, the Review Board shall provide notice to the enemy combatant of the hearing and shall make available to the enemy combatant the written summary prepared by the Designated Military Officer.

         1)   The summary provided to the enemy combatant shall be in a language he understands.

         2)   The summary provided to the enemy combatant shall be provided sufficiently in advance of the hearing so as to permit him to prepare his presentation to the Review Board.

         3)   In no circumstances shall classified information be made available to the enemy combatant.

      b.   Opportunity to be Heard. The enemy combatant shall be permitted to present to the Review Board information on why he is no longer a threat to the United States and its allies in the ongoing armed conflict against al Qaida and its affiliates and supporters, why it is otherwise appropriate that he be released, or any other relevant information.

         1)   The enemy combatant will be permitted to present this information in person at a hearing before the Review Board.

         2)   Members of the Review Board may question the enemy combatant during the hearing.

         3)   If necessary, an interpreter shall be supplied for the combatant's presentation of information to the Review Board.

B.   *Assistance to the Enemy Combatant.* The Review Board shall assign a military officer ("Assisting Military Officer") to assist the enemy combatant in preparing his presentation to the Review Board.

    i.   The Review Board shall select the Assisting Military Officer from a pool of military officers selected by the DCO to serve as Assisting Military Officers.

        a.   The Assisting Military Officer shall meet the same qualifications established for members of the Review Board under Section 2.B.ii.a.

        b.   The Assisting Military Officer and the Designated Military Officer may not be the same person in the review of an enemy combatant.

    ii.   The Assisting Military Officer shall be responsible for explaining to the enemy combatant the nature of his hearing before the Review Board.

    iii.   The Assisting Military Officer shall be permitted to see all information and documentation provided to the Review Board by the Designated Military Officer.

    iv.   The Assisting Military Officer shall be permitted to meet with the enemy combatant prior to the enemy combatant's presentation to the board. If necessary, an interpreter shall be supplied for those meetings.

    v.   If the enemy combatant so elects, the Assisting Military Officer may also present information to the Review Board on behalf of the enemy combatant. If the enemy combatant has made such an election and the Assisting Military Officer believes that it would aid the Review Board's deliberations, the Assisting Military Officer may also, outside the presence of the enemy combatant, comment upon classified information that has been submitted to the Board and that bears upon the enemy combatant's presentation.

C.   *Information from Other Relevant U.S. Government Agencies.* The Review Board shall provide to the Department of State, the Department of Justice, the Department of Homeland Security, and the Central Intelligence Agency notice of the proceedings for the enemy combatant.

    i.   That notice shall be provided in advance of the proceedings for that enemy combatant so as to permit the agencies sufficient time to provide to the Review Board any information they deem relevant prior to the hearing.

    ii.   Any submissions that these agencies elect to provide shall be in written form except in extraordinary cases.

    iii.   In the event that the summary prepared by the Designated Military Officer and provided to the enemy combatant includes information that originated in U.S. government agencies other than DoD, the Review Board must obtain the originating agency's permission to share that information with the enemy combatant in any form.

D.   *Additional Fact-Gathering.* If, after the initial presentation of information, the Review Board believes additional information is necessary before it can make a recommendation, the Review Board may seek additional facts. It may, among other things:

i.   submit written questions to the Designated Military Officer or the Assisting Military Officer;

ii.   request further behavioral assessments of the combatant;

iii. request further questioning of any other combatants who have had contact with the enemy combatant under review while in detention to the extent that the Combatant Commander determines that such questioning is consistent with ongoing intelligence collection; and

iv.   seek other information that may be obtained readily.

E.   *Review Board Recommendations.* The Review Board shall make a written assessment of whether there is reason to believe that the enemy combatant poses a threat to the United States or its allies in the ongoing armed conflict against al Qaida and its affiliates and supporters and any other factors bearing upon the need for continued detention. Based on that assessment, the Review Board shall provide to the DCO a written recommendation on whether detention should be continued.

i.   The Review Board's assessment and recommendations shall be independent, based on the Review Board's review of all reasonably available information.

ii.   The Review Board's assessment and recommendation shall be reached by a majority of the members of the Review Board panel. In the event that a recommendation is not unanimous, any dissenting board member may submit a minority report to the DCO. That report shall take the same form as the written assessment and recommendation to be submitted by the majority.

iii. The Review Board's written assessment and recommendation shall include:

a.   the Review Board's conclusion regarding the threat posed by the enemy combatant;

b.   supporting reasons for that conclusion regarding the threat, including, but not limited to, a summary of information relied upon in reaching that conclusion;

c.   any other reasons that the continued detention of the enemy combatant remains or does not remain in the interest of the United States and its allies; and

        d.   the supporting reasons for the recommendation.

iv.   The written assessment and recommendation shall be provided to the DCO along with the record of the proceedings. Notice of the assessment and recommendation shall also be provided to any U.S. government agency that submitted information to the Review Board.

v.   The determination to continue to detain, release, or seek the transfer of the enemy combatant to the control of another government rests with the DCO. The DCO shall examine whether there is reason to believe that the enemy combatant poses a threat to the United States or its allies in the ongoing armed conflict against al Qaida and its affiliates and supporters and any other factors bearing upon the need for continued detention. Based on that examination, the DCO shall determine whether to continue to detain, release, or seek the transfer of the enemy combatant to the control of another country. He shall give full consideration to the written assessment and recommendation of the Review Board.

vi.   Notification of the DCO's determination will be provided to the Secretary of Defense, the enemy combatant, the Review Board, the relevant government agencies, and to the extent consistent with national security, the State of which the enemy combatant is a national.

F.   *Frequency of Review.* The Review Board shall examine the need for the continued detention of each combatant at least annually insofar as it practicable.

4.   ROLE OF THE DCO

A.   The DCO shall oversee and operate the administrative review process established by this Order.

B.   The DCO may establish as many review board panels as he deems necessary.

C.   The DCO shall, as he deems necessary and appropriate, coordinate his actions and determinations with other U.S. government departments and agencies.

D.   The DCO may seek the assistance of the General Counsel of DoD as appropriate.

E. The DCO shall have the authority to request support, including but not limited to military and civilian personnel, administrative assistance, and logistical assistance, from the head of any DoD component or office to oversee and operate the administrative review process and to accomplish the transfer or release of an enemy combatant. DoD component heads shall promptly provide such assistance. In addition, the DCO may seek the establishment of an executive agency or agencies under DoD Directive 5101.1 to assist him in implementing this Order.

F. The authority granted to the DCO in this Order may not be delegated except with the approval of the Secretary of Defense.

5.   CLASSIFIED INFORMATION

Classified information shall be handled in accordance with all applicable laws and regulations. The DCO should issue implementing guidance to ensure the proper handling and protection of classified information.

6.   OTHER

This Order is neither intended to nor does it create any right, benefit, or privilege, substantive or procedural, enforceable by any party, against the United States, its departments, agencies, or other entities, its officers or employees, or any other person. These procedures involve military authority exercised in the field in time of war. No provision in this Order shall be construed to be a requirement of the United States Constitution or a requirement of any other body of law nor shall this Order be construed to alter the requirements that the law of war imposes. The procedures established by this Order, along with the other procedures described above, have been implemented as a matter of discretion. Because the procedures described in this Order have been instituted as a matter of discretion, the Secretary of Defense may suspend or amend the procedures set forth in this Order at any time.

7.   IMPLEMENTING GUIDANCE

The DCO may, as he deems appropriate, issue guidance to implement this Order.

8.   EFFICTIVE DATE

This Order is effective immediately.

Paul Wolfowitz
Deputy Secretary of Defense

APPENDIX E
Overview
Combatant Status Review Tribunals

In response to last week's decisions by the Supreme Court, the Deputy Secretary of Defense today issued an order creating procedures for a Combatant Status Review Tribunal to provide detainees at Guantanamo Bay Naval Base with notice of the basis for their detention and review of their detention as enemy combatants. Each of these individuals has been determined to be an enemy combatant through multiple levels of review by the Department of Defense. The procedures for the Review Tribunal are intended to reflect the guidance the Supreme Court provided in its decisions last week.

The Supreme Court's Decisions
- The Supreme Court held that the federal courts have jurisdiction to hear challenges to the legality of the detention of enemy combatants held at Guantanamo Bay. In a separate decision – involving an American citizen held in the United States – the Court also held that due process would be satisfied by notice and an opportunity to be heard, and indicated that such process could properly be provided in the context of a hearing before a tribunal of military officers.
- The Court specifically cited certain existing military regulations, Army Regulation 190-8, which it suggested might be sufficient to meet the standards it articulated. The tribunals established under those regulations are relatively informal and occur without counsel or a personal representative. The process is a streamlined process designed to allow for expeditious determinations; in citing it, the Court recognized the military's need for flexibility and indicated that the process might provide all that was needed even for a citizen. Even in a traditional conflict, such a hearing is not provided to everyone who is detained, but only in cases of doubt as to the basis for detention.

The Process – The order issued today creates tribunals very much like those cited favorably by the Court to meet the unique circumstances of the Guantanamo detainees, and will provide an expeditious opportunity for non-citizen detainees to receive notice and an opportunity to be heard. It will not preclude them from seeking additional review in federal court.
- *Notice.* By July 17, each detainee will be notified of the review of his detention as an enemy combatant, of the opportunity to consult with a personal representative, and of the right to seek review in U.S. courts.
- *Personal Representative.* Each detainee will be assigned a military officer as a personal representative to assist in connection with the Tribunal process. This person is not a lawyer but provides assistance to the detainee

330

that is not normally offered in the process cited favorably by the Supreme Court or required by the Geneva Conventions.

- *Tribunals.* Detainees will be afforded an opportunity to appear before and present evidence to a Tribunal composed of three neutral commissioned military officers, none of whom was involved in the apprehension, detention, interrogation, or previous determination of status of the detainee.
- *Hearings.*
  - o The detainee will be allowed to attend all proceedings of the Tribunal except for those involving deliberation and voting or which would compromise national security if held in the presence of the detainee.
  - o The detainee will be provided with an interpreter and his personal representative will be available to assist at the hearing.
  - o The detainee will be allowed to present evidence, to call witnesses if reasonably available, and to question witnesses called by the Tribunal.
  - o The detainee will have the right to testify or otherwise address the Tribunal in oral or written form, but may not be compelled to testify.
- *Decision.* The Tribunal will decide whether a preponderance of evidence supports the detention of the individual as an enemy combatant, and there will be a rebuttable presumption in favor of the Government's evidence.
- *Non-Enemy Combatant Determination.* If the Tribunal determines that the detainee should no longer be classified as an enemy combatant, the Secretary of Defense will advise the Secretary of State, who will coordinate the transfer of the detainee for release to the detainee's country of citizenship or other disposition consistent with domestic and international obligations and U.S. foreign policy.

DEPUTY SECRETARY OF DEFENSE
1010 DEFENSE PENTAGON
WASHINGTON, DC 20301-1010

MEMORANDUM FOR THE SECRETARY OF THE NAVY

SUBJECT: Order Establishing Combatant Status Review Tribunal

This Order applies only to foreign nationals held as enemy combatants in the control of the Department of Defense at the Guantanamo Bay Naval Base, Cuba ("detainees").

a. Enemy Combatant. For purposes of this Order, the term "enemy combatant" shall mean an individual who was part of or supporting Taliban or al Qaeda forces, or associated forces that are engaged in hostilities against the United States or its coalition partners. This includes any person who has committed a belligerent act or has directly supported hostilities in aid of enemy armed forces. Each detainee subject to this Order has been determined to be an enemy combatant through multiple levels of review by officers of the Department of Defense.

b. Notice. Within ten days after the date of this Order, all detainees shall be notified of the opportunity to contest designation as an enemy combatant in the proceeding described herein, of the opportunity to consult with and be assisted by a personal representative as described in paragraph (c), and of the right to seek a writ of habeas corpus in the courts of the United States.

c. Personal Representative. Each detainee shall be assigned a military officer, with the appropriate security clearance, as a personal representative for the purpose of assisting the detainee in connection with the review process described herein. The personal representative shall be afforded the opportunity to review any reasonably available information in the possession of the Department of Defense that may be relevant to a determination of the detainee's designation as an enemy combatant, including any records, determinations, or reports generated in connection with earlier determinations or reviews, and to consult with the detainee concerning that designation and any challenge thereto. The personal representative may share any information with the detainee, except for classified information, and may participate in the Tribunal proceedings as provided in paragraph (g)(4).

d. Tribunals. Within 30 days after the detainee's personal representative has been afforded the opportunity to review the reasonably available information in the possession of the Department of Defense and had an opportunity to consult with the detainee, a Tribunal shall be convened to review the detainee's status as an enemy combatant.

e. Composition of Tribunal. A Tribunal shall be composed of three neutral commissioned officers of the U.S. Armed Forces, each of whom possesses the appropriate security clearance and none of whom was involved in the apprehension, detention, interrogation, or previous determination of status of the detainee. One of the members shall be a judge advocate. The senior member (in the grade of 0-5 and above) shall serve as President of the Tribunal. Another non-voting officer, preferably a judge advocate, shall serve as the Recorder and shall not be a member of the Tribunal.

f. Convening Authority. The Convening Authority shall be designated by the Secretary of the Navy. The Convening Authority shall appoint each Tribunal and its members, and a personal representative for each detainee. The Secretary of the Navy, with the concurrence of the General Counsel of the Department of Defense, may issue instructions to implement this Order.

g. Procedures.

(1) The Recorder shall provide the detainee in advance of the proceedings with notice of the unclassified factual basis for the detainee's designation as an enemy combatant.

(2) Members of the Tribunal and the Recorder shall be sworn. The Recorder shall be sworn first by the President of the Tribunal. The Recorder will then administer an oath, to faithfully and impartially perform their duties, to all members of the Tribunal to include the President.

(3) The record in each case shall consist of all the documentary evidence presented to the Tribunal, the Recorder's summary of all witness testimony, a written report of the Tribunal's decision, and a recording of the proceedings (except proceedings involving deliberation and voting by the members), which shall be preserved.

(4) The detainee shall be allowed to attend all proceedings, except for proceedings involving deliberation and voting by the members or testimony and other matters that would compromise national security if held in the presence of the detainee. The detainee's personal representative shall be allowed to attend all proceedings, except for proceedings involving deliberation and voting by the members of the Tribunal.

(5) The detainee shall be provided with an interpreter, if necessary.

(6) The detainee shall be advised at the beginning of the hearing of the nature of the proceedings and of the procedures accorded him in connection with the hearing.

(7) The Tribunal, through its Recorder, shall have access to and consider any reasonably available information generated in connection with the initial determination to hold the detainee as an enemy combatant and in any subsequent reviews of that determination, as well as any reasonably available records, determinations, or reports generated in connection therewith.

(8) The detainee shall be allowed to call witnesses if reasonably available, and to question those witnesses called by the Tribunal. The Tribunal shall determine the reasonable availability of witnesses. If such witnesses are from within the U.S. Armed Forces, they shall not be considered reasonably available if, as determined by their commanders, their presence at a hearing would affect combat or support operations. In the case of witnesses who are not reasonably available, written statements, preferably sworn, may be submitted and considered as evidence.

(9) The Tribunal is not bound by the rules of evidence such as would apply in a court of law. Instead, the Tribunal shall be free to consider any information it deems relevant and helpful to a resolution of the issue before it. At the discretion of the Tribunal, for example, it may consider hearsay evidence, taking into account the reliability of such evidence in the circumstances. The Tribunal does not have the authority to declassify or change the classification of any national security information it reviews.

(10) The detainee shall have a right to testify or otherwise address the Tribunal in oral or written form, and to introduce relevant documentary evidence.

(11) The detainee may not be compelled to testify before the Tribunal.

(12) Following the hearing of testimony and the review of documents and other evidence, the Tribunal shall determine in closed session by majority vote whether the detainee is properly detained as an enemy combatant. Preponderance of evidence shall be the standard used in reaching this determination, but there shall be a rebuttable presumption in favor of the Government's evidence.

(13) The President of the Tribunal shall, without regard to any other provision of this Order, have authority and the duty to ensure that all proceedings of or in relations to the Tribunal under this Order shall comply with Executive Order 12958 regarding national security information.

h. The Record. The Recorder shall, to the maximum extent practicable, prepare the record of the Tribunal within three working days of the announcement of the Tribunal's decision. The record shall include those items described in paragraph (g)(3) above. The record will then be forwarded to the Staff Judge Advocate for the Convening Authority, who shall review the record for legal

334

sufficiency and make a recommendation to the Convening Authority. The Convening Authority shall review the Tribunal's decision and, in accordance with this Order and any implementing instructions issued by the Secretary of the Navy, may return the record to the Tribunal for further proceedings or approve the decision and take appropriate action.

i. Non-Enemy Combatant Determination. If the Tribunal determines that the detainee shall no longer be classified as an enemy combatant, the written report of its decisions shall be forwarded directly to the Secretary of Defense or his designee. The Secretary or his designee shall so advise the Secretary of State, in order to permit the Secretary of State to coordinate the transfer of the detainee for release to the detainee's country of citizenship or other disposition consistent with domestic and international obligations and the foreign policy of the United States.

j. This Order is intended solely to improve management within the Department of Defense concerning its detention of enemy combatants at Guantanamo Bay Naval Base, Cuba, and is not intended to, and does not, create any right or benefit, substantive or procedural, enforceable at law, in equity, or otherwise by any party against the United States, its departments, agencies, instrumentalities or entities, its officers, employees or agents, or any other persons.

k. Nothing in this Order shall be construed to limit, impair, or otherwise affect the constitutional authority of the President as Commander in Chief or any authority granted by statute to the President or the Secretary of Defense.

This Order is effective immediately.

Paul Wolfowitz

CASE REFERENCES

Abbasi & Anor. v. Sec'y of State for Foreign and Commonwealth Affairs, EWCACiv 1598 (2002).

Armstrong v. Manzo 380 U.S. 545 (1965).

Baldwin v. Hale, 1 Wall 223 (1864).

Bas v. Tingy, 4 U.S. 37 (1802).

Campbell v. Clinton, 203 F.3d 19 (D.C. Cir. 2000).

Case of Hottentot Venus, 13 East 195, 104 Eng. Rep 344 (K.B. 1810).

Chicago & Southern Airlines v. Waterman Steamship Co. 333 U.S. 103 (1948).

Coalition of Clergy v. Bush, 189 F. Supp. 2d 1036 (C.D. Cal. 2002).

Cramer v. United States, 325 U.S. 1 (1945).

Crosby v. Nat'l Foreign Trade Council, 530 U.S. 363 (2000).

Dames and Moore v. Regan, 453 U.S. 654 (1981).

Duncan v. Kahanamoku, 327 U.S. 304 (1946).

Dura v. Reina, 495 U.S. 676 (1990).

E. I. Dupont de Nemours & Co. v. Train, 430 U.S. 112 (1977).

Eisentrager v. Forrestal, 174 F.2d 961 (D.C. Cir. 1949).

Ex Parte Bollman, 8 U.S. (4 Cranch) 75 (1807).

Ex Parte Endo, 323 U.S. 283 (1944).

Ex Parte Merryman, 17 F. Cas. 144 (C.C. Md. 1861).

Ex Parte Milligan, 71 U.S. (4 Wall) 121 (1866).

Ex Parte Quirin, 317 U.S. 1 (1942).

Fuentes v. Shevin, 407 U.S. 67 (1972).

Gherebi v. Bush, No. 03-55785 (9th Cir. 2003).

Hamdi v. Rumsfeld, 542 U.S. __ 2004, 124 S. Ct. 2633, (2004), No. 03-6696.

Hamdi v. Rumsfeld, 316 F.3d 450 (4th Cir. 2003) (*Hamdi III*).

Hamdi v. Rumsfeld, 296 F.3d 278 (4th Cir. 2002) (*Hamdi II*).

Hamdi v. Rumsfeld, No. 02-7338 (4th Circuit Sept. 12, 2002) (Order for interlocutory review).

Harris v. Nelson, 394 U.S. 286 (1969).

Haupt v. United States, 330 U.S. 631 (1947).

Henderson v. INS, 157 F.3d 106 (2d Cir. 1998).

Hirabayshi v. United States, 320 U.S. 81 (1943).

Hirabayshi v. United States, 828 F.2d 591 (9th Cir. 1987).

Holmes v. Laird, 459 F.2d 1211 (D.C. Cir. 1972).

Howe v. Smith, 452 U.S. 473 (1981).

Huynh Thi Anh v. Levi, 586 F.2d 625 (6th Cir. 1978).

In re Yamashita, 327 U.S. 1 (1946).

Johnson v. Eisentrager, 339 U.S. 763 (1950).

King v. Cowle, 2 Burr. 834-854, 855, Eng Rep 587, 598-599 (K.B. 1759).

King v. Schiever, 2 Burr. 765, 97, Eng Rep 551 (K.B.1759).

Kirby v. Illinois, 406 U.S. 682 (1972).

Korematsu v. United States, 323 U.S. 214 (1944).

Korematsu v. United States, 584 F. Supp. 1406 (N.D. Cal. 1984).

Lonchar v. Thomas, 517 U.S. 314 (1996).

Madsen v. Kinsella, 343 U.S. 341 (1952).

Montoya v. United States, 180 U.S. 261 (1901).

Mudd v. Caldera, 134 F. Supp. 2d 138 (2001).

Padilla ex rel. Newman v. Bush, 233 F. Supp. 2d 564 (S.D.N.Y. 2002).

Padilla ex rel. Newman v. Rumsfeld, 352 F.3d 695 (No. 03-2235) (2d Cir. 2003).

Padilla v. Rumsfeld, 352 F.3d 695 (2d Cir.).

Paquete Habana, 175 U.S. 677 (1900).

Powell v. Alabama, 287 U.S. 45 (1932).

Prize Cases, 67 U.S. 635 (1863).

Rasul v. Bush, 215 F. Supp. 2d 55 (D.D.C. 2002).

Rasul et al. v. Bush and Al-Odah et al. v. United States, 542 U.S. __ (Nos. 03-334, 03-343) (2004), 124 S. Ct. 2686 (2004),

Rasul et al. v. Bush and Al-Odah et al. v. United States, 321 F.3d 1134 (D.C. Cir. 2003).

Reid v. Court, 354 U.S. 1 (1957).

Rumsfeld v. Padilla, 542 U.S. __ (2004), 124 S. Ct. 2711 (2004), (No. 03-1027).

Sommersett v. Steward, 20 How. St. Tr. 1 (K.B. 1772).

Talbot v. Seeman, 5 U.S. 1 (1801).

United States v. Awadallah, 349 F.3d 42 (2d Cir. 2003).

United States v. Haupt, 136 F.2d 661 (7th Cir. 1943).

United States v. Mendoza, 464 U.S. 154 (1984).

United States v. Moussaoui, 336 F.3d 279 (4th Cir. 2003).

United States v. Moussaoui, No. 01-455-A (United States District Court, Eastern District of Virginia) October 2, 2003.

United States v. Moussaoui, (No. 03-4792) (4th Cir. 2004).

United States v. Moussaoui, (No. 04-264) (April 22, 2004).

United States v. Rogers, 388 F. Supp. 298 (E.D. Va. 1975).

United States v. Sperry Corp., 493 U.S. 52 (1989).

United States v. Verdugo-Urquidez, 494 U.S. 259 (1990).

Wales v. Whitney, 114 U.S. 564 (1885).

White v. Maryland, 373 U.S. 59 (1963).

Youngstown Sheet and Tube v. Sawyer, 343 U.S. 579 (1952).

CONSTITUTIONAL PROVISIONS

United States Constitution:

Amendment V.

Amendment VI.

Amendment XIV.

Article I, § 8, cl. 1.

Article I, § 8, cl. 10.

Article I, § 8, cl. 11.

Article I, § 8, cl. 10-14.

Article I, § 9, cl. 2.

Article II.

STATUTES, RULES AND REGULATIONS

All Writs Act, 28 U.S.C. § 1651 (a).

Articles of War:
15 H. R. Doc. No. 81-491 (1949).
5 Rep. No. 81-486 (1949).

Classified Information Procedures Act, 18 U.S.C. App. 3 § 7(a), Title 18 United States Code, Section 3731, and Title 28, United States Code, § 1291.

Common Article 3 of the Geneva Convention of 1949.

Convention (No. IV) Respecting the Laws and Customs of War on Land, with Annex of Regulations, October 18, 1907. Annex, art. 1 36 Stat. 2277 T.S. No. 539 (Jan. 26, 1910) (The Hague Convention).

Convention Relative to the Protection of Civilian Persons in the Time of War 6 U.S.T. 3516, T.I.A.S. 3365, 75 U.N.T.S. 287.

Department of Defense Military Commission Instruction No. 1-9, Appendix C5-C13.

Department of Defense Military Commission Order No. 1-4, Appendix C1-C4.

Enemy Prisoners of War, Retained Personnel, Civilian Internees and Other Detainees, Army Reg. 190-9, §§ 1-5, 1-6 (1997).

Executive Order No. 13, 107, 63 Fed. Reg. 68.991 (December 15, 1998).

Executive Order No. 9066, 7. Fed. Reg. 1407 (1942) 56 Stat. 173 (1942).

Geneva Convention III Relative to the Treatment of Prisoners of War, Articles 5, 6 U.S.T. 3316, 75 U.N.T.S. 135 (1949).

Geneva Conventions Relative to POWs at Articles 12, 22.

G. O. 20 of 1847 (Gen. Scott).

H. R. Rep. No. 92-116, 1971 U.S.C.C.A.N. 1435, 1435 ("Judiciary Committee Report").

Joint Resolution of Sept. 18, 2001, Authorization for Use of Military Force, Pub. Law No. 107-40, 115 Stat. 224 (2001).

Manual for Court Martial [MCM], U.S. (1988).

McCoy Papers, *Rules Established by the Military Commission Appointed by Order of the President of July 2, 1942* at 3-4.

Military Order of January 11, 1945, 10 Fed. Reg. 549 (January 16, 1945).

Military Order on the Detention, Treatment and Trial of Certain Non-Citizens in the War Against Terrorism, (November 13, 2001); § 1(a), 66 Fed. Reg. 57, 833 (November 16, 2001).

Opinions:
11 Opins. At. Gen. 297 (1865).
11 Opins. At. Gen. 305 (1865).

Presidential Proclamation of September 24, 1862.

Presidential Proclamation No. 2561, July 2, 1942, 7 Fed. Reg. 5101, 56 Stat. 1964.

Presidential Proclamation No. 7463, 66 Fed. Reg. 48, 199 (Sept. 14, 2001).

Security Procedures for the Protection of Classified Information, 18 U.S.C.A. App. 3 § 9 (West 2000).

The 1977 Protocols Additional to the Geneva Conventions, 16 I.L.M. 1391.

UCMJ, Article 21.

UCMJ, Article 106.

U.S.A. PATRIOT Act, Pub. L. No. 107-56, 115 Stat. 272 (2001).

U.S. Army Field Manual [FM] 27-10, The Law of Land Warfare (1956).

1874 Brussels Convention, Project of an International Declaration Concerning the Laws and Customs of War, August 27, 1874, art 9.

8 U.S.C. § 1534 (c)(1).

10 U.S.C. § 801-950 United States Code of Military Justice.

10 U.S.C. § 956.

10 U.S.C. § 956 (5).

18 U.S.C. § 2441.

18 U.S.C. § 4001(a).

18 U.S.C. App. 3 § 1 et seg.

28 U.S.C. § 2241(a).

28 U.S.C. § 2241(a), (c) (3).

18 U.S.C.A. § 32 (a) (7).

18 U.S.C.A. § 844 (f) (i).

18 U.S.C.A. § 1114.

18 U.S.C.A. § 1117.

18 U.S.C.A. § 2332 a.

18 U.S.C.A. § 2332 b (a) (2).

49 U.S.C.A. § 46502 (a) (1) (A) (a).

BIBLIOGRAPHY

Addicott, Jeffrey F. *Winning the War on Terror: Legal and Policy Lessons from the Past*. Lawyer and Judge Publishing Co., 2002.

Aldykiewicz, Jan E. "Authority to Court Martial Non-U.S. Military Personnel for Serious Violations of International Humanitarian Law Committed During Internal Armed Conflicts," 167 *Military Law Review* 74 (2001).

American Bar Association Task Force on Terrorism and the Law, *Report and Recommendations on Military Commissions*, January 4, 2002.

American Bar Association Task Force on Treatment of Enemy Combatants, *Preliminary Report*, August 8, 2002.

Ashcroft, John. Attorney General. Testimony before the Senate Committee on the Judiciary, http://www.usdoj.gov/ag/testimony/2001/1206/transcriptssenate judiciarycommittee.htm, December 6, 2001.

Barry, John, Michael Hirsh and Michael Isikoff. "The Roots of Torture," *Newsweek,* May 24, 2004.

Bederman, David. *International Law Frameworks*. New York, 2001.

Blum, Vanessa. "Guantanamo Commissions: The Outlines of Justice," *Legal Times*, May 28, 2003.

-----. "Military Lawyers Urge Role for High Court," *Legal Times*, January 21, 2004.

-----. "Powers of Designating 'Enemy Combatant' Outlined," *New York Law Journal*, http://www.abanet.org/natsecurity, March 1, 2004.

-----. "Tribunals Put Defense Bar in a Bind," *Legal Times*, July 15, 2003.

Bradley, Curtis A. and Jack Goldsmith. "The Constitutional Validity of Military Commissions," 5 *Green Bag* 2d 249 (2002).

"Bush Issues Ultimatum to the Taliban, Calls Upon Nations of World to Unite and Destroy Terrorism," *Congressional Quarterly*, September 22, 2001.

Cocco, Mary. "Fair Trial Will Be a Travesty in Terror Cases," *Newsday,* June 3, 2003.

Corwin, Edward S. *President, Office and Powers*. 4th Revised Edition, New York University Press, 1962.

Crona, Spencer J. and Neal A. Richardson. "Justice for War Criminals of Invisible Armies: A New Legal and Military Approach to Terrorism,"*21 Okla. City U.L. Rev.* 349 (1996).

Dean, John. "Military Tribunals: A Long and Mostly Honorable History," *Find Law's Writ*, December 7, 2001.

Devins, Neal. Congress, "Civil Liberties, and the War on Terrorism," 11 *Wm. and Mary Bill of Rights J.* 1139 (2003).

Elwood, John P. "Prosecuting the War on Terrorism," *Criminal Justice Magazine*, Volume 17 Issue 2, Summer 2002.

Ely, John Hart. *War and Responsibility: Constitutional Lessons of Vietnam and Its Aftermath*. Princeton, N. J.: Princeton University Press, 1993.

Evans, Christopher M. "Terrorism on Trial: The President's Constitutional Authority to Order the Prosecution of Suspected Terrorists by Military Commission," *Duke L. J.* 1831 (2002).

Fisher, Louis. "Military Tribunals: The Quirin Precedent," *Congressional Research Service*, March 26, 2002.

Golden, Tim and Eric Schmitt. "General Took Guantanamo Rules to Iraq for Handling of Prisoners," *N.Y. Times*, May 13, 2004.

Gonzales, Alberto. "Martial Justice, Full and Fair," *N.Y. Times*, Nov. 30, 2001.

-----. Memorandum For the President Decision Re: "Application of the Geneva Convention of War to the Conflict with Al Qaeda and the Taliban," January 25, 2002.

Greenhouse, Linda. "Justices to Hear Case of Detainees at Guantanamo," *N.Y. Times*, November 11, 2003.

Hamilton, Alexander. "The Examination," No. 1, 17 Dec. 1801, reprinted in 3 *The Founder's Constitution*, Kurland and Lerner eds., 1987.

Hearing Before the Senate Committee on Armed Services 107th Cong. (2001), Department of Defense's Implementation of the President's Military Order on Detention, Treatment, and Trial by Military Commission of Certain Non-Citizens in the War on Terrorism.

Hearing Before the Senate Committee on the Judiciary, 107th Cong. (2001), The Department of Justice and Terrorism.

Hearing Before the Senate Committee on the Judiciary, 107th Cong. (2002) WL 1722725, Oversight of the Department of Justice, (2002).

Hess, Pamela. "Pentagon: Tribunals to Include Gag Rule," UPI, Pentagon Desk, May 2, 2003.

Hirschkorn, Phil. "U.S. Defends Holding 'Enemy Combatant,'" http://www.cnn.com/2004/LAW /03/18/Padilla, March 18, 2004.

Hirschkorn, Phil and Deborah Feyerick. "Court Weighs 'Dirty Bomb' Suspect's Detention," http://www.cnn.com/2003/LAW/11/17/padilla.appeal/index.html, November 18, 2003.

Katyal, Neal K. and Laurence H. Tribe. "Waging War, Deciding Guilt: Trying the Military Tribunals," 111 Yale L.J. 1259 (2002).

Lacey, Michael D., Maj. "Military Commissions: A Historical Survey, Army Law 41 (2002).

Lewis, Neil A. "Sudden Shift on Detainee," N.Y. Times, December 2, 2003.

-----. "Bush's Power to Plan Trial of Detainees is Challenged," N.Y. Times, January 15, 2004.

MacDonell, Timothy C., Maj. "Military Commissions and Courts-Martial: A Brief Discussion of the Constitutional and Jurisdictional Distinctions Between the Two Courts, Army Law 19, March 2002.

Mahler, Jonathan. "Commander Swift Objects," New York Times Magazine, http://www.NYTimes.com/2004/06/16/magazine/13MILITARY.html, June 13, 2004.

Mauro, Tony. "Historic High Court Ruling is Troublesome Model for Modern Terror Trials," American Lawyer Media, November 19, 2001.

Miller, Arthur S. Presidential Power. Minneapolis: West Publishing Company, 1977.

Military Commissions, 11 Op. Atty Gen. 297; 1865 U.S. AG LEXIS 36 (July 1865).

Military Government and Martial Law. (reprinted in Appendix I). *General Orders*, No. 20 of February 19, 1847.

Mintz, John. "Both Sides Say Tribunal Will Be Fair Trials," *Washington Post*, May 23, 2003.

-----. "Yemeni's Attorney Tries to Halt Tribunal," *Washington Post*, April 8, 2004.

Morin, Richard and Claudia Deane. "Most Americans Back U.S. Tactics: Poll Finds Little Worry Over Rights," *Washington Post*, November 29, 2001.

Navy Admiral in Charge of Abuse Probe, *Chicago Tribune*, http://www. military.com/NewsContent/0,13319,FL_probe_061004,00.html, June 10, 2004.

Newton, Michael A., Maj. *"Continuum Crimes: Military Jurisdiction Over Foreign Nationals Who Commit International Crimes,"* 153 *Mil. L. Rev.* 1, 20 (1996).

New York State Bar Association Coordinating Committee on Federal Anti-Terrorism Measures, *Report on Military Commissions,* June 20, 2002.

Office of White House Press Secretary, Fact Sheet, Status of Detainees at Guantanamo 1 (Feb. 7, 2002).

Operational Law Handbook, JA 422 (Charlottesville 1977).

Oversight of the Department of Justice: Hearing before the Senate Committee on the Judiciary, 107th Cong. 2002 WL 1722725 (2002).

Palmer, Elizabeth A. and Adriel Bettelheim. "War and Civil Liberties: Congress Gropes for a Role," 59 *Cong. Weekly* 2820, Dec. 1, 2001.

Pitts-Kiefer, Samantha A. "Jose Padilla: Enemy Combatant or Common Criminal?" 48 *Vill. L. Rev.* 875 (2003).

President's Address Before a Joint Session of the Congress on the State of Union, *39 Weekly Comp. Pres.* Doc. 109, January 28, 2003.

Rehnquist, William. *All the Laws But One: Civil Liberties in Wartime.* New York: Alfred A. Knopf, 1988.

Rivkin, David B. and Lee A. Casey. "The Law and War," www.Washingtontimes. com/op-ed/20040125-103747-9111r.htm, January 26, 2004.

Rivkin, David B., Lee A. Casey and Darin Bartram. "Bringing al-Qaida to Justice: The Constitutionality of Trying Al-Qaida Terrorists in the Military Justice System," *Heritage Foundation,* Legal Memorandum No. 3, November 5, 2001.

Rose, David. "Guantanamo Bay on Trial," *Vanity Fair,* January 2004.

Rovella, David E. "Tribunal Rules Don't End Debate on Fairness," *National Law Journal,* March 25, 2002.

Rule of Procedure and Evidence 89(c) International Criminal Tribunal for the former Yugoslavia, "A chamber may admit any relevant evidence which it deems to have probative value," IT/32/Rev. 21 (2001).

Shapiro, Martin and Douglas S. Hobbs. *The Politics of Constitutional Law.* Cambridge, Mass.: Winthrop Press, 1974.

Shenon, Philip. "Judges Hear U.S. Appeal in Terror Case," *N.Y. Times,* December 3, 2003.

Staff Statement No. 15, Overview of the Enemy, National Commission on Terrorist Attacks on the United States, June 2004.

Taft William H. IV. "Current Pressures on International Humanitarian Law: The Law of Armed Conflict After 9/11: Some Salient Features," 28 *Yale J. Int'l Law* 319, Summer 2003.

Terrorist Research and Analytical Center, U.S. Dept. of Justice, Terrorism in the United States 1982-1992.

Testimony Before the House Committee on the Judiciary, http://www. usdoj.gov/ag/testimony/2001/agcrisisremarks9_24.htm, September 24, 2001.

Thompson, H. K., Jr. and Henry Strutz. *Doenitz at Nuremberg: A Reprisal.* New York: Amber Pub. Corp., 1976.

U.S. Charges Two at Guantanamo with Conspiracy, *N.Y. Times*, February 24, 2004.

United States Department of Defense News Release. "DoD News Briefing on Military Commissions," March 21, 2002.

United States Department of Defense News Release. No. 908-03, "DoD Announces Detainee Allowed Access to Lawyer," December 2, 2003.

-----. 097-04, "Padilla Allowed Access to Lawyer," February 11, 2004.

-----. 564-04, Guantanamo Detainee Charged, June 10, 2004.

-----. 620-04, "Military Commission Charges Referred," June 29, 2004.

-----. 678-04, "Additional Detainees Charged," July 14, 2004.

Vladeck, Stephen I. "A Small Problem of Precedent: 18 U.S.C. § 4001(a) and the Detention of U.S. Enemy Combatants," 112 *Yale L. J.* 961, January 2003.

Wallach, Evan J. "The Procedural and Evidentiary Rules of the Post-World War II War Crimes Trials: Did They Provide an Outline for International Legal Procedure?" 37 *Colum. J. Transnat'l L.* (1999).

Wedgwood, Ruth. "Al-Qaida, Terrorism and Military Commissions," *American Journal of International Law*, Vol. 96 No 2., April 2002.

Winthrop, W. *Military Law and Precedents* (2 ed. 1920 reprint).

White House Press Secretary, Fact Sheet, Status of Detainees at Guantanamo 1, February 7, 2002.

Writings (Ford ed.) vol. 338, Letter of July 23, 1793: Writings (Hunt ed.).

Yoo, John. Memorandum for William J. Haynes II, General Counsel, Department of Defense Re: "Application of the Treaties and Laws to al Qaeda and Taliban Detainees," January 9, 2002.

-----."Perspectives on the Rules of War," www.sfgate.com/cgi-bin/article.cgi? file=/chronicle/archive/2004/06/15/EDGKJ66AM1.DTL, June 15, 2004.

Yoo, John C. and James C. Ho. "The New York University – University of Virginia Conference on Exploring The Limits of International Law: The Status of Terrorists," 44 *Va. J Int'l Law*, Fall 2003.

Other Authorities (Not cited)

Beattie, Michael and Lisa Yonka Stevens. "An Open Debate on United States Citizens Designated as Enemy Combatants: Where Do We Go from Here?" 62 *Md. L. Rev.* 975 (2003).

Belknap, Michael R. "The Supreme Court Goes to War: The Meaning and Implications of the Nazi Saboteur Case," 89 *Mili. L. Rev.* 59 (1980).

Blackstone, W. *Commentaries on the Laws of England.* Cooley Ed, 1899.

Clemmons, Byard Q. "The Case for Military Tribunals," 49 *The Federal Lawyer* 27 (2002).

Cole, David. "Enemy Aliens," 54 *Stan. L. Rev.* 953 (2002).

Corwin, Edward S. "The War and the Constitution: President and Congress," 37 *American Political Science Review,* 18 (1943).

Crotty, William (ed.). *The Politics of Terror: The U.S. Response to 9/11.* Boston: Northeastern Univ. Press, 2004.

Danelski, David J. "The Saboteurs Case," 21 *J. Sup. Ct. Hist.* 61 (1996).

Dickinson, Laura. "Using Legal Process to Fight Terrorism, Detentions, Military Commissions, International Tribunals, and the Rule of Law," 75 *So. Cal. L. Rev.* 1407 (2002).

Fisher, Louis. *Constitutional Conflicts Between Congress and the President.* Lawrence: University Press of Kansas, 1997.

-----. *Nazi Saboteurs on Trial: a Military Tribunal and American Law.* Lawrence: University Press of Kansas, 2003.

-----. *Presidential War Power.* Lawrence: University Press of Kansas, 1995.

Goldsmith, Jack and Cass R. Sunstein. "Military Tribunals and Legal Culture: What a Difference Sixty Years Makes," 19 *Const. Comment* 261 (2004).

Irons, Peter. *Justice at War: The Story of the Japanese-American Internment Cases.* New York: Oxford University Press, 1983.

Kauper, Paul G. "The Steel Seizure Case: Congress, the President and the Supreme Court," 51 *Mich. L. Rev.* 141 (1952).

352

Kelly, Michael. *Equal Justice in the Balance: Assessing America's Legal Responses to the Emerging Terrorist Threat.* East Lansing: Univ. of Michigan Press, 2004.

Keymann, Philip B. *Terrorism, Freedom and Security: Winning Without War.* Cambridge: MIT Press, 2003.

Mason, Alpheus Thomas. "Inter Arma Silent Leges," 69 *Harv. L. Rev.* 806-838, 1955.

May, Christopher. *In the Name of War: Judicial Review and the War Powers Since 1918.* Cambridge: Harvard University Press, 1989.

Mayer, Jane. "Annals of Justice: Lost in the Jihad," *The New Yorker,* 50, March 10, 2003.

Muller, E. "12/7 and 9/11: War, Liberties, and the Lessons of History," 104 *W. Va. L. Rev.* 1 (2002).

National Institute of Military Justice. *Annotated Guide, Procedures for Trials by Military Commission of Certain Non-United States Citizens in the War Against Terrorism* (2002).

Reveley, W. Taylor, III. *War Powers of the President and Congress.* Charlottesville: University Press of Virginia, 1981.

Roth, Kenneth. "The Law of War in the War on Terror," *Foreign Affairs,* Jan./Feb. 2004.

Rubin, Alfred P. "Applying the Geneva Conventions: Military Commissions, Armed Conflict and al-Qaeda," 26 *Fletcher F. World Aff.* 79 (2002).

Sageman, Marc. *Understanding Terror Networks.* Univ. Penn Press, 2004.

Treanor, William Michael. "Fame, the Founding and the Power to Declare War," 82 *Cornell L. Rev.* 695 (1997).

Wedgwood, Ruth. "After September 11," 36 *New Eng. L. Rev.* 725 (2002).

Woodward, Bob. *Bush at War.* New York: Simon and Schuster, 2002.

Yoo, John C. "The Continuation of Politics by Other Means: The Original Understanding of War Powers," 84 *Calif. L. Rev.* 167-305 (1996).

Zagel, James and Adam Winkler. "The Independence of Judges," 46 *Mercer L. Rev.* 795 (1995).

INDEX

158-161,163,164,167
Stone, Harlan Fisk, (C.J.), 10
Swann, Robert, Lt. Colonel, 74

T

Taft, William H., IV, 84
Taliban, 2,28,30,32-35,45,46,63,94,
102,114,118,129,130,146,151,
153,160,177,179,183,195,199
Taney, Roger B., Chief Justice, 141
Thomas, Clarence, Justice, 156,166
Traxler, William B., Jr., Judge, 107,
108

U

U.S. Court of Appeals for the Second
Circuit, 97-99,113-116,118
United States Court of Appeals for
the Armed Forces, 192
United States Court of Appeals for
the District of Columbia, 36
United States Court of Appeals for
the Fourth Circuit, 90,123,125,
133
United States Court of Appeals for
the Ninth Circuit, 36
USA PATRIOT Act, 181,182

V

Viet Dinh, 119

W

Wesley, Richard, Judge, 98,101,118
Wilkins, William W., Judge, 126
Wilkinson, J. Harvie, Judge, 104
Williams, Karen, Judge, 125
Winter, Ralph, Judge, 39
Winthrop, William, 17,19,21
World Trade Center, 1,124,177,205

Y

Yamashita, Tomoyuki, 7
Yaser Esam Hamdi, 87,120,121,123,
124,127,132
Yoo, John C., 199

358

STUDIES IN POLITICAL SCIENCE

1. David R. Jones, **Political Parties and Policy Gridlock in American Government**
2. Jong-Sup Lee and Uk Heo, **The U.S.-South Korean Alliance, 1961-1988: Free-Riding or Bargaining?**
3. Rachel K. Gibson, **The Growth of Anti-Immigrant Parties in Western Europe**
4. Derek S. Reveron, **Promoting Democracy in the Post-Soviet Region**
5. James R. Hedtke, **Lame Duck Presidents–Myth or Reality**
6. Gerson Moreno-Riaño, **Political Tolerance, Culture, and the Individual**
7. Rosa Gomez Dierks, **Credible Fiscal Policy Commitments and Market Access–Case Studies of Argentina, Chile, and Mexico, 1980-1995**
8. James Biser Whisker, **The Supremacy of the State in International Law: The Act of State Doctrine**
9. Henry Flores, **The Evolution of the Liberal Democratic State with a Case Study of Latinos in San Antonio, Texas**
10. Joseph L. Wert, **A Study of Bill Clinton's Presidential Approval Ratings**
11. Philip Benwell, **In Defence of Australia's Constitutional Monarchy**
12. Janet Campbell, **An Analysis of Law in the Marxist Tradition**
13. Michael J. Zarkin, **Social Learning and the History of U.S. Telecommunications Policy, 1900-1996: Creating the Telecommunications Act of 1996**
14. Herbert P. LePore, **The Politics and Failure of Naval Disarmament, 1919-1939: The Phantom Peace**
15. Matthew T. Kenney, **A Theoretical Examination of Political Values and Attitudes in New and Old Democracies**
16. John Randolph LeBlanc, **Ethics and Creativity in the Political Thought of Simone Weil and AlbertCamus**
17. Terri Jett, **Agenda-Setting and Decision-Making of African American County Officials: The Case of Wilcox County**
18. Bruce A. Carroll, **The Role, Design, and Growing Importance of United States Magistrate Judges**
19. Youngtae Shin, **Women and Politics in Japan and Korea**
20. Geralyn M. Miller, **Changing the Way America Votes–Election Reform, Incrementalism, and Cutting Deals**
21. Georgina Blakeley, **Building Local Democracy in Barcelona**
22a. Peter Baofu, **Beyond Democracy to Post-Democracy: Conceiving a Better Model of Governance to Supercede Democracy: Volume One**
22b. Peter Baofu, **Beyond Democracy to Post-Democracy: Conceiving a Better Model of Governance to Supercede Democracy: Volume Two**
23. Nicolle Zeegers, Willem Witteveen, and Bart van Klink (eds.), **Social and Symbolic Effects of Legislation Under the Rule of Law**
24. Don-Terry Veal, **The Politics of Equity and Growth–A Case Study of Rockford, Illinois**
25. Leonard Cutler, **The Rule of Law and the Law of War: Military Commissions and Enemy Combatants Post 9/11**